GOVERNING THE POST-COMMUNIST CITY

Institutions and Democratic Development in Prague

MARTIN HORAK

GOVERNING THE
POST-COMMUNIST CITY

Institutions and Democratic
Development in Prague

UNIVERSITY OF TORONTO PRESS
Toronto Buffalo London

ISBN: 978-0-8020-9328-8

Printed on acid-free paper

Library and Archives Canada Cataloguing in Publication

Horak, Martin, 1973–
    Governing the post-communist city : institutions and democratic
    development in Prague / Martin Horak.

    Includes bibliographical references and index.
    ISBN 978-0-8020-8328-8 (bound)

    1. Prague (Czech Republic) – Politics and government – 20th century.
    I. Title.

    JS4747.7.A2H67 2007   320.9437'2090511   C2007-905924-4

This book has been published with the help of a grant from the Canadian
Federation for the Humanities and Social Sciences, through the Aid to
Scholarly Publications Programme, using funds provided by the Social
Sciences and Humanities Research Council of Canada.

The author acknowledges the assistance of the J.B. Smallman Publication
Fund and the Faculty of Social Science, The University of Western Ontario.

University of Toronto Press acknowledges the financial assistance to its
publishing program of the Canada Council for the Arts and the Ontario
Arts Council.

University of Toronto Press acknowledges the financial support for its
publishing activities of the Government of Canada through the Book
Publishing Industry Development Program (BPIDP).

Contents

Tables and Figures

Abbreviations

CSSD	Czech Social Democratic Party (Česká Strana Sociálně Demokratická)
DEU	Democratic Union (Demokratická Unie)
HUS	Main Road Network (Hlavní Uliční Sít')
KDU-CSL	Christian Democratic Union – Czechoslovak People's Party (Křest'anská a Demokratická Unie – Československá Strana Lidová)
KSC	Communist Party of Czechoslovakia (Komunistická Strana Československa)
KZSP	Club for Old Prague (Klub za Starou Prahu)
LSNS	Liberal National Socialist Party (Liberální Strana Národně Sociální)
MNV	Local National Committee (Místní Národní Výbor)
NVP	National Committee of Prague (Národní Výbor Prahy)
ODA	Civic Democratic Alliance (Občanská Demokratická Aliance)
ODS	Civic Democratic Party (Občanská Demokratická Strana)
ONV	District National Committee (Obvodní Národní Výbor)
OPP	Department of Historic Preservation (Odbor Památkové Péče)
OSV	Department of Public Relations (Odbor Styku s Veřejností)
OUR	Department of Land Use Decisions (Odbor Územního Rozhodovaní)
PPR	Prague Monument Preserve (Pražská Památková Rezervace)
PROM	Prague Council of Cities and Towns (Pražská Rada Obcí a Měst)

PSSPPOP	Prague Centre of State Monument Preservation and Nature Protection (Pražské Středisko Státní Památkové Péče a Ochrany Přírody)
PUDIS	Design Institute for Transport Engineering Works (Projektový Ústav Dopravně Inženýrských Staveb)
PUPP	Prague Institute for Monument Preservation (Pražský Ústav Památkové Péče)
ROPID	Regional Transit Management System (Regionální Organizátor Pražské Integrované Dopravy)
SD	Free Democrats (Svobodní Demokraté)
SOPMSH	Association of Residents and Friends of the Lesser Quarter and the Castle District (Společnost Občanů a Přatel Malé Strany a Hradčan)
SURPMO	State Institute for the Reconstruction of Historic Sites and Buildings (Státní Ústav pro Rekonstrukci Památkových Měst a Objektů)
SZI	Foreign Investment Section (Sekce Zahraničních Investic)
UDI	Transport Engineering Institute of the Capital City of Prague (Ústav Dopravního Inženýrství)
UGI	General Investment Office of the Capital City of Prague (Útvar Generálního Investora)
UHA	Chief Architect's Office of the Capital City of Prague, renamed URM in 1994 (Útvar Hlavního Architekta)
UNV	Central National Committee (Ústřední Národní Výbor)
UPP	Union for Prague (Unie pro Prahu)
URM	City Development Authority of the Capital City of Prague, formerly the UHA (Útvar Rozvoje Města)
US	Freedom Union (Unie Svobody)
USK	Strategic Planning Section – City Development Authority (Úsek Strategických Koncepcí)
ZKS	Basic Communications System (Základní Komunikační Systém)

Acknowledgments

This study could not have been written without the assistance of many people. I cannot name them all here, but I would like to ackowledge at least a few key individuals. The primary research for this book was conducted, and the initial version of the text written, while I was a doctoral candidate at the University of Toronto. My heartfelt thanks for invaluable encouragement and criticism at this stage go to my mentors and advisers Richard Stren, Peter Solomon, and Blair Ruble. My friends Daniel Mittler and Karen Moore also contributed key ideas at this stage of the work, for which I am very grateful. The research conducted at the doctoral stage received crucial financial support from a four-year Social Sciences and Humanities Research Council of Canada doctoral fellowship.

My research in Prague was aided by the extraordinary generosity of many people whom I interviewed. Although they will have to remain nameless in the interest of safeguarding their confidentiality, their insight and willingness to share information played an irreplaceable role in ensuring that this project came to fruition. Many ideas have found their way into the text as a result of exchanges with colleagues. Among them are Thomas Homer-Dixon, Lawrence LeDuc, Luděk Sýkora, Karel Maier, Timothy Colton, Aurel Braun, and Andrew Sancton. I am in debt as well to several anonymous manuscript reviewers, whose valuable suggestions enabled me to improve the final text substantially. My thanks go as well to Patricia Connor Reid for her outstanding work in redrawing several maps for the book.

Finally, special thanks go to my family: to my parents and grandparents, who passed on to me their love of Prague, their hometown; to my wife Amanda Lynn, whose love and support helps me to be all that I want to be; and to my little son Jacob, for the joy he brings into my life. This book is dedicated to the loving memory of my parents Arnošt Horák (1946–2002) and Helena Horáková (1943–2003) and my grandmother Ada Krupičková (1908–2003).

1 Introduction

Institutional Change and Government Performance in Post-communist Prague

Arriving in the Czech capital of Prague today after twenty years away, the visitor would find the city transformed. The ornate facades and narrow, winding streets of the historic core, mostly grey and crumbling in the late 1980s are now a riot of colour and shine, the local population seemingly swallowed up by crowds of foreign tourists. Once home to a sparse smattering of restaurants and shops, the ancient streets now overflow with garish souvenir stands and stylish pubs, interspersed with the Gap, McDonald's, Giorgio Armani, and countless other imports of Western commerce. Looking closer, beyond the renovated monuments and museums, the visitor would find modern office space lurking behind the facades of medieval burghers' mansions, and the occasional incongruous punctuation mark of a new glass-and-steel office building.

The boom and wealth of Prague is most evident in the city core, but the rest of the capital is also a changed world. New cars clog roads small and large, spilling over onto sidewalks and competing for space with Prague's ubiquitous trams. Vast communist-era public housing projects still form a bone-white ring around the older parts of town, but are now interspersed with a new landscape of supermarkets, retail outlets, and storage depots. Further beyond, on the city's periphery lie villages, tiny weekend cottages, and new single-family housing developments that are slowly creeping outward into the countryside.

Since the fall of communism in 1989, the forces of market-led development have changed the face of the Prague in dramatic ways. Yet there has been another, equally important process of change in post-communist Prague: after half a century of centralized administrative rule, Prague in 1990 regained a democratic system of self-government. The re-emergence of autonomous, democratic local governments is a universal component of the political transformation that has swept East Central Europe[1] since the fall of communism. Defying the predictions of many social scientists, post-communist East Central European countries have consolidated key features of liberal democratic rule at both the national and the local levels. Yet if we look beyond the basic features of liberal democracy, such as electoral pluralism and the rule of law, we find that the quality of democratic policy processes and outcomes – the performance of the region's new democratic governments – varies widely at all levels.

What factors have determined the quality of policy processes and outcomes in East Central Europe and across the post-communist world since 1989? The explosion of scholarly work on post-communist politics suggests many possible answers to this question. Indeed, given the wide array of competing explanations for the former Soviet bloc's 'return to diversity' (Rothschild 1989), much recent research has moved away from the search for general causal factors that might explain the diverse evolutionary trajectories of post-communist politics. Instead, scholars have increasingly been focusing on understanding particular aspects of post-communist politics, such as the development of political party systems and interest groups, or on specific policy spheres, such as the environment or health. This book, by contrast, is based on the premise that it is both possible and useful to analyse the performance of democratic government in post-communist polities in a holistic manner. Tracing the evolution of policy processes and outcomes in Prague across two key issue areas between 1990 and 2000, it suggests that the evolution of local government performance throughout this period was shaped by decisions that local political leaders made during the first year or two after the fall of communism.

Following local government reforms introduced by the national government in 1990, Prague rapidly developed a local government structure that placed strong powers and resources at the disposal of local political elites. The first free local elections were held in November 1990. By 1993 the winners headed a metropolitan government that enjoyed comprehensive powers in key areas of urban policy, owned strategic urban property, and received strong revenues buoyed by a booming local economy. Prague had managed to avoid the basic institutional design problems that complicated the quest for good local government performance across much of the rest of East Central Europe.

Local politics in post-communist Prague presents a puzzle: Despite having a powerful, well-organized local state apparatus, the city's government did not perform well. Local political leaders during the first decade after the fall of communism seemed unable or unwilling to develop and implement systematic policies through open democratic processes in key spheres of public concern. This study focuses in detail on two such policy spheres, transport infrastructure and preservation and development in the historic core. In the transport sphere, local politicians pursued a costly communist-era program of freeway construction in the inner city, even though the program had been a flashpoint for citizen protest in 1989 and continued to face public opposition throughout the 1990s. In addressing issues of historic preservation and development in the city's medieval core, elected officials stuck to an ad hoc, closed-door approach to decisionmaking, despite strong public and administrative pressure to develop systematic policy guidelines. By the late 1990s conflict between government and societal actors over these (and other) issues was endemic in Prague, and disillusionment with local democracy festered on both sides of this divide. The patterns of policymaking that emerged in Prague in the 1990s challenge us to move beyond a focus on the formal structures and powers of the local government. The gap between the resources available to local decisionmakers and the quality of democratic rule in Prague makes this city a critical case to study in advancing our understanding of the factors that influence the performance of post-communist government.

Some scholars sceptical about the ability of new government structures to determine post-communist political outcomes have turned to explanations that focus on the broad societal or attitudinal legacies of communism. This approach yields some useful insights, but does not tell us the whole story. Instead, I argue that the puzzle of poor government performance in Prague can best be explained by examining the broad decisionmaking environment in which the city's political leaders operated immediately following the local government reforms in 1990. Despite the introduction of new state structures, this environment included many organizational elements – such as political parties, civic interest groups, civil service bodies, and legal frameworks – that continued to embody the legacies of past political eras. I suggest that if we broaden our definition of political institutions to include these elements, a picture emerges of a complex and fluid decisionmaking environment populated by conflicting institutional orderings. This environment had a paradoxical effect on the behaviour of political leaders in Prague: It encouraged them to seek simple, short-term solutions to policy problems at the very moment when their influence over the longer-term outcomes was greatest.

This central argument is underpinned by assumptions and insights drawn from the historical institutionalist approach to political inquiry. Recent work suggests that because no single authority controls the overall pace and direction of institutional change in a democracy, state and societal political institutions rarely emerge and develop in a coordinated way. Instead, institutional origins and development trajectories are often asynchronous (Orren and Skowronek 1994: 321). Because institutions embed normative visions that reflect their particular historical origins and evolutionary trajectories, asynchronous institutional change contributes to normative friction or dissonance among institutions in a democratic political system. I call this friction or dissonance institutional incoherence.

While some degree of institutional incoherence is present even in long-established democratic polities, the phenomenon was particularly acute in East Central Europe in the immediate post-communist period, given the extraordinarily rapid political change that followed the collapse of the previous regime. The institutional landscape of early post-communist Prague, for example, included political parties and civic groups that had been designed as vehicles for grassroots anti-communist protest. It also included administrative bodies and legal frameworks that were established during the communist era and that continued to embed that era's norms of bureaucratic rationality and comprehensive planning.

In short, early post-communist political leaders typically inhabited a decisionmaking environment where state and societal institutions were structured to reflect a variety of conflicting norms of political behaviour. This was not the only challenging aspect of the early post-communist decisionmaking environment. The environment was also fundamentally new and unstable. In Prague, and across East Central Europe, political leaders were suddenly confronted with the challenge of pursuing a reform agenda on multiple fronts, and of doing so in a rapidly changing context where the longer-term effects of reform were often difficult to predict.

This combination of institutional incoherence and the unstable character of the decisionmaking environment in Prague produced the paradox outlined above. In the absence of established policy practices, political leaders faced critical decision points in individual policy areas – moments when they had to make decisions that would have an extraordinary influence over future political outcomes. The new, unstable, and normatively incoherent decisionmaking environment encouraged political leaders to make decisions based on short-term incentives. Lacking a clearly dominant normative framework for policymaking and confronted with multiple issues requiring decisions, Prague's early post-communist leaders felt overwhelmed by conflicting demands and priorities. As a result, they tended to seek the most immediately available short-term solutions to problems in individual policy areas. In an environment where many pre-democratic institutions remained in place, the available short-term solutions were not always compatible with the longer-term development of systematic and open policy-making.

This paradox played itself out in different but parallel ways in the two policy areas that I examine in this book. In the area of transport infrastructure, the city's politicians faced acute public pressure at the beginning of the 1990s to scale down the inner-city freeways program initiated during the communist era. Any such change, however, would have involved reforming Prague's transport planning institutions, which had survived the fall of communism and were strongly committed to the freeways program of the 1980s. Shying away from the complexities of reform, political leaders chose in 1991 to press ahead with but slight modifications to that program and to shut local civic activist groups out of the policymaking process. In the area of preservation and development, implementing the consensus in favour of a systematic policy for the historic core would have meant engaging in a complex process of devising goals and implementation mechanisms appropriate in the context of a private real estate market. In the absence of regulations governing conflicts of interest, the emerging property market offered political leaders the promise of immediate personal financial gain if they acted as intermediaries for real estate developers. Swamped by complex governing tasks, Prague's politicians in the 1990s turned in increasing numbers to the latter course and abandoned the quest for systematic policies for the preservation and development of the historic core.

Once these critical decisions about direction and process had been made in each policy sphere, they became difficult to reverse. In the two policy spheres examined in this study, distinct but parallel processes of 'increasing returns' (Pierson 2000a) began to entrench the consequences of early choices in the institutional landscape of post-communist Prague. In the area of transport infrastructure, a deep mistrust developed between politicians and bureaucrats, on the one hand, and civic activists on the other. Administrative institutions remained technocratic in orientation, while civic groups retained their protest focus and became politically isolated. Over time, the sunk costs of freeways construction grew, further reinforcing the existing policy orientation and the state-centred decisionmaking processes that reproduced it. With regard to preservation and development of the historic core, politicians and civil servants developed vested interests in maintaining a closed, ad hoc style of policymaking that maximized room for their discretion, and this in turn impeded the emergence of structures that could support systematic and open policymaking. In this manner, the critical decisions made early in the transformation had negative effects on the quality of democratic rule in Prague, effects that were felt throughout the rest of the 1990s.

The story of early decisions and their longer-term consequences in Prague has broader implications for our understanding of post-communist political transformations. It suggests that outcomes have been shaped neither by new state structures nor by the legacies of communism alone, but that they have also been significantly influenced by the way in which new and old institutions *interacted* to create a uniquely challenging decisionmaking environment in the early post-communist period. While Prague's early post-communist political leaders had unprecedented opportunities to shape future policy outcomes, the nature of the institutional context in which they were embedded encouraged them to focus on finding simple, short-term solutions to policy problems. Critical decisions made in individual policy areas during the early 1990s set in motion processes of increasing returns that entrenched the consequences of these decisions for the longer term.

To characterize the evolution of government performance in post-communist Prague as a tragedy of missed opportunities would be too simplistic, however. Democratic development there is by no means over. Towards the end of the 1990s a combination of factors – including the rise of a new local political party and changes to national legislation – began to put pressure on the city's leaders to improve performance. Yet the patterns of policymaking developed in the early post-communist period proved hard to change, and as of the year 2000 – the end of the study period for this book – these new pressures had led only to a few incremental changes. Once the initial period of institutional flux had passed, agents interested in improving government performance in Prague faced institutional and collective action obstacles to change that are all too familiar to those who study politics in long-established democracies.

The rest of this chapter lays out the theoretical and methodological framework upon which the argument is built. I begin by briefly explaining why I have chosen to adopt explicit evaluative standards of government performance and how I conceptualize these standards in light of existing work. I then review some of the early systemic explanations for post-communist political outcomes and use these as a springboard for developing a historical institutionalist framework for analysis, one that draws attention to the coexistence of new and old institutions in early post-communist political systems. From theory I move to the issue of case selection, discussing the merits and limitations of investigating broader issues in democratic development through a case study of local government. A brief review of the rich history of Prague's urban development comes next, followed by an introduction to the two policy areas detailed in this study – transport infrastructure and preservation and development in the historic core. I conclude the chapter with a few words on how the data for this project were gathered.

Beyond Transition: Assessing the Performance of Post-communist Government

As Robert Putnam pointed out more than a decade ago, 'the undeniable admixture of normative judgments in any inquiry about performance ... has made most scholars over the last forty years reluctant to pursue such questions' (1993: 63). Political scientists have tended to leave explicit assessment of government performance to public policy analysts well versed in the technicalities of one particular issue sphere, and the volume of political science literature that assesses the overall performance of democratic governments is correspondingly small.[2] Even if political scientists are reluctant to put them on the table, the discipline nonetheless is full of implicit normative biases, and studies of post-communist politics are no exception.

The concepts of 'transition' and 'consolidation' that dominated much writing on post-communist politics until the late 1990s rested on the premise that achieving a stable democratic order was the desired end of post-communist transformations. Since stable democracy was the goal, transition and consolidation were typically defined as stages in a process that has a definable end. Although definitions varied, transition in this literature most often meant the period between the fall of the old regime and the successful completion of the first free elections. Consolidation was usually said to be complete once democratic institutions enjoyed broad popular and elite support and were thus stable for the foreseeable future.[3]

Behind many early analyses of post-communist politics, then, was a preoccupation with the normative goal of stable democracy. The work of scholars of post-communist transition and consolidation has significantly advanced our understanding of the factors that shape post-communist political trajectories. The focus on stability, however, has left open the question of the *quality* of the democracies emerging in many post-communist states. Yet, as Herbert Kitschelt and his colleagues caution, in the longer run the stability of democratic rule may depend significantly on the '*quality of democratic interactions and policy processes*, the consequences of which affect the legitimacy of democracy in the eyes of citizens and political elites alike' (1999: 1, emphasis in original). As many post-communist states successfully developed the basic features of democracy, analysts began to turn their attention to the quality of democratic rule.

Mapping the sheer diversity of post-communist democracy is the subject of some of this recent work. John Dryzek and Leslie Holmes, in their book entitled *Post-Communist Democratization* (2002), examine twelve former Soviet bloc countries and China. Dryzek and Holmes identify fourteen qualitatively different political discourses that combine in various ways to reflect distinct degrees and paths of democratization. Other studies consider particular aspects of post-communist democratic development. Herbert Kitschelt and his co-authors, in *Post-communist Party Systems* (1999), take the emergence of programmatic political parties as one important goal of democratic development, and then explore the factors that encourage or discourage it in Hungary, Poland, Bulgaria and the Czech Republic. In her recent book *From Elections to Democracy* (2005), Susan Rose-Ackerman assesses 'policy-making accountability' – the robustness of the connection between policymaking and public preferences – in post-communist Hungary and Poland. Collectively, such recent studies illustrate the broad range of outcomes that are possible under the rubric of democracy, and contribute to the shift away from teleological accounts of transitions to democracy. This study of Prague joins a growing literature (Pickel 2002; Ekiert and Hanson 2003) that adopts the term 'transformation' to capture the ongoing and essentially open-ended nature of political change in the post-communist world.

Even as the normative focus has shifted from democratic stability to the quality of democracy, standards of democratic quality are often implied rather than made explicit. Moreover when they are explicit, they usually pertain to one aspect of democracy. Kitschelt focuses on the development of programmatic party systems, Rose-Ackerman on the character of the policy process beyond the electoral sphere. Most analysts of post-communist politics avoid altogether the language of 'government performance.'[4] The reasons for this are not hard to see: Given the diversity of political outcomes in post-communist states, there is a reluctance to impose evaluative standards that privilege some outcomes over others. Furthermore, scholars rarely agree on broad evaluative standards. Indeed, as Nikolai Petro reminds us (2004: 7-9), the earlier literature on transition and consolidation faced considerable difficulty in defining what democracy was in the first place, to say nothing of assessing the performance of governments that may be said to be democratic. The literature on government performance in established democracies likewise espouses a variety of incommensurable standards of performance.[5]

Nonetheless, since the field of post-communist political studies is full of implicit judgments about the quality of the region's nascent democracies, the reluctance of many analysts to develop explicit standards of government performance can amount to obfuscation of the object of analysis. We cannot avoid the issue of assessing the quality of post-communist democracy without denying the normative concerns that drive much of this research in the first place. The challenge is to formulate a conception of democratic government performance that can be assessed empirically, that is broad enough to capture the multidimensional nature of democratic rule, and that does not measure post-communist polities up against practically unattainable or ideologically narrow benchmarks.

The conception of government performance that I use in this study rests on a rather minimalist definition of democracy itself. Democracy is taken to mean the existence of institutionalized electoral pluralism, supported by basic political and civil rights – such as the right to free association and due process – and a functioning legal apparatus that protects these rights. This minimalist definition leaves much room for variation in the quality of policy processes and outcomes in individual policy areas, and this is where the evaluation of government performance comes in. My conception of government performance is designed to assess the quality of democratic rule consistently across multiple issue areas. The primary authority for making governing decisions in democratic political systems is vested in elected political leaders, and the conception of performance used here therefore centres on the decisionmaking behaviour of political leaders.[6] To try to move beyond the disparate array of performance measures developed by past evaluative studies of government performance, I ground my conception in the work of contemporary theorists on liberal democracy, drawing especially on Robert Dahl's 1989 volume entitled *Democracy and Its Critics*.

In his influential study of regional government performance in Italy, Robert Putnam distinguishes between two aspects of performance: effectiveness, or 'getting things done,' and responsiveness to societal demands (Putnam 1993: Chapter 3). This distinction reflects two basic axes along which the quality of any democracy varies: its *output* and the *processes* that lead to this output. Most writers who explicitly conceptualize performance focus primarily on evaluating the quality of outputs. A wide range of criteria for what constitutes good outputs has been proposed. Among the most common criteria are efficiency or 'value for money,' equity, and innovation (see, e.g., Putnam 1993; Fried and Rabinowitz 1980). Yet how do we choose which, if any, to prioritize? Focusing on efficiency tends to marginalize non-economic goals (Painter 1995); focusing on innovation may champion the hasty copying of inapplicable strategies from other settings (Keating 1991); and focusing on equity brings up the ideologically charged question of how far to go in using the policy process to mitigate inequalities among citizens. Each standard has serious pitfalls, and in choosing such substantive measures of performance we impose an external standard of the common good upon governments that are, by definition, supposed to be built on popular preferences (Dahl 1989: 305; Shapiro 1996: 121).

We can however, identify one standard of output that does seem to be universally valued in modern democracies, both established and emerging. Whatever the substantive content of outputs, all democratic governments are expected to produce and implement *policy*, as opposed to making ad hoc decisions. Policy is 'a course of action or plan' (Parsons 1995: 14) that allows governments to establish priorities among competing substantive visions of the common good and thereby to manage public conflict over these visions.[7] In assessing the performance of local government in post-communist Prague, I will therefore look at the extent to which political leaders govern in a *systematic* fashion in individual policy spheres. Do they develop broader priorities and goals that can guide individual decisions in a policy sphere? If so, do individual governing decisions reflect these broader priorities and goals? Focusing on systematic rule does not mean that we should expect post-communist governments to set rigid long-term policies in what is often a rapidly changing environment. It does mean that to govern well, political leaders must embed individual decisions in a broader context of goals and priorities.

The ability to govern systematically is one measure that we will use to assess the performance of post-communist government. But democracies must also pay close attention to the process through which policies are produced. A well-performing democratic government forges its policies in ways that are systematically *open* to input from societal actors (Dahl 1989: Chapter 10). Much of the literature on government performance ignores or downplays this aspect of performance.[8] Putnam (1993) and Kathryn Stoner-Weiss (1998), for example, both measure responsiveness through public satisfaction with policy. Levels of public satisfaction are, of course, important to democratically elected leaders, but they tell us little about the democratic quality of policymaking. After all, it is entirely possible to imagine (although more difficult to actually find) a dictatorship that enjoys strong public support because it has produced broadly acceptable solutions to policy challenges.

How, are we to assess the openness of a government to societal preferences? An obvious place to start is with the character of electoral processes. Dahl notes that elections are the one arena of democracy in which the voice of each citizen has equal weight (Dahl 1989: Chapter 20). The availability of substantively different policy platforms at election time gives citizens an important avenue of input into the governing process. This is the logic that motivates researchers such as Kitschelt et al. (1999) to focus on the growth of programmatic political parties after the fall of communism. In Prague, the presence or absence of alternative electoral programs offers one indicator of the city government's openness to societal input.

Although the positive potential of programmatic electoral competition is undeniable, it is by no means the only avenue for public input into policy processes, and it is not always the most important one. Substantively differing electoral programs have been slow to emerge in some cases (Kitschelt et al. 1999), especially at the local level of government. Nikolai Petro, in his study of regional government in contemporary Novgorod, Russia, argues that high-quality democratic rule emerged without programmatic political parties. Petro cautions us against assuming that such parties 'are the only effective vehicles for interest articulation and aggregation' (2004: 59). In the absence of programmatic parties, Petro suggests, governments can still effectively pursue open policymaking by reaching out to local civic groups and the general public in policy processes between elections.

Rose-Ackerman (2005) argues that openness to societal interests at the level of individual policy processes is critical even if voters do have the opportunity to choose among competing programs. There are many ways to elaborate and implement electoral programs, and difficult choices have to be made among alternatives. Lacking voting equality between elections, citizens face what Dahl calls 'gross inequalities' in resources and information, and these inequalities tend to skew actual policy outputs towards the interests of powerful actors in government and society (1989: Chapter 20). The extent to which political leaders make the effort to minimize such inequalities by fostering open policy processes is a second indicator of the openness of government to the preferences of the citizenry. The less electoral processes provide voters with meaningful policy choices, the more critical the existence of open policy processes becomes. As we will see in Chapter 4, Prague did not develop strong programmatic electoral competition in local politics until 1998, making policy processes the most significant mechanism for public input through much of our case study period. To assess the openness of policy processes in Prague, I look at the extent to which political leaders attempted to include in decisionmaking those directly affected by an issue, be they members of mobilized civic interest groups or the general public, and at the extent to which decision processes were transparent and information on decision options and their implications was made public.

Systematic government and open government do not necessarily go hand in hand. A government may make systematic policies while operating in a manner divorced from societal preferences, while a political system that includes programmatic electoral competition and open policy processes may produce governments that are unable to define and implement systematic policies. In Chapter 2 we will see that when local state structures are weak, there is often a trade-off between systematic and open government. At the same time, however, this book is based on the premise that the development of government that is both systematic and open *is* possible.

Numerous case studies of cities in various parts of the world indicate that local government that performs well according to the criteria elaborated above is achievable (see, e.g., Borja and Castells 1997). They show that our two aspects of performance can be mutually supporting: Open process can lend legitimacy to decision outputs and facilitate their implementation, while the practice of systematic policymaking can encourage societal involvement in governing processes. The broader context in which political leaders operate in the cities studied is very different from the post-communist context, however. We turn our attention now to the debate over which features matter most for the emergence and performance of democracy in the post-communist context.

The Study of Post-communist Politics: Institutions vs Legacies?

The sudden and unanticipated collapse of communist regimes across the Soviet bloc in 1989–91 spurred a flood of academic research. Some authors focused on retrospectively explaining the mass mobilizations against communism that social scientists had so patently failed to predict. Most, however, rushed to predict what was to come next and to prescribe the optimal route to a market economy and democracy. The dominant concern was whether and how post-communist states could successfully build stable democratic regimes from the ashes of the old political order. Although the focus of this study of Prague is the performance of a post-communist democratic government, rather than the emergence of stable democracy itself, a selective review of earlier research on post-communist politics highlights some broad themes that we can draw on in constructing an analytical framework for the study.

The field of 'transition studies' was initially heavily populated by scholars who had written on democratization elsewhere in the world, and who brought with them an institutional design perspective. For these scholars of comparative transitions, the fall of communism seemed to present a unique opportunity to apply knowledge from earlier democratization processes in the developing world and southern Europe. A core premise of this school was that 'there is a "best practice" in democracy building that can be applied across regions' (King 2000: 157) and that democracies could thus be 'crafted' (DiPalma 1990) with the right set of institutional reforms. Basic constitutional arrangements – such as legislatures, executives, and electoral laws – needed to be designed using experience from other democratizing countries. Once these arrangements were in place, political actors would adapt their strategies rationally to the new environment, and stable democracy would emerge (Geddes 1997).[9]

The early institutional design school focused on identifying constitutional arrangements that organized political power in ways that would encourage democratic consolidation. Parliamentary systems of government, with their concentration of power in one directly elected body, were deemed superior to presidential systems, which created a dangerous potential for conflict between presidents and legislatures (Linz 1994). Electoral systems based on closed party lists put together by party members were considered to be better than Westminster-style single-member plurality systems, since the former would encourage the rise of program-based parties rather than populist leaders (Geddes 1997). In other words, the belief was that if the basic constituting rules of democracy were appropriately designed, post-communist countries would rapidly develop stable democratic systems.

The development of post-communist politics since the early 1990s suggests that the early writers on institutional design were right in at least one key respect: The choice of constitutional rules clearly does make a difference for political outcomes. For example, Juan Linz's argument about the superiority of parliamentary over presidential democracy remains compelling, since the countries that adopted presidential institutions have had more trouble consolidating stable democratic rule than those that chose parliamentary institutions (Ekiert 2003: 108–10). Yet the early work on institutional design soon came under fire for at least two important reasons: its inadequate explanation of the drivers of institutional choice and its inability fully to explain differing political trajectories under similar constitutional rules.

Proposing that certain basic institutional arrangements are superior to others begs the question of what conditions support the adoption of these superior institutions. Here the institutional design literature has been criticized for producing 'excessively shallow' explanations (Kitschelt 2003: 68–73) that pay inadequate attention to contextual factors. Early authors on institutional design often argued that the new constitutional order was the result of an elite negotiation process, the outcome of which depended on the relative power of democratizing elites vis-à-vis the communist old guard (DiPalma 1990; Shugart 1997). This argument, derived from studies of transitions from military rule in Latin America and southern Europe, does not entirely fit with the reality of post-communist cases. In most countries the transition from communism was initiated by mass mobilization processes that created a stronger popular mandate for radical change than in most transitions from military rule (Bunce 2003: 172). But post-communist polities often initially lacked a 'successor elite' with a clearly defined program for change, since civil society organizations in these countries had been subject to more comprehensive state control than is the case in most military dictatorships (Elster, Offe, and Preuss 1998: 11–14).

In seeking to explain constitutional choices in a more contextually grounded manner, even researchers working from an institutional design perspective have been led beyond analysis of elite negotiations. Jon Elster, Claus Offe, and Ulrich Preuss produce convincing evidence that the design of basic constitutional rules matters a great deal to the successful consolidation of post-communist democracy, and in concluding in their study of four former Soviet-bloc countries submit that, ultimately, post-communist institutional choice itself depends to a significant extent on the pre-existing 'social and cultural capital' of a society (1998: 306–7). It seems that a convincing account of the initial institutional choices made in post-communist polities must look beyond the analytical framework presented by early theorists of post-communist institutional design.

Critics of the institutional design school point out that although the form of basic governing institutions clearly does matter, it is by no means the whole story, as post-communist countries with similar formal governing structures have followed very different paths of democratic development. Responding to this reality in a seminal essay on post-communist Russia, Stephen Holmes advances a different institutional argument to explain the difficulties of democratic consolidation. He argues that the success or failure of democratic consolidation may have less to do with the *form* of government institutions than with the presence or absence of a strong state that can back up the formal powers of political leaders with tangible resources. Whether authorities can reliably extract taxes from the population, whether the law is enforceable – such questions are crucial to democratic consolidation (Holmes 1996).

Some early analysts turned away entirely from the emphasis on government institutions and the state and argued that broad social and cultural traits inherited from the past were the principal determinants of post-communist political outcomes. Primarily long-time students of communist politics, these scholars criticized comparative transitions scholars for whom 'the past is irrelevant, as are any circumstances beyond the immediate context of the problem at hand' (Reddaway and Glinski 2001: 65). Ken Jowitt, the most influential early critic of the institutional design school, identified a number of 'Leninist legacies' that he believed would have a lasting impact on political development in the region. He argued that a political culture of passivity and intolerance would produce a political environment conducive to populist politics; a 'flattened' social structure – in which the material interests of various social groups were ill-defined – would provide a poor basis for the development of program-based parties. As a result of these and other social and cultural legacies, Jowitt asserted, political leaders lacked a constituency for seeing genuine democratic reforms through, both at the institutional and at the policy level. He predicted that 'most [post-communist transitions] will fail, and of those that succeed many will have predominantly antidemocratic-capitalist features' (1992: 208).

The focus on social and cultural legacies provided an antidote to the teleological bent of comparative work on transitions, but, its initial formulation by authors such as Jowitt has also come in for criticism. First, its predictions about the prospects for post-communist democracy were clearly too pessimistic. In response, some authors point out that the social and cultural legacies of communism are not uniformly negative. For all their anti-democratic characteristics, communist regimes did modernize many societies, introducing democracy-enabling social features such as mass education and mass communications (Ekiert 2003). In some cases elites, or what Jan Kubik calls 'cultural entrepreneurs' (2003: 343–4), have been able to draw upon pre-communist legacies to build popular support for democratic development. For example, Petro shows that in Novgorod, regional leaders drew on the popular idea of Novgorod as a bastion of democracy in medieval times to build support for present-day democratic reforms (2004). A similar interpretation, detailed in Chapter 2, helps to explain the initial institutional choices in post-communist Prague, where the pre-communist experience of metropolitan government was used effectively by policymakers to break a stalemate on local government reform in 1990.

This is a second difficulty with arguments based on assumptions about broad social and cultural legacies. In contrast to the institutional design approach, the legacies approach often produced 'overly deep' explanations in which causal mechanisms were underspecified (Kitschelt 2003). In other words, it was often left unclear exactly *how* broad features such as mass political culture and social structure translated into political outcomes. Kubik (2003) and Petro (2004), who focus on the agency of cultural entrepreneurs, suggest that this difficulty can be overcome. Analysts must move beyond simply describing inherited features of the social and cultural landscape, and pay attention to the contemporary mechanisms through which these features gain causal power.

How can the early work on institutional design and on social and cultural legacies inform an analysis of the performance of democratic government in post-communist Prague? Each approach has clear shortcomings; nonetheless, two useful points emerge. First, the design of basic state institutions clearly influences political outcomes. Although the literature on institutional design emphasizes the impact of these institutions on the emergence of stable democracy, institutional design also has implications for the quality of rule in those polities where the basic features of democracy have emerged. By structuring the formal powers and resources at the disposal of political leaders, state institutions either expand or shrink the menu of policy options available to political leaders. As we will see in Chapter 2, even within long-established democracies local political leaders who have to work with in the confines of a weak and/or fragmented local government apparatus often face insurmountable obstacles to governing both systematically and openly. Second, the legacies approach reminds us that neither institutional design itself, nor the subsequent evolution of post-communist polities, operates in a historical vacuum. Any serious consideration of the performance of post-communist governments must take into account the enduring presence and potential causal impact of the residues of communist, and possibly even pre-communist, political development.

To state that both new institutional arrangements and historical legacies matter does not tell us enough. What kinds of institutions and legacies matter most, and when and how might they influence the performance of post-communist democracies? For early scholars of post-communist institutional design, the institutions that mattered most were the basic constitutional structures of the state. Yet these provide only a broad frame work within which governing processes take place. To assess fully the impact of institutions on the performance of government we need a finer-grained account, one that looks both beyond and beneath basic state structures. For early legacies analysts, the legacies that mattered most were broad social and cultural ones. Yet these were not the only residues of the past inherited by post-communist polities. To assess when and how institutions and legacies might matter for government performance in post-communist Prague, we need to think about both 'institutions' and 'legacies' somewhat differently than the early literature did. We will build upon insights from some recent work on post-communist politics, and frame these insights in terms of a historical institutionalist approach to political inquiry.

A Historical Institutionalist Framework for Analysis

Since the 1980s, mainstream political science has rediscovered institutions. Temporarily marginalized by a behaviouralist approach to research that focused on the social and economic bases of political behaviour, institutions are now once again broadly acknowledged as key factors that influence political outcomes. Institutionalism in political science comes in several varieties, each underpinned by different starting assumptions about what institutions are and how they affect the behaviour of political actors (see Koelble 1995). The literature on institutional design discussed in the previous section usually employed assumptions drawn from the rational choice variant of institutionalism, which takes institutions as the strategic context within which rational political actors operate. By contrast, this case study of Prague joins a small but growing body of work on post-communist politics using a historical institutionalist approach (see e.g., Johnson 2001; Ekiert and Hanson 2003). Historical institutionalism provides a framework for analysing influences on the performance of post-communist governments that can steer a middle road between the ahistorical bent of early work on institutional design and overly deep historical analyses of social and cultural legacies.

Among historical institutionalist scholars there is some debate over the basic question of what counts as an institution. In this book I focus on explicitly *political* institutions, blending Peter Hall's (1986) broad definition with a narrower one favoured by Karen Orren and Stephen Skowronek (1994).[10] Political institutions, as I use the term, are formally organized elements of the political system, inside and outside the state, that do not arise spontaneously, but that are designed deliberately for a certain set of political purposes. Political institutions include state organizations such as legislatures and bureaucracies; impersonal 'mediating' structures created by the state, such as legal frameworks; and societal organizations such as political parties and interest groups. This definition of political institutions takes us beyond the constitutional focus of early work on institutional design in post-communist countries. To maintain analytical coherence, it excludes all structures that are not consciously designed for political purposes.

Insofar as they constitute organizations with members, institutions structure the actions of their members.[11] Unlike purely social organizations such as, say, sports clubs, however, political institutions are designed to influence behaviour beyond their own bounds – they are 'other-directed' (Orren and Skowronek 1994: 325). As a result, 'the matrix of incentives facing most political actors is shaped, not by a single set of institutions, but by a combination of interlocking institutions' (Hall 1986: 260). For example, although the behaviour of bureaucrats is shaped by the structure of administrative organizations, it is also influenced by broader legal frameworks, as well as by the actions of politicians and members of interest groups who are in turn embedded in their own distinct positions in the institutional configuration that makes up the political system.

In contrast to rational choice institutionalism, historical institutionalism holds that institutions affect the behaviour of actors in two basic ways. Institutions provide a strategic context that distributes power and resources in a way that makes certain goals more or less feasible, but as purposive entities, institutions are also structured to reproduce norms regarding legitimate and appropriate political behaviour (Orren and Skowronek 1994: 326). By distributing incentives such as money, power, prestige, and recognition in accordance with these underlying norms, institutions help to define what action is seen as desirable (Thelen and Steinmo 1992: 7–9).[12] In other words, institutions provide actors with power and resources that influence the *feasibility* of certain forms of political action, and they also provide actors with a set of incentives that influence the *desirability* of certain forms of political action.

Conceptualizing political institutions and their impact in this way allows us to move beyond the constitutional focus of the institutional design approach and to develop a fuller account of the institutional factors that shape the performance of post-communist governments. The basic constitutional structure plays an important role in shaping political outcomes, because it is the primary variable that determines the formal powers and resources available to political leaders. If state structures divide political power among competing actors (as presidentialism has the potential to do, according to institutional design scholars), or if state structures are too weak to back up formal powers with tangible resources (as Stephen Holmes argues was the case in early post-communist Russia), systematic and open government may simply be unattainable. Yet, even if basic state structures do make systematic and open government feasible in principle, there is no reason to expect that politicians will find it desirable to pursue systematic, open rule in practice. What political leaders decide to do is influenced by the broader overall configuration of state and societal institutions.

Although they do not use historical institutionalist language, Juan Linz and Alfred Stepan do underline the importance of this broad configuration of institutions in their volume entitled *Problems of Democratic Transition and Consolidation* (1996). They argue that while constitutional arrangements are key to the initial emergence of democracy, successfully consolidated (i.e., stable) democracies must be supported by appropriate institutional forms in a number of 'arenas' of political activity, including civil society, political parties, the administrative apparatus, the legal system, and the economy. Like constitutional structures, these arenas provide political leaders with important resources that help to make systematic, open government feasible. For example, in order to govern systematically political leaders need an administrative apparatus that can reliably evaluate the costs and benefits of various policy options. In addition, these arenas also embed norms of political behaviour. In doing so, they produce a matrix of incentives that helps to shape the desirability of systematic and open rule. For example, if political leaders encounter civil society organizations that expect to be treated as partners in policy dialogue with state actors, and if they are also embedded in a political party system that operates on the basis of programmatic competition, they will face incentives to govern openly, or else encounter civil society opposition and potential defeat in elections (Linz and Stepan 1996: Chapter 1). The feasibility and desirability of systematic and open rule are influenced by an institutional configuration that extends far beyond the basic constitutional structures of the state.

If a well-performing government depends on a broad configuration of supportive state and societal institutions, the obvious question is: How can this configuration emerge in the post-communist context? Of course, in concrete terms the answer to this question is different for every polity. We can, however, develop a theoretical framework to organize our thinking about this question, by again turning to historical institutionalism. Because institutions influence both the feasibility and the desirability of political action, historical institutionalists argue that institutions tend to be quite difficult to change and that the options for endogenous change are 'path dependent' – they are limited in scope to what is feasible and desirable within the existing configuration. As a result, most historical institutionalist analyses have treated institutions mainly as independent variables, that is, enduring organizational elements that shape the behaviour of political actors. But, as Colin Hay and Daniel Wincott point out, the approach also has the potential to develop powerful insights about the dynamics of institutional change (1998: 955–7).

The model of institutional change used by most historical institutionalists to date is Stephen Krasner's 'punctuated equilibrium' (Krasner 1984). Because of its durable and path-dependent nature, Krasner argues, an institutional configuration usually remains in place until it is in fundamental discord with underlying social and economic conditions or until it faces a major external shock. At this point, the old institutional configuration collapses, ushering in a relatively short period during which multiple paths of future development are open – what many authors call a 'critical juncture' (Pierson 2000a). During a critical juncture, the absence of a firmly entrenched political order means that political actors have an extraordinary amount of influence over the future development of the polity. Once the fundamental institutional choices have been made, actors quickly adapt to the new rules of the game, and a new political order emerges.

Krasner's model of punctuated equilibrium has been further developed by some contemporary historical institutionalists. These authors rely on a distinct set of assumptions about individual rationality as they theorize the dynamics of punctuated equilibrium. They reject the assumption that agents always act instrumentally and have full information about the consequences of their actions. Instead, they see the rationality of actors as 'bounded.' Although actors pursue their aims as best they can, they have only a limited ability to deal with complex situations, and they often have incomplete information about the context for, and the consequences of, their actions (Simon 1985). In complex situations, actors engage in 'satisficing' behaviour: Rather than choosing the best possible outcome, they choose an one that satisfies their immediate interests given the information limits and cognitive limits they face. Furthermore, since actors have limited tolerance for ambiguity, they seek to routinize behaviour – that is, to develop rules and norms that allow them to make sense of complex situations (North 2005).

Working with the assumption of bounded rationality, Paul Pierson presents two important lines of argument about institutional change that extend Krasner's punctuated equilibrium model. One line of argument proposes three reasons we cannot view institutional design during critical junctures as a wholly rational-instrumental process. First, the political actors who design institutions do not usually work on a blank slate, but are often influenced by norms of appropriateness or structural models drawn from the institutional and cultural history of their polity (Pierson 2000b: 478). Second, even if they disregard past influences and focus solely on resolving the institutional design challenges of the present, the time horizons of actors are typically shorter than the lifespan of the institutions that they are designing. This is particularly the case during critical junctures, when the fluidity of the political context makes predicting future outcomes especially difficult, and actors may heavily discount future considerations in favour of short-term objectives (ibid.: 480–3). As we will see, this issue of short time horizons is critical to understanding the paradox of poor government performance in post-communist Prague. Finally, even if actors do think long term when they design new institutions, the complexity of any institutional setting means that actors cannot foresee all results, and the new institutions are likely to have unanticipated future effects (ibid.: 483–6).

Pierson's second line of argument also deploys assumptions about bounded rationality to explain why institutions designed during a critical juncture tend to endure, even if they do not produce the intended effects. In doing so, he sharpens our understanding of the concept of 'path dependence' often used by historical institutionalists. Pierson points out that political institutions – and especially the fundamental constitutional structures of a state – are *designed* to be difficult to change (Pierson 2000a: 262; 2000b: 490–1). Furthermore, he submits, changing institutions might be unattractive to political leaders. Institutions take time and energy to set up, so change has considerable costs. In addition, boundedly rational actors must expend considerable effort to learn how to operate within a given set of institutions, and once they have done so, change becoms less appealing. Since institutions embed normative orientations, actors tend to develop normative commitments to them, making change even less attractive. A variety of 'increasing returns' processes thus tends to discourage change once a given set of institutions has emerged (2000a, 2000b).

Early writers on institutional design in post-communist polities did not use the language of punctuated equilibrium explicitly; nevertheless, their account of systemic political change closely paralleled Krasner's model. Most significantly, these writers share with Krasner the assumption that once the fundamental constitutional choices had been made, political actors would adapt to them quickly and a durable new political order would emerge. Pierson's work on increasing returns processes provides theoretical support for the view of institutional change as a process that begins with the design of new institutions during a critical juncture and is followed by path-dependent development. But, Pierson's attention to the limits of rational institutional design also suggests that actors might not choose functionally optimal constitutional rules in the first place. Working with norms and models inherited from the past, with short time horizons, and with an inability to foresee future outcomes, political actors might choose rules that do not support the emergence of a well-functioning democracy but endure nonetheless. Other authors make use of similar ideas to account for the emergence of varied – and sometimes problematic – constitutional arrangements in the post-communist world (see, e.g., Stanger 2003).

How does the punctuated equilibrium model hold up when we look at the broader configuration of state and societal institutions that shape government performance? Even a brief look at post-communist politics on the ground reveals that a key assumption of this model – that the *entire* configuration of state and societal institutions in a political system rapidly adapts to the emergence of a new constitutional order – is empirically inaccurate. A growing body of studies has identified a range of *institutional* legacies that survived the collapse of communist regimes. In examining subjects such as political party development (Kitschelt et al. 1999), civil service reform (Verheijen 1999), and the evolution of social policy (Inglot 2003), researchers observe that post-communist institutions bear strong traces of their communist or even pre-communist origins.

How can we square the persistence of such institutional legacies with punctuated equilibrium? We could argue that the punctuated equilibrium model is not useful for analysing post-communist transformations. David Stark takes this route in his work on economic reform, arguing that post-communist transformations should be seen as gradual evolutionary processes in which the continued existence of institutional legacies keeps multiple paths of future development open for an extended period (Grabher and Stark 1998). This case study of Prague takes a different view. As we will see in chapters 4 and 5, following a short initial period of flux, institutions in Prague tended to stabilize and further change became more difficult. Yet, the new institutional order that emerged in post-communist Prague was not a fully coherent alternative to what had come before, but rather contained an uneasy mix of old and new institutional elements.

To explain how and why some elements of the communist institutional order survived the early post-communist period in Prague, we need to unpack the idea of 'critical juncture' and develop a finergrained account of the dynamics of institutional change during this time. Although 'critical juncture' is a useful overall label for a period of rapid institutional change, there is, in fact, a certain fuzziness to the idea.[13] In particular, there is no clear dividing line between a period of critical juncture and the subsequent consolidation of a new institutional order. If we look at early post-communist politics up close, what we see is an initial period of flux that was *incrementally* resolved into a new institutional ordering through an accumulation of discrete decisions made by political actors. A critical juncture can thus be usefully reconceptualized as a period of flux marked by a *series* of non-simultaneous critical decision points, whose cumulative resolution results in the construction of a new political order.

Let us look in more detail at the rationale behind this reconceptualization. Some authors make a distinction between 'politics about constitutions' and 'politics within constitutions' in the post-communist transformation process. Although in some cases post-communist constitutional change has been a lengthy process (see Stanger 2003), in most cases, including that of local government in Prague, basic state structures underwent major reform very soon after the fall of communism. Most post-communist polities quickly moved beyond the critical decision point at which one path of constitutional development was chosen over others. The transformation of state and societal institutions at the sub-constitutional level, however has tended to be a slower process.

As Orren and Skowronek (1994) argue in their work on American politics, even in established democracies the broad set of state and societal political institutions rarely emerges at once or changes as a single unit, because no one set of actors controls the overall pace and direction of institutional change; instead, the formation and development of institutions are typically *asynchronous*. There are at least two reasons that asynchronous institutional change is likely to be particularly pronounced early on in a post-communist transformation process. First, although post-communist legislators can directly shape the development of many political institutions, including legal frameworks and administrative bodies, as actors whose capacity for rational-instrumental action is limited or 'bounded,' they might not have the cognitive ability to pursue simultaneous institutional reform on many fronts in a turbulent environment. Second, they might be understandably reluctant to engage in major legislative or administrative reform before constitutional questions are settled, lest their achievements be swept away.[14]

Even after basic questions of state structure have been resolved, post-communist political leaders thus initially operate in a context that includes institutions inherited from the past. In other words, even if the key choices regarding constitutional design have been made, decision-makers face multiple critical decision points at the level of 'politics within constitutions,' and these might remain unresolved for some time. In every major policy sphere, early post-communist political leaders are confronted with basic choices about legislative, policy, and/or administrative reforms that will shape the terrain for future government performance. The 'critical juncture' period of early post-communism thus involves a *series* of critical decisions that have to be made at two levels – that of constitutional design, and that of institutional design in individual policy spheres.

Reconceptualizing critical junctures as a series of critical decision points leads us away from a simple punctuated equilibrium model of institutional change. We can now think of the movement from critical juncture to new institutional order as a multi-stage process. The resolution of each critical decision point places another piece in the puzzle of a new institutional order, but no *single* decision can usher in the rapid and wholesale 'seismic shift' of punctuated equilibrium. In other words, institutional change is asynchronous, and political institutions born of differing eras typically coexist for some time during a process of transformation. This reframing can move our analysis of the factors that shape early post-communist politics beyond the less than satisfying dichotomy between institutional design and social and cultural legacies. Early post-communist political leaders in East Central Europe were embedded in an institutional configuration that included *both* new constitutional structures (once these had been adopted), *and* a variety of older political structures – the institutional legacies of earlier political eras.

Working with the conceptualization of institutional change that we have outlined, we can propose an answer to the question of how a broad institutional configuration supportive of good performance can develop: The development of such a configuration is influenced by the way in which post-communist political actors – and in particular political leaders with access to the formal levers of power – deal with a series of critical decision points that face them after the collapse of an old political order. These critical decision points include the design of new constitutional rules, but they also include the design or redesign of institutions in a wide variety of policy spheres. In every case, political leaders face a range of choices with different implications for the eventual emergence of a well-performing democracy. The obvious question that comes next, then, is: What factors increase the likelihood that early post-communist political leaders choose institutional paths that support good democratic performance?

One place to look for an answer to this question is in the character of the institutional legacies that exist during the critical juncture. This is precisely what some of the recent writing on post-communist institutional legacies examines. Although none of this work uses the language of performance, much of it implicitly asks: To what extent did inherited institutions in any one policy sphere or political arena need to be changed in order to support the consolidation of a well-performing democracy? The answers are, of course, highly varied, but Grzegorz Ekiert makes two general observations. First, in most cases the institutional legacies of communism were partly but not wholly incompatible with democratic development. In many cases institutions could be reformed rather than scrapped altogether. Second, countries that had experienced significant liberalizing reforms before the fall of communism tended to inherit legacies that were more amenable to democratic development than countries that had little or no history of reform (Ekiert 2003: 111–12).

This case study of Prague supports Ekiert's generalizations. Early post-communist Prague inherited some institutions – such as a professional bureaucracy – that could, with reform, be assets for the process of democratic governing. The absence of significant political reform in Prague prior to 1989, however, meant that, even after the initial local government reforms of 1990, many local institutions – both state and

societal – retained features that made them ill-suited to a well functioning democracy. Comprehensive reform strategies were needed to trans-
form the many communist-era state institutions that remained; such
strategic reforms might in turn have helped spur the transformation of
societal institutions, such as political parties and civic interest groups.
Yet, as we shall see, Prague's early political leaders did not always pursue comprehensive reform strategies, even though the necessary powers and resources were at their disposal. To understand why, we need to
look beyond the character of individual institutional legacies, at the
overall character of the early post-communist decisionmaking environment.

Following initial reforms to state structures, post-communist decisionmakers in Prague were embedded in a mixed configuration of old
and new political institutions. Alongside new state structures were
institutions that had changed little since the communist period, such as
the civil service, and institutions that had emerged during the period of
anti-communist mobilization, such as political parties and civic interest
groups. Each institution reflected the norms of political behaviour
appropriate to the period in which it emerged. The net result was a
decisionmaking environment that embedded a variety of conflicting
norms of political behaviour – what I call an 'institutionally incoherent'
political environment. Orren and Skowronek (1994), in their discussion
of asynchronous institutional development, suggest that some degree
of institutional incoherence is present in all democratic political systems; however, the speed with which communism collapsed in Europe
ensured that the structural and normative incompatibilities among
institutions were particularly acute in the early years after communism.
Furthermore, the decisionmaking environment that initially emerged
was highly fluid and unstable. This environment confronted political
leaders with many simultaneous reform challenges and meant that the
longer-term consequences of alternate reform strategies were difficult
to predict.

The analysis presented in the rest of this book is guided by two
main questions that follow from this characterization of the early
post-communist decisionmaking environment. The first question is:
What impacts did the character of this environment have on the
behaviour of political leaders in early post-communist Prague? I will
argue that Prague's local politicians reacted to their unstable and
institutionally incoherent environment by seeking simple, short-term
solutions in making the critical decisions that they faced in key areas

of urban policy. In a context where many pre-democratic institutions remained in place, these short-term solutions did not always bode well for the emergence of systematic and open policymaking. The second question is: What were the longer-term impacts of this decision-making behaviour? I argue that increasing returns processes ensured that the decisions made during the early post-communist period entrenched Prague's initially incoherent mix of institutional forms for the longer term, frustrating the development of systematic and open government in Prague throughout the rest of the 1990s. We will explore these two questions in detail starting in Chapter 3. At this point, let us turn to some methodological issues, and introduce the case of Prague.

Case Selection: Why Study Prague?

In conducting a case study of post-communist politics in Prague, I depart from the dominant tendency of post-communist political research, which focuses on national-level politics in the study of democratic development. The emphasis on national politics is natural, because most of the basic decisions shaping the course of post-communist democratization are made by national governments. Yet there are also important empirical reasons to study democratization at the local level. Moreover, if we select our case carefully, a local study can contribute to our understanding of post-communist transformation processes more generally. In this section, we will look in turn at the empirical and the methodological rationales for studying politics in Prague in the 1990s.

The focus on national-level studies leaves a gap in our knowledge of politics in East Central Europe. The literature on local government in the region is written largely from the perspective of public administration or policy studies. The usual emphasis is on either formal changes in the structure of the local state or policy developments in a single issue area.[15] Only a few studies, notably Harald Baldersheim and colleagues (1996) and Gabor Soos, Gabor Toka, and Glen Wright (2002), explore the development of local democracy in East Central Europe in a systematic way.[16] Both of these volumes gather a wealth of data about local politics and government, but the multitude of variables mentioned and the absence of case studies make these works valuable primarily as reference volumes rather than as causal analyses. With the exception of one unpublished study (Brunnell 2000), there is no detailed English-language case work on the dynamics of local democracy in Poland, Hungary, or the Czech or Slovak republics. This gap in our knowledge is particularly significant because throughout the region local governments emerged as major sites of political activity soon after the fall of communism.

During the communist period, local government structures in East Central Europe were the lowest tier in a centralized administrative system controlled by the parallel structures of the Communist Party. Local administrators and functionaries had sometimes gained substantial de facto autonomy from national government by the 1980s, but local councils were little more than rubber-stamp bodies for administrative and Communist Party decisions (Coulson 1995: 7–9). After the fall of communism, the region's national governments instituted wide-ranging local reforms to make municipalities self-governing. The aims were essentially two-fold. First, the reforms were seen as a way of building democracy 'from the grassroots' by dismantling the legacy of hierarchical, centralized communist rule. Second, they were seen as a way of relieving national governments of the responsibility for managing some difficult policy areas, such as public housing and social assistance, and instead placing this responsibility with a level of government that could be more responsive to local needs and preferences (ibid.: 10–11).

The local government reforms that swept East Central Europe in 1990 introduced freely elected municipal councils and gave municipalities the right to own and manage their own property. The reforms also transferred to municipal councils sole or partial responsibility over substantial areas of policy (Table 1.1). Broadly speaking, these responsibilities stayed the same across the region in subsequent years, with the exception of Poland, where municipalities took on increased responsibility for education in the mid 1990s (Levitas 1999).

In the sphere of social services including health, welfare, and education, responsibilities are usually shared with the national government, although the degree of municipal responsibility varies across the region.[17] In all cases, however, national governments have retained significant control over the regulation of service standards, so municipalities typically have little say in policy making. By contrast, in the sphere of physical goods and services – such as physical planning, roads, and public infrastructure – local councils often have primary responsibility for policymaking as well as delivery, within a broad framework established by national laws (see Coulson 1995; Baldersheim et al. 1996; Lev-

Table 1.1. Sole or shared responsibilities of East Central European municipal governments after 1990

	Czech Republic	Hungary	Poland	Slovakia
Preschools	x	x	x	
Primary schools	x[a]	x	x[b]	
Secondary schools	x			
Health care	x[c]	x		
Social welfare	x	x	x	
Public housing	x	x	x	
Physical planning	x	x	x	x
Public transport	x	x	x	x
Streets and roads	x	x	x	x
Garbage collection	x	x	x	x
Water provision	x	x	x	x
Sewage treatment	x	x	x	x
Fire protection	x	x	x	x
Local police[d]	x	x	x	x

Source: Adapted and updated from Baldersheim et al. 1996: 28–9.
[a] Maintenance of school buildings only.
[b] Optional until 1996 (Levitas 1999).
[c] Local clinics only.
[d] Many small municipalities do not have a local police force.

itas 1999). The many new responsibilities of local governments in East Central Europe greatly increased their importance as sites of political activity during the 1990s.[18] By 1999 total local government spending in four East Central European states averaged 27 per cent of all government spending in these countries, which is close to the average of 28.7 per cent for local government in the four largest Western democracies.[19]

National governments in East Central Europe quickly recognized that local government can play important roles in supporting the development of democracy. Local government can alleviate national fiscal and policy overload, train a new generation of democratic political leaders, and provide space for political involvement by citizens at a level that is accessible and close to their daily concerns (Baldersheim and Illner 1996: 4; Kirchner and Christiansen 1999: 1–3; Zsamboki and Bell 1997: 178–80). To fulfil these functions, however, local government must perform reasonably well, something that cannot be taken for granted. By studying the links between institutional change and performance, we can better understand the factors that might prevent local government from fulfilling its potential contribution to the broader development and consolidation of democracy.

This study of Prague in the 1990s also has broader theoretical ambitions. The case of Prague can serve as a microcosm within which theories of democratic development produced by scholars of national politics can be evaluated and refined. In relying on insights from local politics to draw inferences about democratic politics at other levels of government, the study follows a small but often-cited body of political research that includes Robert Dahl's *Who Governs?* (1961) and Robert Putnam's *Making Democracy Work* (1993). Any study of local government that claims to have broader relevance must confront the issue of whether local and national political systems are comparable. This study is based on the premise that they can indeed be comparable, but that comparability depends on the questions we ask and the cases we select.

Perhaps the most fundamental difference between national and local governments is that local governments lack sovereignty. This limits the range of questions that we can ask at the local level if we seek to 'scale up' our insights to national politics. We cannot, for example, scale up insights about the design of basic state institutions, since the basic structures of the local state are usually designed by higher levels of government. To understand the factors that shape local state institutions, we have to examine multilevel political processes that have no clear parallel at the national level. While local interests and local history did shape Prague's post-communist state structures, the final decisions about local government reform were made at the national level. Had they not been, the local state in post-communist Prague might have looked quite different.

We cannot generalize, therefore, about the dynamics of post-communist constitutional design from a local case. If we select the case carefully, however, a local study can give us much insight into the factors that shape the *quality* of democratic rule in the post-communist world. One advantage of studying government performance at the local level is that a local polity may be easier to study holistically. It is no coincidence that explicit studies of government performance usually focus on local politics.[20] Because the scale and scope of local government are more restricted than those of national government, local politicians typically face a narrower range of critical governing issues and deal with a smaller set of actors. This makes holistic studies of performance more feasible at the local than at the national level. The feasibility factor is all the more important if one adopts an approach to explanation that examines change in political processes over time, which adds another layer of complexity to the analysis. However, to speak to broader theoretical concerns, we cannot go too far in the interest of feasibility. The political unit we choose to study must be large enough to contain a range of institutions and actors broadly analogous to those present in a national polity. Studying a large city such as Prague, with its complex set of legislative, executive, administrative, legal, partisan, and civic institutions, allows us to draw more convincingly generalizable inferences than studying a smaller municipality would.

A brief look at the literature on local and urban politics in established democracies suggests that even in large municipalities, local politics is qualitatively distinct from national politics, however. For one thing, the performance of urban governments in established democracies tends to be lower than the performance of their national counterparts (Keating 1991). Scholars often connect these performance problems to the weakness of the local state. Subject to strict jurisdictional, fiscal, and territorial limitations on their authority, urban municipalities often lack the powers and resources that might allow systematic and open government to develop. For us to scale up our insights, our case study must be one in which the local state is uncommonly strong. Prague, as we have already noted, is such a case, since it rapidly developed a resource-rich metropolitan government after the fall of communism. The contrast between the power of the local state and the shortcomings of government performance in Prague makes it a 'critical case,' one that we can use to explore influences on government performance above and beyond the basic design of state structures. We will return to the broader implications of this in the final chapter. Right now, let us sketch a backdrop for the study by briefly looking at the history of urban development in Prague up to the end of the communist period.

Ten Centuries of Urban Development in Prague

For hundreds of years Prague has been the urban hub and governing centre of the Czech lands, its fortunes as a city closely tied to the fortunes of the Kingdom of Bohemia and, later, the Czechoslovak state. Founded as the royal seat of the Přemyslid dynasty in the ninth century, Prague developed in the late Middle Ages into a conglomerate of three autonomous municipalities: the Old Town (Staré Město), the Lesser Quarter (Malá Strana), and the Castle District (Hradčany). During the reign of Charles IV in the fourteenth century, when Prague became seat of the Holy Roman Empire, the city grew rapidly, reaching a population of about 50,000. In 1348 Charles founded the New Town (Nové Město), the first major planned urban development on the territory of Prague (Hrůza 1992, Ledvinka 2000). It was also at this time that many of the Gothic structures that still grace Prague's historic core were built.

In the late sixteenth century, Prague enjoyed another boom under the Habsburg Emperor Rudolf II, who made the city his imperial residence. A layer of Renaissance architecture was added to the tapestry of historic buildings already in place. During the following 250 years, Prague was gradually downgraded to the status of a provincial city in the Habsburg Empire. Although its historic building stock survived several wars and occupations and grew to encompass outstanding examples of Baroque and Classicist architecture, the city grew slowly, and in the early nineteenth century it was still largely confined to the walled perimeter delineated by Charles IV in 1348.

This began to change during the latter half of the nineteenth century, when industrialization spurred rapid growth. Prague became the major manufacturing centre of the Czech lands, and the population of the metropolitan area more than quadrupled between 1850 and 1920, from about 170,000 to about 730,000 inhabitants (Hrůza 1992: 80–1). A ring of dense suburbs, characterized by four- or five-storey walk-up apartments laid out in planned fashion along rectangular street grids, arose around the walls of the historic medieval town. In the late nineteenth century the city walls were torn down, uniting the new suburbs with the old core. Although most of the core retained its old building stock, a major and highly controversial redevelopment scheme involved the tearing down of the entire medieval Jewish ghetto and its replacement with expensive apartment blocks at the end of the nineteenth century (Maier, Hexner, and Kibic 1998: 33–8).

Escaping significant damage during the First World War, the city continued to grow during the 1920s and early 1930s as the capital of the newly independent Czechoslovak Republic. By 1940 the population of the urban area had surpassed one million. Parts of the medieval New Town underwent significant redevelopment to accommodate modern banking and commercial interests, although much of the historic building stock remained intact. New lower-density suburbs of single-family houses grew up between and around the dense apartment blocks of the late nineteenth century. Although plans for major development of the city's roads infrastructure foundered, a dense network of trams was extended throughout the city (Maier, Hexner, and Kibic 1998: 41–4).

In contrast to most other major East Central European cities, the physical fabric of Prague survived the Second World War and Nazi occupation largely intact, due to the early incorporation of the Czech lands as a protectorate of the German Reich in 1939. The war years and the post-1948 communist regime's initial focus on developing rural areas brought urban development in Prague nearly to a standstill between 1940 and the late 1950s (Maier, Hexner and Kibic 1998: 49; Sýkora 1995). Combined with a lack of housing construction during the pre-war Depression years, this stagnation resulted by the late 1950s in a severe housing crisis. This was subsequently addressed through the construction of massive, uniform state-owned high-rise housing estates, modelled on the Soviet template of the *mikroraion* (micro-region), on open land surrounding the city (Smith 1996). Overall, housing of this type for over half a million Prague residents was built between the 1950s and the 1980s (Sýkora 1995: 323).

The older areas of the city experienced very little change during the communist era. As Jiří Musil points out, the abolition of a market in land in communist cities made location an 'almost irrelevant economic variable,' and city centres often saw 'far fewer physical and functional changes ... than [those in] cities of similar size in countries with market economies' (1993: 901). With a few notable exceptions, the older parts of Prague saw little demolition or construction. Instead, the high costs of upkeep for older building stock meant that many such buildings fell into disrepair, and large amounts of residential and commercial space in the historic core were abandoned or came to be used for storage (Sýkora 1993: 284–5). The 1980s renovation of a small number of historic monuments in the city centre did little to offset such losses.

The lack of upkeep of older buildings reflected the low priority given by the communist regime to public goods and services in general – these were classified as 'non-productive' sectors in an economic system that focused on continually increasing production (Enyedi 1996: 115; Maier, Hexner, and Kibic 1998: 87). Such underinvestment meant that Prague accumulated significant deficits in the maintenance not only of housing, but also of public utilities such as water, sewers, and lighting. One partial exception to this was transport. In line with its collectivist philosophy, the communist administration focused heavily on the development of public transit, during the 1970s and 1980s a high-capacity Metro (subway) system was built to complement existing tram and bus lines. Roads infrastructure also saw significant, although less

Figure 1.1. Urban zones of Prague

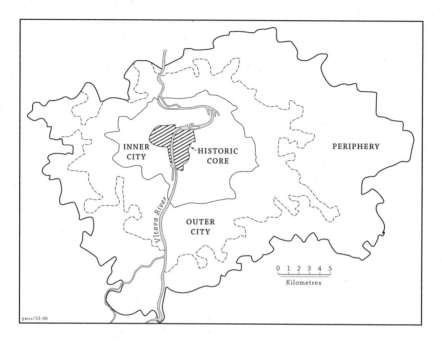

Source: Adapted and redrawn from Hrůza 1992: 78.

intensive, investment with the partial construction of a freeways network in the 1980s.

By the end of the communist period the urban fabric of Prague
reflected the influence of centuries of development. In 1990 the city was
by far the largest urban centre in what was soon to become the Czech
Republic. With about 1.2 million inhabitants, Prague had about three
times the population of the Czech lands' second-largest city, Brno, and
more than twice that of Bratislava, the capital city of the Czechs' federal
partner, Slovakia. Centuries of growth had produced a city with four
clearly differentiated urban zones; these are shown in Figure. 1.1.

The boundaries of the first zone, the historic core, correspond to the
city walls built by Charles IV in the fourteenth century. The historic
core straddles the Vltava River, nestled in a basin rimmed by steep hills.
Although it comprises only 1.6 per cent of the city's total area, it has the
largest contiguous collection of historically valuable buildings in East

Central Europe, an eclectic mix of Gothic, Renaissance, Baroque, and Classicist architecture. In 1990 it housed just over 60,000 people or about 5 per cent of the city's population, far below the historical peak of 170,000 achieved in 1900 (City Development Authority 2000: 11). Given the dilapidated state of most buildings in 1990, the residents tended to be elderly and poor (Musil 1987). At the same time, however, most of the city's high-paying professional jobs, as well as most of its government and cultural institutions, were located here. About 200,000 people, one-third of the city's total workforce, were employed in this small area (Hrůza 1992: 79).

The second zone, the inner city, comprises the apartment-block suburbs and villa districts that were built between about 1850 and 1940. Much of the inner city sits high above the historic core, on the hills that surround the medieval centre. Covering about 15 per cent of the city's total area, the inner city in 1990 housed about half of Prague's population. While the social character of its residents was mixed, as elsewhere in the city much of the housing stock was in need of major maintenance and repair work. The inner city also provided about 300,000 jobs in a wide variety of industrial and service positions, or 45 per cent of all employment in Prague (Hrůza 1992: 79).

The outer city forms a third distinct urban zone in Prague, comprising nearly 40 per cent of the city's metropolitan area. It is characterized by large-scale high-rise housing developments built between the 1950s and the 1980s, interspersed with parks, fields, and woodland. In 1990 this part of the city housed over 40 per cent of its population. While the population here remained socially mixed, the inexpensive, assembly-line technologies used to build the area's housing estates ensured that here, too, maintenance of housing was quickly becoming a problem.[21] About 200,000 people worked in the outer city in 1990, but most of this work was concentrated in a few large industrial zones on the eastern edge of Prague. Many of the housing estates lacked basic amenities and had the character of 'dormitory suburbs' for residents who commuted to work elsewhere (Hrůza 1992: 79). The periphery, administratively joined to the city during the communist era, forms the final urban zone of Prague, and covers about 40 per cent of the city's territory. In 1990 the periphery was a landscape of agricultural land, forest, and parkland, dotted by villages that housed about 50,000 people (ibid.: 79–80).

Despite decades of policy privileging the development of smaller urban centres, Prague in 1990 remained the administrative, cultural and educational hub of the Czech Republic, and dominated the country's trade and commerce.[22] This was reflected in the overrepresentation of associated employment sectors in the city. With about 12 per cent of the Czech Republic's population, Prague had 29 per cent of the country's jobs in finance and insurance, 57 per cent of the research jobs, and 77 per cent of jobs in foreign trade (Dostál and Hampl 1994: 39). It was this privileged position in the Czech political and economic system, interacting with national market reforms in the early 1990s, that would produce in Prague the rapid urban changes described at the beginning of this chapter. Such rapid changes were not unique to Prague. The dominance of East Central European capital cities in their respective national contexts contributed to extraordinary changes in all of these cities soon after the fall of communism. Let us look at some of them and the policy challenges that they produced, to set the stage for an examination of the politics of transport and development of the city centre in Prague.

The Challenges of Urban Development in East Central European Capitals

Across the industrialized world, the management of urban development is at the heart of what local political leaders in cities do. The levers of social and economic policy are largely under the control of higher levels of government, but urban governments play a crucial role in managing social and economic change through their control over the physical fabric of the cities. Since the reforms of 1990 East Central European local and urban governments, too, have conformed to this pattern. Although control over social and economic policy has remained partial and uneven, they have gained primary responsibility for regulating physical development and for providing physical services such as transport, drinking water, and waste disposal.

In the 1990s the governments of capital cities in East Central Europe faced broadly similar challenges in these new fields of responsibility. East Central European capitals are what central-place theorists in geography call 'dominant capital cities.' Warsaw, Budapest, Prague, and Bratislava are the largest urban centres in their respective countries. In all cases except that of Warsaw, their population is greater than the combined population of several of the next-largest urban centres in the country.[23] Throughout decades of communist policy privileging industrial development and the growth of smaller urban centres, these cities maintained diversified economic bases that included large service and knowledge-based sectors (Dostál and Hampl 1994).

With their well-educated workforces and concentration of govern-

Table 1.2. Capital city per capita GDP as a percentage of national
per capita GDP, 1995–97

	Warsaw (Poland)	Budapest (Hungary)	Prague (Czech Rep.)
1995	136	181	184
1996	144	185	186
1997	150	187	190

Source: Eurostat 2001 data tables.
Note: Figures for Warsaw include all of the Mazowieckie region,
an area substantially larger than metropolitan Warsaw itself.

ment and financial services, these cities quickly became gateways for foreign capital and engines of the region's emerging market economies (Dostál and Hampl 1994). In all four cities, unemployment levels remained well below national averages throughout the 1990s,[24] while per capita GDP was well above average (see Table 1.2). The attractiveness of these cities for domestic and foreign capital has been reflected in the rapid rise of employment in the financial and other business sectors, which has offset a decline in industrial employment that came with post-communist economic reform (Sýkora, Kamenický, and Hauptmann 2000, Bárta 1998).

The prosperity of post-communist capital cities in the context of an evolving market economy produced two key sets of policy challenges in relation to urban development – the regulation of real estate markets and the provision of public infrastructure investments long neglected by the communist regime. In the early 1990s national initiatives to liberalize prices and privatize real property transformed the character of real estate development in East Central European capitals. Comprehensive government management of the housing, retail, and office sectors gave way to a system dominated by the market initiative of private investors. The change was especially dramatic in the non-residential property sector, where prices and rents were liberalized very quickly, and where investor interest was greatest because of the rapid development of commercial activity (Sýkora and Šimoničková 1994; Sýkora 1998; Ghanbari-Parsa and Moatazed-Keivani 1999).[25]

The opening of the real estate market produced pressure for the commercial development of property with high market values, whether prime office space in historic city centres or open space near major roads on the urban periphery. This pressure frequently led to conflict between private developers and local residents joined by defenders of historic and/or environmental values – what Marcuse (1996) calls conflict between the 'exchange value' and the 'use value' of urban space. The frameworks for real estate liberalization and privatization were introduced by national governments, but management of the ensuing conflicts through planning and regulation instruments was put on the shoulders of local political leaders. Elaborating and implementing priorities for managing real estate development has thus been a key challenge for local governments in East Central European capital cities.

The capitals' newfound prosperity also heightened the need for investments in public infrastructure. During the communist era the focus on industrial productivity resulted in chronic underinvestment in key elements of urban infrastructure such as housing, transport, water supplies, and waste treatment (Enyedi 1996: 115–16).[26] After 1989 local governments, encouraged by national legislation, attempted with varying degrees of success to divest themselves of the fiscal burden of public housing through large-scale privatization schemes (see, e.g., Bodnar 1996; Hegedus and Tosics 1998). However, in other areas of provision of public infrastructure local government retained a leading role.

Changes in patterns of consumption associated with prosperity, such as increased automobile ownership and higher production of consumer waste, put growing pressure the aging public infrastructure. This led to intense controversies over public investment priorities in the 1990s. Infrastructure development projects such as freeways and waste disposal sites frequently faced opposition from environmental interests and groups of adversely affected local residents (Judge 2000; Enyedi 1999; Pickvance 1996), challenging local political leaders to develop and implement investment priorities that balanced the demands of growth with concerns about the quality of life.

In this study of politics in Prague between 1990 and 2000, two issue spheres that embody the broad urban development challenges just outlined are examined in detail. These are the construction of Prague's freeway system and the regulation of preservation and development in Prague's historic core. The decision to examine these particular two issue spheres was guided by three considerations. First, because good performance of democratic government involves openness to citizens' interests, I chose policy spheres that were the subject of significant public concern at the beginning of the 1990s. Second, because the broad challenges outlined above relate to two distinct functions of local government – the regulation of market activity and the provision of physical services – I chose one sphere to represent each function. Finally, because my assessment of performance focuses on the actions of local political leaders, I chose two policy spheres over which they, rather than political actors at higher levels of government, had primary authority. This consideration led me to exclude from my study the overall issue of housing, which, although clearly an important aspect of urban development, remains subject to extensive national intervention in Prague and across East Central Europe. By tracing how local politicians responded to policy challenges in these two issue spheres through the 1990s, this study builds a dynamic account of the factors that influenced the performance of the municipal government in Prague after the fall of communism.

Collecting the Data

Before we turn to our detailed account of politics in post-communist Prague, a few words about data collection are in order. As a case study in political development, this book relies on somewhat different data than a variables-oriented analysis would. Variables-oriented analyses usually focus on establishing cause and effect by looking at how certain factors (variables) correlate across a range of different cases at one particular point in time. Although this study does examine two separate policy spheres, and engages in comparisons with other cities described in previously published literature, the main consideration used here to determine cause and effect is the interplay of various factors over time (1990–2000) in one city. To acquire reliable data on this interplay, evidence was gathered from a variety of sources.

Most of the primary source material for this book comes from two research trips to Prague (January and February 2000 and May to November 2000), and it includes written documents, print media reports, and interviews with key actors in municipal politics. Although some archival research was conducted, the political upheaval of the early post-communist period meant that many official records have been misfiled or lost. As a result, much of the documentary evidence for this analysis comes directly from interview subjects. It was largely through their generosity that I was able to collect several dozen studies and reports, as well as an invaluable store of memos, letters, minutes, and fact sheets. Reports from the print media are a second major source of information. Drawing on a variety of print and electronic archives of daily and weekly newspapers, I surveyed a total of 946 articles from twenty-nine publications, dating as far back as 1983 but focusing on the 1990–2000 period, with three main aims in mind: to identify key issues and actors, to generate ideas about possible links between patterns of institutional change and the behaviour of political leaders, and to gather background information on the public face of municipal politics that could serve to inform interviews.

Interviews with key actors in municipal politics, which were conducted in Czech, are a major source of the primary evidence for this project. I identified an initial set of about twenty interview subjects – politicians, administrators, and representatives of local civic interests – through my analysis of the print media; additional subjects were selected on the basis of recommendations by earlier interviewees. A total of forty-three interviews with forty-two individuals were conducted between June and November of 2000 (see Appendix). The interview process served three main purposes: filling in information about institutional structure and institutional change that was missing in the written record; gaining access to 'inside accounts' of political and policy processes; and perhaps most importantly, collecting information on the actors' understanding of their own actions and motivations, their perceptions of other actors in local politics, and their political priorities and attitudes. Responses were analysed with reference to these three basic aims. In the interest of obtaining open responses on potentially sensitive topics, I chose to conduct all interviews anonymously. When citing interviews in the text, I therefore keep identifying elements to a minimum. Where some identification is relevant to the information being provided, I identify subjects only in terms of general descriptive categories such as 'transport planner' or 'executive board member' to preserve confidentiality.

2 The Structure of Government in Prague: Building a Strong Local State

Prague's Contemporary Local Government in Comparative Perspective

In 1990 new national governments across East Central Europe introduced sweeping local government reforms that established a local political autonomy long absent from East Central European politics. Local government soon became a significant focal point of political activity. Nowhere were the new responsibilities of local authorities put to the test more rapidly than in the capital cities, where the impact of national market reforms was immediate and profound. To meet the challenges of urban development in post-communist capitals such as Prague, local political leaders needed to have at their disposal strong and well-organized powers and resources. In many cases East Central European national governments did not follow through on the local government reforms of 1990 in a way that would have provided political leaders in the capital cities a strong local state apparatus.

Working from an institutional design perspective, the literature on local and urban government in post-communist East Central Europe devotes much of its attention to this problem. After all, as Stephen Holmes (1996) observes, democracy cannot succeed if governments lack the resources and scope of authority to produce public goods and services. Two aspects of local institutional design stand out as particularly important for the region's capital cities: the need for strong, autonomous fiscal resources and the need to secure a citywide concentration of authority in policy areas where a citywide coordination of governing tasks is required. Evidence from both Western and East Central European contexts suggests that if either of these institutional features is absent, local politicians face trade-offs with regard to systematic and open policymaking that worsen the prospects for strong local government performance. Fortunately, in the 1990s local government in Prague was substantially better off on these two fronts than its counterparts elsewhere in East Central Europe.

Local governments the world over often lack fiscal autonomy that is commensurate with their policy responsibilities, and as a result they are dependent to varying degrees on external funding. As many writers on Western local and urban politics point out, a democratic local government without sufficient revenue sources of its own often faces a trade-off. If it chooses to maximize its reliance on its own sources of revenue, it will in the process limit the range of policy initiatives that it can pursue. If it chooses to seek resources from external actors – such as national governments or the business community – to pursue a more fiscally demanding governing agenda, this agenda may become hostage to external interests, thereby limiting openness to the preferences of local citizens (Leo 1996: 91; Stone 1989).

Prior to 1990 the local state structures of East Central Europe depended almost entirely on national sources of revenue. Local finances were components of the national budget, and transfers from national accounts made up the majority of local revenues. Whether as grants for specific purposes or subsidies from the annual national budget, these transfers gave national governments strong control over local policymaking (Baldersheim and Illner 1996: 11). Throughout the region, the 1990 local government reforms were accompanied or followed by financial reforms that decreased transfers from national governments and increased the fiscal autonomy of municipalities.

As Table 2.1 shows, transfers from national governments as a share of local revenues decreased markedly in post-communist East Central Europe in the 1990s,[1] although there were major differences among countries. In Poland fiscal reforms in 1990 immediately made central transfers a minority source of local revenue, but these later grew again as local governments took on greater responsibilities for social services (Levitas 1999). By contrast, in the Czech Republic analogous reforms did not come into effect until 1993, but they had an immediate and lasting impact. By the late 1990s the dependence of Czech municipalities on fiscal transfers was far below the Western average of 35 per cent to 45 per cent (Keating 1991: 63). In Hungary the fiscal reform process and its effects were much more gradual, and at the end of the 1990s local governments remained strongly dependent on such transfers (see also Hegedus 1999).

Table 2.1. Central transfers as a percentage of total local government revenues, 1991–99

	1991	1992	1993	1994	1995	1996	1997	1998	1999
Poland	25.5	30.5	28.1	30.3	29.4	33.0	32.3	34.1	39.7[a]
Hungary	67.0	61.6	64.1	63.0	59.8	55.1	50.9	50.1	49.3
Czech Rep.	86.0	78.7	30.3	27.6	26.8	37.5	24.7	23.7	22.0
Prague	75.3	63.9	29.8	12.7	12.5	21.3	18.7	16.7	15.8

Sources: Adapted and calculated from International Monetary Fund 2000, Levitas 1999, Bosáková 1999, Czech Statistical Office 1993, 1994, Prague budget documents.
'Central transfers' equal targeted grants plus general subsidies from national government.
[a] Includes the new *voivod* (regional) level of government.

The pattern of Prague's dependence on transfers (also shown in Table 2.1) broadly mirrored the pattern across the Czech Republic. After 1993, however, the city's dependence was well below the national average, as well as below the averages in neighbouring states. Buoyed by its strong economy, Prague reaped the fiscal benefits of guaranteed proportions of national taxes (primarily income tax), stipulated in the 1993 reforms, and these monies rapidly replaced national transfers as the dominant source of municipal revenue. The rates of such taxes – a major source of local government finance across East Central Europe – were subject to national control, limiting the extent to which the city could determine its overall level of revenues. Nonetheless, the rapid decline in transfers meant that from 1993 on Prague's political leaders were freer to choose how the city spent its money than were their counterparts elsewhere in the region.

Fiscal autonomy is of limited benefit to local political leaders if the sum of the fiscal resources they can muster does not match the breadth of their responsibilities. As discussed in Chapter 1, the responsibilities of local governments across East Central Europe vary by country, and they changed significantly in Poland during the 1990s. As a result, we cannot easily compare the fiscal strength of municipalities across the region by comparing total per capita expenditures. We can, however, get an approximate picture of relative fiscal strength by looking at two measures: the proportion of total expenditures spent on capital investments (mainly on physical infrastructure), as opposed to operating expenditures, and annual per capita capital investment figures (see Table 2.2).

Low and/or rapidly decreasing proportions of capital investment

Table 2.2. Capital investments of local government as a percentage of total expenditures

	1991	1992	1993	1994	1995	1996	1997	1998	1999
Hungary	16.4	19.3	19.3	22.7	17.2	15.9	19.4	19.9	17.6
Poland	26.0	23.5	25.4	18.6	19.3	19.0	20.7	19.9	13.2
Czech Rep.	30.8	39.3	35.2	37.1	38.2	30.7	33.8	32.9	31.4
Prague	34.6	49.9	43.9	49.1	45.9	40.4	41.1	42.0	33.0
Budapest	12.8	16.2	19.2	21.0	20.6	16.2	13.5	16.6	15.6

Sources: Adapted and calculated from International Monetary Fund 2000, Bosáková 1999, Levitas 1999, Czech Statistical Office 1993, Ebel and Simon 1995, Prague and Budapest budget documents.
Of the drop in capital investment of Polish municipalities between 1993 and 1994, 3%–4% is due to differing definitions of 'capital investments' used in Levitas 1999 (1991–93 figures for Poland) and International Monetary Fund 2000 (1994–99 figures).

are often a sign of local fiscal weakness and stress. In the immediate aftermath of the 1990 local government reforms, local political leaders in East Central Europe universally complained of insufficient finances (Swianiewicz et al. 1996). Data on capital investments tell a more complicated story. Municipalities in Hungary and in Poland spent similar proportions of their budgets on capital investment in the 1990s: 18.6 and 20.6 per cent, respectively. Despite the complaints of local politicians, this compares favourably with Western figures. In the late 1990s, municipalities in Germany, Britain, France, and the United States spent on average 16.7 per cent of their budgets on capital investments (International Monetary Fund 2000).

The real contrast here, however, is between Hungary and Poland and the Czech Republic. Czech municipalities averaged a much stronger 34.8 per cent of total expenditures as capital investment. This difference is even more pronounced if we look at the capital cities; Table 2.2 presents figures for Prague and Budapest.[2] Capital investment as a proportion of Budapest's expenditures tended to be somewhat below Hungary's averages in the 1990s, but in Prague it was far above Czech national figures.

Compelling as these differences are, the overall higher proportions of capital investment in the Czech Republic might partly be explained by the fact that Czech municipalities do not fund primary education, a major outlay for local governments in Poland and Hungary. Yet municipalities in Poland, Hungary, and the Czech Republic all have similar responsibilities for provision of physical infrastructure, the

Table 2.3. Municipal capital investment per capita (in U.S.$)

	1991	1992	1993	1994	1995	1996	1997	1998	1999
Hungary	79.76	118.66	122.74	158.49	107.34	93.51	115.16	122.69	109.72
Poland	28.80	29.11	34.90	38.50	49.80	67.77	76.30	81.37	88.95
Czech Rep	n.a.	n.a.	105.30	139.4 5	184.13	186.15	155.74	156.19	159.95
Prague	n.a.	n.a.	225.34	314.41	374.56	359.55	296.72	301.24	252.08
Budapest	48.82	71.37	81.76	95.23	97.82	71.69	70.72	87.78	84.74

Sources: Adapted and calculated from International Monetary Fund 1999, 2000, Bosá-ková 1999, Levitas 1999, Czech Statistical Office 1993, 1995, 1997, Ebel and Simon 1995, Prague and Budapest budget documents.
Exchange rates used for calculation are annual averages for each data year.

dominant component of capital investment by local governments. We may therefore approach fiscal strength from another angle, comparing per capita capital spending in absolute terms; these data are shown in Table 2.3.[3]

By this measure, Hungary's municipalities appeared to be substantially wealthier than their counterparts in Poland in the 1990s, although still not as wealthy as Czech ones. In the city comparison Prague once again clearly emerges on top. In per capita investment terms, it was much wealthier than the average municipality in the Czech Republic, Poland, or Hungary, and clearly outpaced Budapest, the region's largest capital city. Indeed, on average it invested almost as much per capita in the 1990s as Western local governments did: U.S.$302.97, compared with an average of U.S.$387.13 for local governments in the four largest Western democracies.[4] In terms of fiscal autonomy and health, Prague's local government rapidly emerged as one of East Central Europe's strongest.

Post-communist East Central European urban governments experienced another key institutional design problem: the territorial fragmentation of authority. The reforms of 1990 were followed by widespread municipal territorial fragmentation. In large measure this was a natural reaction by newly elected local politicians to the history of centralized administrative rule during the communist era (Baldersheim et al. 1996: 25–6). Nevertheless, the negative impact of excessive fragmentation on the quality of urban development policy outweighed any anticipated benefits in terms of enhanced local democracy.

Many authors, especially those writing in the American public choice tradition, defend such fragmentation asserting that it enhances openness to public preferences in distinct parts of the city (see Ostrom et al. 1988). While the debate is by no means closed, evidence from a wide variety of cases suggests that with respect to metropolitanwide urban development issues this goal is often undermined by other problems stemming from fragmentation. Small municipalities rarely have sufficient resources for large-scale infrastructure investment. Furthermore, a multiplicity of decisionmaking bodies may lead to deadlock on issues – such as transport – that cross fragmented municipal boundaries (Keating 1991: Chapter 5). If fragmented governments are to overcome this deadlock, they must delegate authority to specialized bodies, compromising their openness to the local citizenry. Like fiscal weakness, metropolitan fragmentation may produce a trade-off between pursuing systematic policies and remaining open to local preferences.

In the 1990 reforms, the capital cities of East Central Europe were treated as unique cases whose structure was designed independently of the structure of other municipalities. All of the region's capital cities came out of the 1990 reforms with multi-tier local structures that included a citywide level of government and at least òne subsidiary level of district or borough government. In most cases, the net result was a fragmentation of municipal authority that hampered the emergence of systematic, open government. Let us look at Budapest and Warsaw as examples, and briefly contrast them with the case of Prague.

Budapest was divided into twenty-three boroughs in 1990, and each had the status of an independent municipality. The boroughs were granted the right to issue construction permits and became owners of land and housing units (Enyedi 1999: 6). A directly elected council for the whole city was to coordinate development through land use planning. This division of responsibilities soon led to deadlock on metropolitan issues. Gabor Demszky describes but one of many such instances: 'A famous case was a planned sewage treatment plant for which the municipality assigned an area in the master plan but the district [borough] refused to accept. Under those circumstances, it was a problem without a solution: the municipality did not allow any other use of the assigned area, while the district did not issue a building permit for the plant' (1998: 68).

In an effort to address such difficulties, the governing system in Budapest was significantly centralized in 1994. The city council's powers in urban development were expanded to include planning that was binding on the boroughs; and the city got some control over borough budgets. But another problem of fragmentation remained: Budapest proper is surrounded by seventy-eight suburban municipalities. Until 1996 there was no coordination of urban development between the city and the suburbs, and conflict over priorities was endemic. In 1996 new national legislation created the Budapest Metropolitan Development Council as a coordinating body. This council was dominated, however by appointed members from national ministries, and thus accountability to the local public was sacrificed in the name of coordinated development (Enyedi 1999: 7–8).

Warsaw also came out of the 1990 reforms without an effective concentration of urban development powers at the citywide level. The City of Warsaw, which – like Budapest – does not cover the entire metropolitan area, was initially divided into seven boroughs that each had independent municipal status. As in Budapest, these boroughs owned property and had responsibility for most urban services and construction approvals. The city council for all of Warsaw, which had responsibility for urban planning, was indirectly elected from the ranks of borough councillors, leading to frequent conflict within the council among divergent borough interests (Suraszka 1996: 375; Judge 2000: 11).

In 1994 the Polish government reorganized Warsaw, increasing the size of the central borough and dividing it into seven districts, each with its own council and power over issuing construction permits (Judge 2000: 37). Metropolitan Warsaw now had another level of local government, which further fragmented authority over urban development. In 1999 regional reforms carried out with a view to Poland's European Union membership introduced yet another new level of elected local government, the *powiat*, or county. The new county covered the same geographical territory as the City of Warsaw, but had its own powers, mostly in the field of social services. Throughout the 1990s the metropolitan area also had a *voivod*, or regional, council with responsibility for regional planning. Warsaw thus had five levels of sub-national government, each with some responsibilities for urban development. The result was extremely slow policymaking and frequent deadlock (Judge 2000).

By contrast, Prague's post-communist local government structure was characterized by a much greater concentration of authority. In the 1990 reforms Prague became a single municipality with a directly elected city council. The municipal boundaries encompassed all of Prague's urbanized and suburban area, as well as a substantial portion of the surrounding countryside. The council elected from its ranks an executive board and the mayor, and these wielded much of the city's day-to-day decision making power. As Annemarie Hauck Walsh submits, in her classic comparative study of urban government, 'concentrated executive power facilitates progress in coping with urban-development problems,' because large, infrequently meeting city councils tend to get overwhelmed by micromanagement in the absence of strong executives (1969: 105).

The 1990 reforms subdivided Prague into fifty-seven boroughs of widely varying size, and gave each its own elected council but did not make them independent municipalities. The city subsequently delegated administration of a number of services – most notably with regard to public housing – to the boroughs, but it maintained control over urban development. The city alone could own property and approve land use plans, although use of considerable property and the right to approve detailed development plans for specific areas were delegated to the boroughs. Planning permits and construction approvals were officially issued by municipal administrative bodies, but the executive board had the power to organize these bodies and appoint their personnel, which gave it an important indirect level of control.

In sum, post-communist Prague rapidly developed one of the most fiscally powerful local governments in East Central Europe, with a concentration of urban development powers at the citywide level. Why and how did this happen? If we look at the political conditions under which the local government reforms were carried out there is no immediately apparent answer. On the contrary, starting in 1990 the Czech national government espoused an agenda of radical, centrally led market reform that had little place for strong local government, and in the Czech Republic as a whole the local reforms of 1990 resulted in extreme municipal fragmentation.[5] These forces had an impact on the evolution of local government structures in post-communist Prague, but they were counteracted in crucial ways by the city's long history of strong metropolitan governing institutions.

Origins and Growth of Prague's Local Government to 1939

Prague was never a typical East Central European municipality. The capital and largest city in the Czech lands, Prague for centuries had institutions whose scale and scope of operations surpassed those of most other municipalities in the region. By the same token, it was perennially torn both between the quest for local autonomy and the desire of higher levels of government to curtail its autonomy, and between internal fragmentation and the search for a unified administration that could govern the development of the whole city. The interaction between these two tensions to a large extent shaped the development of the city's local government structures until 1939.

The origins of self-government in Prague date back to the thirteenth and fourteenth centuries, when four autonomous towns emerged – the Old Town, the Lesser Quarter, the Castle District, and the New Town – each governed by its own town council. During the next four hundred years the formal powers of the town councils waxed and waned, depending on the strength of their political influence vis-à-vis higher levels of government. Repeated attempts to unify the towns failed because of either infighting among local elites or intervention from higher levels of government afraid of the political and economic power of a unified city (see Ledvinka 2000: 13–29; Ledvinka and Pešek 1990: 4).

The successful unification of Prague's four medieval towns finally occurred in 1784, when the Habsburg Emperor Ferdinand I decreed their union as part of his empirewide drive to modernize administration. The new city council was placed under imperial supervision; in 1797 it was abolished altogether, ushering in five decades of absolutist administrative rule. During the first half of the nineteenth century Prague developed the foundations of a modern, professionalized civil service which came to be called the Magistrát (Ledvinka 2000: 63–6). This modern administrative apparatus – one that had the capacity to govern an emerging industrial metropolis – was, paradoxically, a consequence of the Habsburg imperial project of curtailing local political autonomy.

The revolutions of 1848 that shook the very foundations of Habsburg authority brought renewed self-government to Prague, within the framework of a new Municipal Code that applied to all of the Czech lands. The city's propertied burghers regained the right to elect a city council (*Zastupitelstvo*) with autonomous powers, which in turn elected from its ranks an executive board (*Rada*)[6] and the mayor (*Primátor*). In addition to basic responsibilities such as the budget and appointments to the Magistrát, Prague's autonomous powers (sometimes called 'own powers') included most areas directly pertaining to urban development – such as property management and the construction and maintenance of roads, lighting, sanitation, and water systems. When the Habsburg administrators introduced a Building Code in 1866, Prague and the suburbs that had started to spring up around it were given autonomous control over construction and urban planning

(Maier, Hexner, and Kibic 1998: 34). In addition to implementing council decisions on all of the above matters, the Magistrát carried out 'transferred powers' on behalf of the imperial administration. It received funding for the latter – which included keeping birth, death, and marriage registers and managing conscription and tax collection – from the imperial government and was subordinate to it in terms of policy in these areas of competence (Ledvinka 2000: 69).

During the next seventy years of rapid urban growth, Prague's civil service apparatus grew quickly to meet the needs of the new industrial metropolis. The city founded a series of municipal enterprises, such as the gasworks, the waterworks, and the tram service (see Horáček 1998: 177–215). The need to fund associated infrastructure investments led the city not only to borrow extensively, but also to get involved in large-scale speculative real estate dealings. By far the largest and most controversial of these was the decision in the 1890s to raze the medieval Jewish ghetto in the centre of the Old Town and redevelop the area as a high-end residential zone (Ledvinka 2000: 90–6).[7]

By the late nineteenth century, booming new suburbs stretched far beyond the medieval boundaries of Prague, and the city frequently ran up against geographical limits to its power to manage development. Both the city and the suburban municipalities increasingly made use of urban planning and design instruments, but there was little coordination among them. In the 1890s the city launched a campaign to annex the suburbs, whose total population was about to surpass that of Prague proper. The suburbs enjoyed the proximity of city services that they did not have to pay for, so they resisted annexation (Ledvinka and Pešek 1990: 4–5). With only a couple of exceptions, Prague's suburbs remained autonomous until after the First World War.

By 1920 Prague's suburbs themselves had begun to feel a need to coordinate planning and services with the city, and local opposition to annexation weakened (Ledvinka and Pešek 1990: 5–6). In this context, the newly independent Czechoslovak national government that emerged after the First World War issued the Law on Greater Prague in 1920. The city's administrative area expanded almost ten-fold to cover the entire metropolitan agglomeration. The new metropolis was governed by a two-level structure, with power centralized at the citywide level. Greater Prague became a single municipality comprised of nineteen boroughs, each with an elected council. But the powers of the boroughs were minimal and their budgets depended on the budget of the city (Ledvinka and Pešek 1990: 6).

The new City of Prague had a city council, now elected through universal suffrage, and from its ranks the city council elected an executive board and the mayor (Ledvinka 2000: 74–5). The distinction between own powers and transferred powers was retained, with both being administered by a Magistrát whose employees and structure were set by the city council. The new system was decidedly council–centred, with all significant 'own power' decisions directly in the hands of the council and its standing committees, as opposed to the executive board. The city retained autonomous control over a wide range of functions relating to urban development, including: municipal finances and property management; the provision of transport, sewage, lighting, water and other physical infrastructure; and the granting of building permits (Ledvinka and Pešek 1990: 6).

The national government was anxious to see Prague develop in a way that befitted its new status as a national capital, so the new practice of urban planning was taken out of local hands. In 1920 the national government established the State Commission for Regulation, a body appointed by and responsible to the national Ministry of Public Works. It was this body, rather than Prague's city council and the Magistrát, that developed the first overall land use plan for Prague (Maier, Hexner, and Kibic 1998: 41). Thus, 'the most significant legal document for urban development was beyond the control of local authorities ... the city's construction administrators could not make autonomous decisions regarding any territory in Greater Prague, and had to seek the Commission's approval for every intervention' (Ledvinka 2000: 106).

The commission emerged in a context of a local public politicized over preservation issues in the wake of the razing and redevelopment of the Jewish Ghetto at the turn of the century. Not responsible to local politicians or local public opinion, the commission found itself the target of widespread criticism when it unveiled its master plan for Prague in 1929 – complete with ambitious proposals for a new network of high-capacity roads and large modern buildings in the historic core. As a result, Prague's first master plan was never approved and few of its elements were realized (Maier, Hexner and Kibic 1998: 41). Prague's urban growth continued to be regulated in piecemeal fashion. In the historic core, new development was almost completely banned in three districts (the Old Town, the Lesser Quarter, and the Castle District) and strictly regulated in the fourth (the New Town). Prague's rapid growth during this period largely reached outward, and the core retained most of its old building stock.

Despite its lack of planning powers, Prague's city council was heavily involved in managing urban development throughout the interwar years. Under the leadership of Mayor Karel Baxa, who headed a coalition of political parties that governed the city uninterruptedly between the world wars, Prague further developed its municipal enterprises and launched a program to acquire municipal property. By 1936 the city had some 120 municipal enterprises and owned 679 buildings (including theatres, schools, hospitals, libraries, and rental housing units), close to a thousand pieces of urban real estate, and dozens of tracts of field and forest (Ledvinka and Pešek 1990: 8, 98).

This property brought the city some revenue. But Prague's large-scale infrastructure development program – which included the construction of rental housing, schools, and social welfare institutions (Horáček 1998: 300) – required massive investment. Throughout the interwar years, the city got a substantial proportion of its revenues from a wide range of local fees and taxes, most notably the rental tax and the property transfer tax (Ledvinka 2000: 93). These sources did not cover the city's capital investments, however, and municipal officials turned to long-term borrowing to raise funds for their ambitious construction program (Horáček 1998: 300).

Prague under Communist Rule

The Nazi occupation of 1939–45 brought an end to Prague's self-government, and elected politicians were replaced by Nazi appointees. Liberated in 1945 after six years of occupation, Prague failed to fully regain its local autonomy. Anxious to put ideals of popular democracy into practice and to abolish vestiges of Habsburg administrative rule, the first postwar democratically elected Czechoslovak government introduced major local government reforms. Prague lost the dual system of own and transferred powers, while the boroughs were renamed districts and lost their limited autonomy. All local government power was formally vested in the hands of a citywide Central National Committee (Ústřední Národní Výbor, UNV), consisting of an assembly and an executive board. In contrast to the interwar years, most powers of decision were given to the executive board (Ledvinka 2000: 85).

Originally meant to strengthen the role of local elected officials vis-a-vis the state administration by abolishing transferred powers, in practice this unified system of local authority paved the way for a transition to a local state managed by the Communist Party of Czechoslovakia

(KSC) and national government ministries. This transition began even before the communist coup in February 1948, since Prague's first post-war UNV assembly had not been elected, but rather appointed as a transitional body by the national government (Ledvinka 2000: 85). After the coup, the country's new communist leaders replaced most non-communist local politicians with communist political appointees chosen by the Ministry of the Interior. Formal elections did take place in 1954 and every three years thereafter, but henceforth all candidates were preselected by the KSC. Nearly four decades of Communist Party domination of the city's representative bodies followed (Horáček 1998: 450–2).

Intent on making Prague's local institutions into efficient instruments for building a new socialist order, the new regime at first retained the highly centralized model of decisionmaking introduced in 1945, with most powers of decision vested in the UNV's executive board. This system was now fully integrated as one of fourteen regional (*kraj*) administrations in a unified national system of administration, and lost all self-government powers. The assembly and executive board were directly subordinated to the national cabinet. Prague's administrative bodies, no longer called the magistrate, were subordinated to national ministries. The city lost its autonomous sources of revenue, and its budget became wholly dependent on national subsidies. Prague was redivided into sixteen districts, each governed by a District National Committee (Obvodní Národní Výbor, ONV) that had very limited powers. Informally, all of these bodies were also controlled by the parallel structures of the KSC, producing the classic communist-era 'dual subordination' of local political bodies to both higher levels of government and parallel party structures (Ledvinka 2000: 86–7).

After five years, the executive-centred character of this system proved to be too cumbersome, producing an overload of responsibilities at the top. Reforms at the end of the Stalinist period in 1954 strengthened the formal powers of the UNV assembly vis-à-vis the executive board. Another reform initiative in 1960 redivided the city into ten districts, renamed the UNV the Prague National Committee (Národní Výbor Prahy, NVP), and further increased the assembly's formal powers by introducing a system of standing committees (*komise*) under assembly control. This system, illustrated in Figure 2.1, remained unchanged until the end of communist rule (Ledvinka 2000: 86–7).

In practice, such structural reforms had little impact on the exercise of power. The NVP assembly and executive board remained dually subor-

Figure 2.1. Formal lines of authority in Prague at citywide level, 1960–89

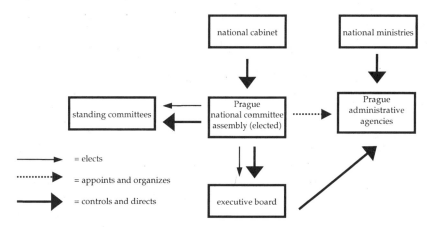

Source: Adapted in simplified form from Grospič 1983.

dinated to higher levels of government and to the parallel structures of the KSC (not shown in Figure 2.1) until 1989. De facto, these bodies were the primary arms of Communist Party authority in the city. The composition of the last NVP assembly before the 1989 revolution underlines the point. The assembly had 207 deputies, of whom 70 per cent were KSC members, 15 per cent were members of smaller parties under KSC control, and the rest were 'independents' who had been hand-picked by KSC officials (calculated from Prague National Committee 1989).

Despite the tight control over representative bodies, over the years, higher-level authorities and Communist Party officials slowly stepped back from micromanaging the city's affairs. As a result, Prague's administrative bodies gradually developed substantial autonomy in policy development and implementation. The massive nationalization of property that followed the communist coup in 1948 and 1949 had officially eliminated the City of Prague as a corporate property holder. In practice, though, most formerly municipal land and enterprises remained municipally managed, the stock augmented further by confiscated private holdings (Ledvinka 2000: 98). During the late 1950s the management of many other services, such as public housing, was decentralized from national ministries to the citywide national committee (UNV) or the district national committees (ONV) (Ledvinka

2000: 99, 108). By 1960 city administrative bodies and municipally run enterprises managed the majority of social and economic services in Prague, with the exception of industrial enterprises.

Despite this decentralization, until the early 1960s planning was still the responsibility of national ministries, resulting in a cumbersome asymmetry in which city affairs were administered locally but planned nationally (Ledvinka 2000: 87). The national government addressed this issue in 1961 by assigning urban development and planning powers to the City of Prague. This change opened the door to the creation of many new Prague-level planning and development institutions. A new Chief Architect's Office (Útvar Hlavního Architekta, UHA) was given full responsibility for formulating and overseeing the implementation of master plans for Prague's development. The General Investment Office (Útvar Generálního Investora, UGI) was created to manage the many municipal construction companies. A host of specialized planning and development agencies, such as the Transport Engineering Institute and the Prague Centre of State Monument Preservation and Nature Protection, also sprang up (Ledvinka 2000: 108).

During the remainder of the communist era, this conglomeration of of planning, investment, and construction institutions continued to expand, through many organizational changes. Along with the expansion of municipally managed services, such as housing, health, education, and retail, this brought the total number of municipal employees in Prague up to a staggering 154,000 by 1975 – or more than 25 per cent of the city's entire workforce (Ledvinka 2000: 100). Political decisions within the Communist Party, channelled through local assemblies and executive boards, continued to provide the initial impetus for major urban development projects, such as Prague's massive housing estates and the subway system. Administrative bodies remained dually subordinate to both national ministries and the Communist Party, which controlled the purse strings for projects through the unified system of national accounts. During the 1970s and 1980s, however, the KSC increasingly took an arm's-length approach to governing urban development, and the city's planning and investment bureaucracy acquired correspondingly increased control over urban development policy.

This relative autonomy is clear from the recollections of long-time bureaucrats interviewed for this project: 'We often had trouble convincing political representatives of the merits of a project,' recalled a transport planner, 'but once we had succeeded in doing that, we pretty much had free rein to develop it ... The only common problem was a lack of funds to finish what we had started' (Interview 29). 'Overall, I'd say that as professionals we got more respect from politicians during the old regime than now,' observed one former preservation official. 'There was the occasional nonsense that we fought in vain, like the destruction of the Těšnov railway station. In general, though, I'd have to say that our opinions were taken seriously' (Interview 19).[8]

Throughout the communist era, development was guided by a series of detailed land use plans that dictated zoning and infrastructure development for the entire territory of Prague. Again, the broad outlines of these plans were set by national Communist Party priorities, but the details were increasingly left to local planners and administrators. An initial plan from 1953 remained largely unrealized, but the 1964 plan successfully introduced a policy of mass housing development on the city's outskirts that stayed in place through the rest of the communist era. The 1975 master plan furthered this policy of outward growth, coordinating Prague's development with that of the surrounding region. By the time the last communist-era plan was passed in 1985, fiscal constraints had led to a scaling back of development initiatives, and the plan focused mainly on completing the many housing and transport projects already under way (Maier, Hexner, and Kibic 1998: 51, 54–7). The planned outward growth of the city was accompanied by further territorial expansion. A total of fifty-one surrounding municipalities were annexed to Prague in two waves, in 1967 and in 1974. This increased the city's total area about three-fold, to 496 km^2, and placed sizeable rural areas within its boundaries (Blažek et al. 1994: 76). The historical growth of Prague's municipal boundaries to this point is shown in Figure 2.2.

The geographical expansion of the city produced a complicated three-tier administrative structure. The annexed municipalities, reduced in number from fifty-one to forty-six through some amalgamations, retained their local national committees (Místní Narodní Výbory, MNV) with basic control over local affairs. The ten already-existing district national committees (ONVs) were charged with administering additional functions for adjacent MNVs. In the late communist era, there was the Prague National Committee (NVP), which had most citywide planning and development powers; ten ONVs that administered social service functions, such as public housing and schools, for their own territory and that of the MNVs; and forty-six MNVs, which had limited local power over items such as community centres, parks, and shop licences (Blažek et al. 1994: 77–8).

By 1989 the local state in Prague was larger and possessed more resources than ever before. Its central organizing feature was a three-

Figure 2.2. Historical growth of Prague's municipal boundaries

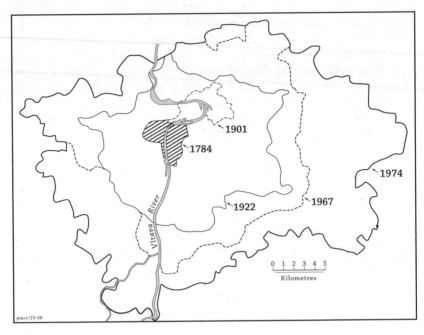

Source: Adapted and redrawn from Hrůza 1992: 77.

tier system of administrative institutions that planned and delivered urban development and public services in the context of a centrally directed economy. The influence of the Communist Party in Prague was exercised primarily through a system of national committee assemblies (one NVP, ten ONVs, and forty-six MNVs), all subordinate to the national government. Over time, the KSC became less involved in the day-to-day governing of the metropolis, creating significant space for the autonomous activity of urban development administrators working, for the most part, at the citywide level. The existence of this powerful set of institutions would have a strong impact upon the reconstitution of local self-government after 1989.

The Rebirth of Local Self-Government: The 1990 Law on Municipalities

In November 1989 the wave of popular mobilization against East Central Europe's communist regimes reached Czechoslovakia. Within a few short weeks the country's political elites, no longer able to rely on all–important Soviet military support, gave in to the demands of hundreds of thousands of protesters who packed the streets of Prague and other major cities. Roundtables between KSC leaders and representatives of the opposition umbrella group, Civic Forum, hammered out power-sharing agreements through which Civic Forum would replace 45 per cent of Communist Party delegates in national and local representative bodies with its own activists, producing interim assemblies that would govern until the first free elections in late 1990.

In Prague the process of replacing communist delegates in the local assemblies took place at all three levels (NVP, ONV, and MNV) in February 1990. Free local elections were scheduled for that November. But the first order of business was a fundamental reform of the basic structures of local government, a task that the still valid Czechoslovak federal constitution of 1969 delegated to the Czech National Council, the representative assembly for the western half of the Czechoslavak federation. As it was across East Central Europe, the re-establishment of autonomous local government in the Czech lands was seen as an integral part of the transition to a democratic political order. For Prague two key laws laid down much of the basic framework for the development of a self-governing city: the Law on Municipalities (no. 367/1990), and the Law on the Capital City of Prague (no. 418/1990).

The Law on Municipalities was passed in September 1990 and came into force on the day of the first free local elections, 24 November 1990. It laid out the broad framework for local government, within which a specific law for Prague was worked out. In designing the law, the Czech National Council worked with the chairs of regional administrative bodies, representatives of the Association of Cities and Towns (Svaz Měst a Obcí), and Prague's first post-communist mayor, Jaroslav Kořán (Lidové Noviny 1990a). Intent on overturning the communist-era model of local administration, the drafters of the law turned to the tradition of pre–Second World War local government.

The Law on Municipalities abolished the communist-era system of national committees dually subordinated to the national government and the Communist Party. It re-established municipalities as legally autonomous entities, entitled to own property and to prepare their own budgets (par. 4),[9] and once again, it granted 'own powers' to them. Own powers included: managing physical services such as water, lighting, roads, and sanitation; managing municipal property;

collecting and setting rates of local fees (laid out in a separate law, discussed below); keeping public order; and managing certain limited aspects of health, social services and education. In addition, for the first time since the downfall of the Habsburg Empire, the power to approve land use plans was vested in elected municipal officials (par. 14.1, par. 36.1).

As it had been before 1939, the primary responsibility for managing the municipality's own powers was given to directly elected municipal councils (*Zastupitelstva*). These councils, which were to hold meetings open to the public, were given power to approve all major own power municipal decisions, including the creation of municipal enterprises and the sale or acquisition of property. They could pass by-laws (*vyhlášky*) in all areas pertaining to the municipality's own powers. In addition, city councils were to approve land use plans, elect from their ranks an executive board (*Rada*) and the mayor (*Starosta* in smaller municipalities and *Primátor* in large cities), and decide which councillors, if any, would be employed on a full-time basis (par. 36.1).

Compared with the governing structure in Prague before the Second World War and the communist-era structure after 1960, the Law on Municipalities increased the powers of the executive board. This concentration of power in the executive reflected the concern of the legislation's drafters with encouraging effective and cohesive local leadership (Lidové Noviny 1990a). Executive boards, which would meet behind closed doors, were given responsibility for the day-to-day management of municipal affairs, including the right to control and direct the activity of administrative bodies in areas of municipal jurisdiction. In addition, they had personnel and organizational control over the municipal civil service as a whole, including the right to create new departments and appoint their heads, and the right to appoint the municipal secretary, that is, the chief administrative officer. Executive boards also were given the right to create and appoint standing committees, which had been creatures of the city council during the pre-communist period (par. 45).

The drafters of the law were concerned as much with promoting the development of political parties at the local level as they were with encouraging effective and cohesive local leadership (Lidové Noviny 1990a). As a result, they shied away from introducing a strong-mayor model of government. Instead, they turned to Czech historical precedent and reintroduced the model of a mayor as 'first among equals.' Like the executive board, the mayor was to be elected from among the ranks of the city councillors, and had only a few powers separate from those of the board as a whole, involving ceremony, external representation, and emergencies (pars. 52–55). Czech municipalities would thus be run by a strong but collective executive body, which offered relatively little independent power to mayors.

The Law on Municipalities also re-established the responsibility of municipalities to carry out the 'transferred' tasks delegated to them by the national government. As had been the case before 1939 these functions were to be paid for by the national government and were subject to regulation and review by national ministries. They were, however, to be administered by the same bureaucracy as areas of municipal jurisdiction (par. 21.2, 21.3). In large cities such as Prague, the municipal bureaucracy regained the traditional designation of 'Magistrát.' Local politicians were given no policymaking power in areas of transferred competence. Significantly, however, executive boards would have the potential to influence decisions in areas of transferred power indirectly, through their control of personnel appointments and the organizational structure of municipal administrative bodies. Furthermore, through responsibility for land use planning instruments, councils also gained opportunities to influence the way in which many transferred powers, such as land use permits and historical preservation controls, were exercised.[10] The lines of authority in Czech municipalities according to the Law on Municipalities are shown in Figure 2.3.

In specifying the range of transferred powers to be delegated to the municipal level, legislators ran up against the issue of differentiation between small and large municipalities. During the communist era, small municipalities had been governed by local national committees (MNV), medium-sized ones by district national committees (ONV), and larger cities by city national committees (such as Prague's NVP). In each case, the administrative bodies of these units had had different sets of powers. Furthermore, the communist state had been divided into administrative regions, which were now abolished, since they were seen as symbols of a bloated bureaucratic machine (Geussová 1990). The Law on Municipalities created out of this complexity two categories of municipalities with different transferred powers. Small municipalities that had had MNVs retained MNV-level powers. Larger municipalities that had had ONVs or city NVs received ONV-level powers and some, although not all, regional–level powers (par. 60). Prague, however, was in a unique position among municipalities; it was the only municipal unit whose

Figure 2.3. Formal lines of authority according to the 1990 Law on Municipalities

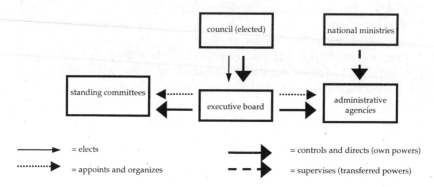

boundaries covered all of what had been a region. The precise assignment of powers transferred to Prague was left open, as it would be dealt with in a separate new Law on the Capital City of Prague.

The Rebirth of Local Autonomy: The Law on the Capital City of Prague

In Prague, the process of preparing the new Law on Municipalities raised little debate or controversy. Instead, during the spring and summer of 1990 the city's interim political representatives focused on the preparation of the Law on the Capital City of Prague. All interested parties agreed that Prague ought to return to the pre-communist tradition of being governed by a separate law that reflected the city's unique status. Opinions differed greatly, however, on the shape that this document should take. The key controversy was over whether Prague should be governed in a centralized or decentralized fashion.

This controversy pitted politicians and bureaucrats from the ONVs and MNVs against representatives of the NVP and the national government. ONV and MNV politicians, assembled in the Prague Council of Cities and Towns (Pražská Rada Obcí a Měst, PROM), argued that in the new era of democracy Prague needed to be governed in a decentralized way so that it could be responsive to the wishes of the local citizenry. This position was supported by some citizens' groups that had emerged out of the anti-communist protest of 1989 (Pešek, Pithartová, and Pospíšilová 1990). These 'decentralists' proposed that Prague be a confederation of independent municipalities, bound together only by voluntary cooperative agreements (Ledvinka and Pešek 1990: 9).

By contrast, representatives of Prague's interim NVP and many national legislators claimed that the decentralists – at least the ONV and MNV politicians among them – were less interested in local democracy than in preserving their newly found positions of power (Interview 33). They argued that the historical record in Prague demonstrated the superiority of a strong centralist model. In the summer of 1990, the Prague council of the Civic Forum movement issued an endorsement of this centralist vision:

> While there is certainly no quick recipe for fixing [Prague's] accumulated problems, historical experience does provide us with a relatively optimal model for the organization of Prague and for finding a way out of the crisis of a neglected metropolis: a return to the successful interwar model of Greater Prague as a single municipality ... we dare say that only a strong executive board heading an integrated metropolis will be a sufficiently strong partner for the Czech and Federal governments, and for large international investors in negotiations over the conditions of their functioning on the territory of Prague. Only an internally strong city government can rationally manage city property (assuming the city's property will be returned by law) and thoughtfully link property investment to satisfying the needs of the city and its boroughs. (Ledvinka and Pešek 1990: 9–10)

Accordingly, the interim NVP assembly drafted a law on Prague, which was endorsed by the Czech government in August 1990. It reinstated the interwar model of Prague as a single municipality divided into boroughs, which would have elected councils but would not have municipal status, meaning that they could not own property and would not have a right to autonomous sources of revenue (Czech National Council 1990). Although the draft did propose to grant boroughs a few autonomous powers, it raised a storm of protest from decentralists (Lidové Noviny 1990b; Pospíšilová 1990). They complained that boroughs would be dependent on the city for their property and budgets, and accused the drafters of the law of behaving paternalistically towards citizens who were assumed to 'not [be] ready to manage their own affairs' (Pešek et al. 1990).

As a result of this outcry, PROM was invited to help develop a second draft. Historical arguments regarding the importance of a unified municipal unit once again won out over decentralist objections. 'We had modern historical experience on our side, and that was an argument that couldn't be ignored,' says one Prague politician who was involved in the drafting process. 'The decentralists only had Prague's distant past, which wasn't exactly very relevant to the needs of a modern metropolis, as well as some fairly obvious self-interest' (Interview 41). In addition, advocates of centralism pointed to the activities of some long-time ONV and MNV bureaucrats after the fall of communism as evidence of their 'real' motives for embracing decentralization. They noted the proliferation in 1990 of cases in which ONV or MNV staff took advantage of the inexperience of new local politicians to profit from managing state property under their control and argued that only a centralized system of local government could introduce clear accountability and put a stop to such practices (Šindelářová 1990, Plechát 1990). In the end, the Law on the Capital City of Prague, passed in October 1990, retained a local government structure strongly centralized at the metropolitan level.

The new law – which, like the Law on Municipalities, came into force on 24 November 1990, the day of the first free local elections – made Prague a single municipal unit with a city council, executive board, mayor, and bureaucracy (Magistrát), set up in accordance with the Law on Municipalities (par. 1).[11] The city was divided into fifty-six boroughs, whose elected and administrative institutions were organized according to the Law on Municipalities, but which lacked municipal status. Borough boundaries corresponded with those of ONV and MNV units during the previous regime (par. 2). This continuity with past boundaries was a concession to ONV and MNV politicians and administrators, who if they could not have powerful boroughs were at least dead set against amalgamations or boundary changes (Interview 11). The net result was that Prague had many more boroughs than it had had during the interwar years. They varied immensely in terms of population, from nearly 144,000 to a mere 218 inhabitants. The former ONVs formed a cluster of large, urban boroughs with over 30,000 people each, while the former MNVs formed a ring of small boroughs around them (Blažek et al. 1994: 81).

As a municipality, Prague got all of the standard own powers of Czech municipalities. The law granted boroughs some of these powers, most notably the power to approve development programs (but *not* land use plans) for their territory,[12] develop their own budgets, establish and manage enterprises, and manage property delegated to them by the city. Other powers could be delegated to boroughs by the city by way of a city charter (*statut*) to be passed later on by the city council (par. 8, par. 24). Boroughs could not actually own property and had no access to autonomous sources of revenue. The division of property and revenues between the city and the boroughs was also left to codification in the city charter (par. 20).

Prague was the only territorial unit that had also been a region before 1990. The drafters of the Law on the Capital City took advantage of this fact to mandate continuity in the structure of transferred powers in the city. City administrators got the full range of what had been regional powers (par. 14), and Prague thus gained the most powerful local administration in the post-communist Czech Republic. Borough offices formerly at the ONV level got ONV-level powers, while borough offices at the MNV level got MNV- level powers (par. 14). In other words, the Law on the Capital City of Prague retained the three-tier administrative system introduced in 1974, in which administrative bodies in the ten large boroughs carried out functions for their own territory, as well as for the territory of adjacent small boroughs that had more limited administrative powers. As was the case with own powers, the city council had the discretion to decentralize more transferred powers in the future through the mechanism of the city charter (par. 20).

Even though the Law on the Capital city of Prague established a strong metropolitan authority, some analysts argue that the city still experienced the territorial fragmentation that was characteristic of other post-communist East Central European capitals. Wisla Suraszka groups Prague with Budapest, Bratislava, and Warsaw as a typical East Central European capital city in which boroughs got 'vast prerogatives' after the fall of communism, and 'the city government found it increasingly difficult to cope with [their] aspirations' (1996: 375, 379). Since Suraszka bases her interpretation partly on interviews with city-wide political leaders, this conclusion is understandable. Following the municipal elections in November 1990 (see Chapter 3), these politicians faced pressure from the boroughs to further to decentralize powers and resources. But a closer look at the sphere of urban development reveals that most key powers and resources remained citywide.

The Law on the Capital City gave boroughs autonomous powers to manage property delegated to them by the city, but the city remained the sole owner of municipal property. Even before the scope of the city's property became clear (see below) the boroughs demanded the delegation of municipal property on their territory (Lidové Noviny

1991b). Passed by the city council in June 1991, Section II of the city charter did delegate the management of much property to the boroughs. It generally consisted of existing physical amenities and services – such as schools, parks, recreational centres, and most significantly, the city's massive public housing base. By contrast, despite strong objections from borough politicians the city retained control over most of its valuable open land, and included in the charter provisions for regaining control of property that it might need for urban development (Lidové Noviny 1991a, 1991b).

By retaining control over strategic municipal property, the city council retained the resources necessary to complement its power to approve land use plans for the city. Furthermore, most urban development bodies, including land use planning and historical preservation offices, remained at the citywide level. Although these were formally state administrative bodies operating in areas of 'transferred power,' the citywide executive board could strongly influence their functioning by exercising its personnel and organizational powers over them. In the case of planning bodies, in fact, 'transferred' status was little more than a formality, because the city council had to approve any planning documents that they produced.

The development permits process, another 'transferred' area of competence, also remained largely centralized at the citywide level. In the Czech Republic's municipalities, development approvals are a two-step process: first, a planning permit that confirms that a project is in accordance with the municipal land use plan must be granted; then, a building permit approving the technical details of the project must be issued. In post-communist Prague, the planning permit office remained at the citywide level, where elected officials could influence its decisions both by approving land use plans and by making decisions about staffing and organizational structure. Building permit offices were partly decentralized, with permits for most structures issued by administrative bodies in the city's ten large boroughs. The building permit office for all major transport-related construction (freeways, as well as tram and subway lines) remained at the citywide level, however (Interview 15). In all cases, in addition to their personnel and organizational control over the civil service institutions at their level of government, elected officials at both the city and the borough levels had a right to participate in planning and construction permit proceedings, and to appeal decisions made in these proceedings to national ministries (Interview 15).

Throughout the early 1990s, borough politicians continually pressed the city to delegate more transferred powers (see Votoček 1994). Longer-term stability in the division of transferred powers came in 1994, when the city council passed the relevant section of the city charter (by-law 38/1994). The result of several years of political wrangling between the city and the boroughs, this document further complicated Prague's administrative system. It created *four* tiers of boroughs with differing transferred powers, in contrast to the two recognized in the Law on Municipalities (by-law 38/1994). Some urban development powers were decentralized – for example, the number of building permit offices was expanded to twenty-six (Interview 15). However, despite this lower-tier complexity, most key urban development powers remained at the citywide level.

One way to assess the balance of power between the city and the boroughs in post-communist Prague is to look at their relative shares of total municipal expenditures. Although figures are not available for all of the 1990s, those for the middle of the decade show a clear concentration of resources at the citywide level (Table 2.4).

Furthermore, borough budgets remained heavily dependent on the redistribution of municipal revenues by Prague's city council, considerably weakening the boroughs' fiscal autonomy (Bosáková 1999). If low expenditures by the boroughs and their budgetary dependence indicate a lack of resources at the borough level, however, we need also to examine the fiscal position of post-communist Prague as a whole. If the city as a whole did not develop strong fiscal resources, the formal powers of politicians would have been of limited use in managing the challenges of post-communist urban development.

Fiscal Health and Autonomy

We saw at the outset of this chapter that Prague in the 1990s was one of the most fiscally powerful cities in East Central Europe. However, this was not the case immediately after the fall of communism. The Law on Local Fees (no. 565/1990), passed in December 1990, was a first step towards re-establishing autonomous sources of revenue for municipalities. It entitled them to collect and set rates for a variety of local charges, including fees on alcohol and tobacco sales, hotels, and public parks. The range, however was restricted by a Czech government anxious to limit public spending in the context of the transition to a market economy (Interview 21). As a result, local fees in the 1990s were responsible for a much smaller proportion of total municipal revenues

Table 2.4 Shares of total expenditures by City of Prague and its boroughs (%)

	1993	1994	1995	1996	1997
City of Prague	70.9	74.5	75.6	71.8	79.6
57 boroughs	29.1	25.5	24.4	28.2	20.4

Source: Data taken from Bosáková 1999.

than they had been during the pre-communist era – less than 2 per cent on average (Bosáková 1999; Prague budget documents).

As we saw above, the Law on Municipalities also gave the city the right to manage its own property. In many East Central European municipalities, selling municipal property became a major, although clearly unsustainable, strategy for dealing with fiscal stress in the early 1990s (see, e.g., Devas 1995). Prague, however, chose to sell relatively little of the extensive property that it got in 1991 and 1992, and rental income from municipal holdings did not meet expectations (Hospodářské Noviny 1993). As a result, revenues from municipal property peaked at 7.4 per cent of total revenues in 1993, and generally formed only a minor component of overall budgets in the 1990s (Bosáková 1999; Prague budget documents).

In contrast to the pre-communist era, the majority of Prague's revenues in the 1990s came from sources other than local fees and the management of municipal property. Until 1993 the national treasury remained the dominant source. In 1990 the communist-era practice of financing municipalities through targeted grants was replaced by a system of general-purpose subsidies, with the aim of increasing municipal discretion over spending (Dušková 1997: 30). In 1991 and 1992 the vast majority of Prague's revenues came from such subsidies (see Table 2.1), but these were subject to yearly negotiation, leaving the city vulnerable to changes in national priorities. Preparing the budget involved lengthy haggling with the national government over subsidies, which usually were lower than the city had hoped (Kvačková 1991a).

The scope of Prague's fiscal outlays was changing in 1991 and 1992 with the ongoing privatization of some municipal services. As a result, we cannot usefully compare budget totals for the late 1980s and early 1990s to assess the fiscal health of Prague. Indirect evidence suggests that the city did experience a fiscal crunch in 1991 in particular. In this year, work on many major infrastructure projects in the city slowed significantly because of the lack of money (Lidové Noviny 1991c; Handl 1992). Overall, the proportion of the city budget spent on capital investments in 1991 was substantially lower than it became in subsequent years (see Table 2.2).

Prague's fiscal autonomy and health both got a strong boost with the introduction of a new local finance system at the beginning of 1993. Shared national taxes, rather than subsidies, became the key source of municipal revenues. Prague was given the right to keep 100 per cent of all personal income taxes and property taxes collected on its territory. Rates of these taxes were set nationally, so the city was not able to influence the volume of these all–important sources of revenue. In comparison with the interwar years, during which Prague had got much of its revenues from local taxes whose rates it could set, the city's power to determine its revenue was thus weaker. Nonetheless, the city's dominant source of revenue was now much more stable than it had been during 1991 and 1992, and the money could be spent as the city wished.

For the remainder of the 1990s, Prague received between 50 per cent and 75 per cent of its total revenues from shared national taxes (Bosáková 1999; Czech Statistical Office 1999; City of Prague budget documents). By far the more significant of the two national taxes that the city received was the personal income tax, because property taxes remained little more than symbolic. As a result of Prague's prosperity in the 1990s, revenues from personal income taxes grew quickly, contributing to a 20 per cent rise in the real revenues of the city between 1994 and 1996 (calculated from Bosáková 1999).

In 1996 the national government once again intervened. It altered the local finance system to decrease regional disparities in revenue resulting from differential income tax bases. Thirty per cent of personal income taxes collected in Prague now went to the national government, and were replaced by 20 per cent of corporate income taxes, distributed by population rather than by place of collection (Blažek 1996). This change, while beneficial to the Czech Republic's poorer municipalities, had a negative impact on Prague, which lost about 10 per cent of its revenue base (Dušková 1997: 30).

By this time, Prague had built up sufficient physical assets and was fiscally sound enough that it could issue long-term bonds on the international market. In the later 1990s local politicians, pointing to the extensive use of bonds in pre–Second World War Prague, increasingly turned to this strategy to raise funds for investment in infrastructure. An initial bond issue in 1994 – the first international bond issue made by any East Central European city – was gradually used during subsequent years to fund roads and housing projects, and it was followed by a second issue in 1999 (Čápová 1994; Paroubek 1999). In this way, Prague was able to maintain a level of capital investment that was the envy of other cities in the region (Tables 2.2 and 2.3).

Rebuilding the Municipal Property Base

The right to own and manage property was returned to Czech municipalities through the 1990 Law on Municipalities. How much property they would have remained an open question, as the processes of postcommunist property transfer had not yet begun. Consequently, securing a strong property base became a priority for the Civic Forum government that came out of Prague's elections of November 1990. Despite the national government's intention to place most property in private hands, Prague managed to take advantage of its historical record of property ownership and property management to secure a strong municipal property base.

During the communist era, the scope of municipally managed property in Prague had grown to encompass the majority of land, buildings, and non-industrial enterprises. In formal terms, however, this property was owned by the state, and the NVP, ONVs, and MNVs had no right to dispose of it freely. In 1990 the reintroduction of municipal autonomy was supposed to be accompanied by a new Law on Municipal Property that would delimit the scope of property to be transferred. As had happened with the Law on the Capital City of Prague, the first draft of the Law on Municipal Property ran into trouble.

Prepared by the Ministry of Finance in consultation with the Association of Cities and Towns, the draft law proposed a de facto continuity with the communist era, transferring to municipalities all property and enterprises previously managed by their respective MNV, ONV, or city national committee administrations (Weiss 1991). However, such a massive transfer would have placed most state property aside from industrial enterprises in municipal hands, crippling the national government's planned privatization program. As a result, the draft died before it reached the Czech National Council, and a Law on Municipal Property was not passed before the first municipal elections.

During the following two years, the transfer of property to municipalities was subordinated to the twin national goals of restitution and privatization of property (Weiss 1991). Academic analysts of politics in post-communist Prague, most notably Luděk Sýkora, have seen the precedence given nationally to restitution and privatization as fundamentally weakening ability of local government to control urban space (1994: 1158). In comparison with the communist era, when municipal administrations had comprehensive control over everything from the location of shops to the allocation of state flats, this claim is certainly true. Restitution – the return of buildings, land, and businesses to their pre-1948 owners or their heirs – started in 1991, and quickly transferred much property, including up to 70 per cent of the housing stock in some inner-city boroughs, to private owners (Sýkora and Šimoničková 1994). In 1991 and 1992 small businesses not subject to restitution were privatized, taking some 2,500 shops out of municipal control (Sýkora 1993: 285). Together with the deregulation of rents and land prices these processes helped produce the transformation to market-led urban development desired by the national government.

For a local government now operating in an emerging market economy, Prague nonetheless secured extensive property holdings in the early 1990s. The city got a first wave of property through the Law on Municipal Property, passed in amended form in April 1991. For land and buildings the new law used 1948 as its reference date and returned to municipalities real estate that they had owned at the time of the communist takeover. For Prague, which had built up a strong property base during the interwar years, this meant the return of hundreds of buildings and large tracts of land. 'In a very important sense, we were lucky that [interwar] mayor Baxa had acquired a lot of property for the city,' remarked one planner interviewed for this project. 'The property we managed during communism was up for grabs, but with the rest of it we could tell [national legislators]: look, if individuals who lost property [during the communist era] should get it back, why shouldn't the city?' (Interview 8).

In the Old Town and the Lesser Quarter alone the city regained ownership of about 150 pieces of property, including key public buildings such as concert halls and libraries, as well as the majority of the historic core's scarce and lucrative vacant building lots (Schreib 1991). Prague also recovered 20 square kilometres of empty development sites on the outskirts of the city's built-up areas, which amounted to about 10 per cent of all open land within municipal boundaries (Kvačková 1996a). Despite some initial difficulties in documenting the extent of Prague's historic property (Schreib 1991), within a couple of years the city had recovered the great majority of its prewar buildings and land.

In addition, the Law on Municipal Property gave municipalities ownership of all state housing not subject to restitution. Although much housing in the older parts of Prague was restored to its owners, overall the city ended up with ownership of over 70 per cent of state housing, or about 50 per cent of all housing in the city (calculated from Eskinasi 1995: 535). Much of this was in the communist-era housing estates, which fell almost entirely into municipal hands. Unfortunately for the city, the national government did not relinquish control over rents as part of this transfer of housing. While some deregulation was allowed, rents in most communist-era housing estates remained minimal throughout the early 1990s. In combination with the high upkeep costs of these poorly constructed buildings, rent control made housing a fiscal liability, rather than a useful asset, for the borough officials who controlled the housing stock (Eskinasi 1995; Horak 1998).

In contrast to land and buildings, municipal enterprises were not automatically transferred to the city by the Law on Municipal Property. Rather, they were slated for privatization by the national Ministry of Privatization. The city could compete with private investors for the right to own entire enterprises or to acquire specific assets from enterprises slated for liquidation (Večerní Praha 1991b). This process got off to a rocky start in 1991. City councillors were divided on the issue of how much property the city should keep, with some arguing that acquiring extensive municipal property amounted to 'municipal socialism' and undermined the national goal of building a market-based economy. Bureaucrats, for their part, were often slow to produce the documentation needed for a transfer of title (Večerní Praha 1991c). In the meantime, the national government privatized many formerly municipal enterprises (Kuncová 1994).

After some months of debate city councillors voted in late 1991 to request the transfer of extensive enterprise property, with the aim of privatizing some, while keeping a controlling share of ownership in key municipal enterprises (Večerní Praha 1991c). Subsequently, most physical services were successfully transformed into joint stock companies in which the city owned a controlling share. These included the transit service, road repair, sewage, water, and sanitation companies (Information Centre of the Department of External Affairs 2000; Dušková 1997).[13]

In addition, the city filed several hundred requests for individual buildings or land belonging to municipal enterprises slated for liquidation, such as the old communist-era housing construction firms

(Kvačková 1992). Despite frequent conflict with the Ministry of Finance over what property the city should get, one former executive board member asserted that 'individual decisions by the ministry ultimately brought us the most valuable property in terms of urban development' (Interview 9). Indeed, one single transfer in 1992 alone brought the city open land for development worth some Kc 100 billon (U.S. $3.7 billion). As of 1997, the city estimated its fixed assets at Kc 181 billion (U.S. $6.7 billion) and had Kc 43 billion (U.S. $1.6 billion) in shares in thirty-six companies, making it one of the largest property owners in the Czech Republic (City of Prague 1998; Kvačková 1996b; Achremenko 1997; Dušková 1997: 37).[14]

Conclusion: History and Contemporary State-Building in Prague

At the citywide level, the municipal government in post-communist Prague quickly developed the strong base of powers and resources that local politicians needed to systematically govern urban development on the basis of local preferences. Although in some respects the structure of the local state was by no means ideal – for example, some administrative functions were divided in a complex fashion among different categories of boroughs – in general, post-communist Prague avoided the twin problems of fragmentation and fiscal weakness that plagued other post-communist East Central European capitals. The city owed this outcome in large part to historical precedent. Prague's history of metropolitan government and its ownership of extensive property in the pre-communist era gave power to those who argued for a strong, resource-rich metropolitan authority, blunting the impact of interests that favoured municipal fragmentation and the wholesale privatization of municipal property. An extensive network of administrative bodies inherited from the communist era meant that the city could continue to execute a wide range of transferred powers without having to engage in extensive development and reorganization of the municipal civil service.

The development of local government structures in post-communist Prague provides support for those who claim that early writers on post-communist institutional design tended to ignore important historical variables. As we saw in Chapter 1, institutional design theorists argued that 'relative power balances and bargains struck between a few elite actors provide a central explanation for the shape of the new institutional framework' (Crawford and Lijphart 1997: 15). More recent work suggests that the range of institutional options considered and the choices made among them were strongly influenced by past institutional histories. Some authors point to the shape of communist institutions as a powerful influence on post-communist institutional design (Bunce 1999; Stanger 2003), while others suggest that post-communist decisionmakers drew on 'institutional patterns re-membered and reflexively adopted from the storehouse of their national history' (Elster et al. 1998: 295; see also Petro 2004). Both of these factors are evident in the case of Prague.

Although the interaction of local and national political elites clearly shaped Prague's post-communist government structure, those who argued for a strong metropolitan Prague gained the advantage by being able point to the city's pre-communist governing traditions. The strong, centralized administrative apparatus inherited from the communist era bolstered the centralists' position by making a transition to their vision of a metropoliton authority more feasible. In short, pre-communist and communist-era history mattered a great deal to the contemporary shape of Prague's local state, both by providing historical templates of successful institutional forms and by leaving behind a legacy of existing institutions that the designers of Prague's post-communist government structures could build on.

Like most analyses of post-communist institutional design, this examination of the origins of contemporary municipal government in Prague focuses on state institutions and on the way in which these structure the powers and resources available to political elites. It thereby isolates the structure of state powers and resources from the broader configuration of political institutions that make up the local political system. A strong state is a necessary condition for the emergence of systematic and open rule, but as we saw in Chapter 1, it is not a sufficient condition. A broad configuration of institutions – including administrative structures, legal frameworks, the political party system, and the civic interest group system – affects the prospects for good government performance. Many of these institutions tend to change at a slower pace than basic state structures. Even after the 1990 local government reforms, Prague's political leaders operated in a broad environment filled with a disparate mix of old and new political institutions. The characteristics of this environment, and their implications for the decisionmaking behaviour of political leaders, are the subject of the next chapter.

3 Institutions and Political Actors in Early Post-communist Prague

Making High Performance Desirable: Incentives, Coherence, and Stability

The basic structure of the state has a major impact on the prospects for good government. Largely because of the historical legacy of local government in Prague, the structures developed in the early 1990s gave municipal politicians strong powers and resources. In principle at least, these gave Prague's political leaders an advantage over their counterparts elsewhere in the region in their prospects for developing systematic policies that responded to the needs and interests of the citizenry. In other words, a strong local state made strong performance more *feasible* in post-communist Prague. Nonetheless, as we will see in detail in chapters 4 and 5, local government performance in the City of Prague remained quite poor throughout the 1990s.

This chapter lays the groundwork for understanding the puzzle of poor performance of local government in Prague. It does so by examining the character of the broader institutional environment in which the city's political leaders were situated immediately after the local government reforms of 1990. The structure of the state is by no means the only institutional element that shapes government performance. Although a strong state can provide many of the powers and resources that make systematic, open rule feasible, political leaders are embedded in and react to a much broader matrix of state and societal political institutions. This broader matrix can provide additional resources to political leaders, but it does more than this: It also generates incentives that make the pursuit of systematic, open rule more or less *desirable* for politicians. All political institutions are designed to embody and reproduce norms of political behaviour. As a result, they generate incentives that privilege certain forms of behaviour over others. These incentives take the form of material or non-material rewards – such as money, re-election to office, prestige, or public recognition – that accrue to political actors if they behave in accordance with the norms embedded in a given institution or set of institutions. Both the feasibility and the desirability of systematic, open rule are thus affected by a matrix of institutions that reaches far beyond the basic structure of the state.

To illustrate how a broad matrix of state and societal institutions can support well-performing democracy, let us return to the work of Juan Linz and Alfred Stepan, first mentioned in Chapter 1. They argue that consolidated democracy is supported by five 'arenas' – five institutionalized spheres of political life beyond the basic constitutional structures of the state (1996: 7). Linz and Stepan label these arenas: Economic society, rule of law, political society, civil society and useable bureaucracy. In a well-performing democratic polity, either national or local, each of these arenas of political life provides resources and incentives that encourage politicians to pursue systematic, open rule. Let us look at how each arena can contribute to strong government performance in an ideal-type democratic polity.

In the literature on post-communist politics, attention is often paid to 'economic society' – the institutions of a regulated market economy – as a crucial set of supports for democratic rule. There is justification for this claim, since a well-functioning democracy in the context of a state-run economy is difficult to imagine. As Linz and Stepan point out, at least some degree of economic pluralism in necessary to provide 'a material base for the pluralism and autonomy of civil and political societies.' Economic pluralism is thus a sine qua non of modern democratic rule (Linz and Stepan 1996: 14).

The direct incentives that economic pluralism generates for political leaders are often problematic, however. Economic pluralism produces political actors with unequal resource endowments, and thus unequal political power beyond the ballot box. Dominant economic actors – such as property developers in urban politics – have financial and organizational resources that make them attractive policymaking partners for governments. But if politicians rely heavily on these resources, they face incentives to close policymaking to other actors. Furthermore, the competitive nature of business interests leads them to prefer confidentiality in the conduct of their affairs, further discouraging open process (Painter 1995). A wealth of comparative research shows that if other democratic political institutions are not robust, economic pluralism rapidly produces closed government that serves the narrow interests of economic elites.[1] In a well-functioning democracy, the incentives for political leaders produced by economic inequality must be kept in check by the institutions in other arenas of political life.

The arena that Linz and Stepan call the 'rule of law' plays an especially central role in this respect. Defined as a 'hierarchy of laws, interpreted by an independent judicial system and supported by a strong legal culture in civil society' (1996: 10), the rule of law is a basic precondition for the ordered political life of a democracy that functions well. Moreover, we can identify some characteristics of laws themselves that might directly encourage leaders to govern openly and systematically. First, laws can foster transparency by mandating public consultation in policy processes, disclosure of information by state authorities, and the like. Openness is further supported by a legal separation between public and private spheres through provisions, such as conflict-of-interest legislation, that mitigate the potentially problematic relations between dominant economic interests and political elites. Finally, laws can encourage both open and systematic rule by streamlining decisionmaking processes, thereby encouraging both political and bureaucratic elites to invest more energy and resources into dialogue with civic interest groups and into policy implementation (Walsh 1969).

What Linz and Stepan call 'political society' is characterized in most established democratic polities by a plurality of political parties. While political parties are not always present in democratic urban politics, where they do exist they may give important positive incentives to political leaders. By providing institutional venues that can support the creation of coherent alternative electoral platforms, as well as the resources necessary to mount successful campaigns on the basis of these platforms, political parties can provide institutional infrastructure for the emergence of programmatic electoral choices. The existence of such choices tends to enhance the openness of policy processes by providing politicians with cues about broad public preferences. Furthermore, partisan programs provide a basis on which voters can collectively hold political leaders to account in future elections, giving them an incentive to govern systematically and openly in the interim.

In the late communist era, the term 'civil society' was used in East Central Europe primarily to refer to pockets of independent societal organization and resistance to communist rule (see Krygier 1997: 60–

64). In established democracies, by contrast, civil society – defined as the realm of 'self-organizing groups ... relatively autonomous from the state' (Linz and Stepan 1996: 7) – plays a crucial supportive role. Although some authors claim that this role can be played by all groups autonomous of the state (see Putnam 1993: Chapter 6), incentives for political leaders are most directly generated by those civil society organizations that explicitly aim to influence government policy: interest groups, community groups, and social movement organizations.

As Martin Krygier puts it, 'particularly in democracies, leaders seek, at least, to appear to behave in ways they expect that voters want. They have to *know* what these expectations are, and they have to have reasons to *care* about them' (1997: 87; emphasis in original). A dense network of organized societal interests representing a wide range of political demands produces this information on what the citizenry wants, and generates pressure on political leaders to satisfy those preferences. It provides information from which governing priorities can be developed and functions as a check on the exercise of power between elections (ibid.: 87–8). Furthermore, insofar as interest groups have strong organizational or financial resources and are willing to pursue negotiation with state authorities, they may provide politicians with incentives to institutionalize open policy processes to secure additional resources.

At the most basic level, a 'useable bureaucracy' in the post-communist context means one with 'the effective capacity to command, regulate, and extract'(Linz and Stepan 1996: 11). Such a bureaucracy affords political leaders the resources needed to govern systematically by helping to develop and maintain stable, long-range policies. In a democracy that works well the bureaucratic apparatus also has features that encourage politicians to govern openly. First, it functions as a crucial conduit of information on societal interests and the implications of policy options. Relaying data on these factors, it presses political leaders to consider the impacts of decisions, provides them with feedback on the results of past policies, and produces venues in which societal preferences can be aired during the policy process (Keating 1991: 51). Second, it functions flexibly enough to implement changing political priorities, allowing politicians to adapt their policies to changing circumstances and public preferences.

In sum, in an ideal-type democracy a number of distinct institutional arenas supply crucial incentives and resources that encourage political leaders to govern in a systematic and open way. Further, our ideal institutional configuration has two overall, or 'systemic,' characteristics that influence the behaviour of political leaders: It is *institutionally coherent* and it is *stable*. It is institutionally coherent in that the norms embedded in different political institutions, while not necessarily identical, are broadly compatible with each other. It is stable in that major institutional shifts are rare and change tends to happen incrementally, if at all. Let us unpack these ideas a bit.

In the ideal institutional configuration we have outlined, the norms embedded in various institutional arenas are not identical, since different arenas have different political functions. For example, useable bureaucracies tend to emphasize systematic, stable policy orientations, while civil society organizations tend by their very nature to place a premium on open governing processes. The system does form a coherent whole, however: an overarching commitment to the value of systematic and open democratic politics exists in all of these arenas, despite the differences in emphasis. The normative orientations of various political institutions are thus complementary, rather than mutually conflicting. The coexistence of institutions with complementary normative orientations promotes the stability of the system: Pluralist economic institutions provide an indispensable material base for political pluralism, as well as a material base of resources on which the state can draw; the rule of law produces social order, which allows institutions such as political parties and interest groups to develop and flourish; a strong civil society provides the political basis for the growth of a plurality of programmatic political parties; and so on. Such links are manifold, and give an established democratic political system considerable stability and resilience in the face of new policy challenges and evolving public preferences.

How do institutional coherence and stability affect the behaviour of political leaders? Let us start with the idea introduced in Chapter 1 that politicians are 'boundedly' rational. They cannot absorb more than a set amount of information; they have a limited tolerance for complexity, and they seek overarching normative frameworks to guide their decisionmaking behaviour. Insofar as these assumptions are valid, it follows that a coherent and stable institutional system will improve the ability of political leaders to govern *strategically* – that is, to systematically consider alternative courses of action and their possible consequences. As Harry Eckstein points out, if the 'forms, norms, and practices' of authority in state and society are highly dissimilar, political actors experience 'cognitive strain' in moving among various institutional arenas of politics (1998: 10–11, 18–19). Conversely, a normatively coherent institutional configuration helps orient politicians as to their basic purposes in governing and minimizes the cognitive strain that they face in making decisions. If an institutional system is unstable, political actors must continually learn new rules and practices, and they may find it impossible to predict the future consequences of their actions (Pierson 2000b). Stability, conversely, minimizes learning costs and promotes attention to longer-term time horizons in decisionmaking.

In an ideal-type democratic polity, a broad range of institutions helps to make systematic and open government feasible and desirable. In addition, the coherence and stability of the institutional configuration maximizes the ability of actors to govern strategically – that is, to consider alternative courses of action and their future implications. As we shall see, however, early post-communist Prague was decidedly *not* an ideal-type democratic polity, despite the emerging strength of the local state. In Chapter 1, we noted that across the broad configuration of institutions influencing government performance not all of them change simultaneously during times of systemic transformation. Even after the basic questions of state design have been settled, politicians are usually situated in a configuration of institutions that includes many holdovers from past political eras. Systemic change is a multi-stage, asynchronous process, marked by an initial period of flux – a critical juncture – that is resolved into a new institutional order through a series of political decisions. This gives political leaders *multiple* opportunities to engage in institutional design in the early days of a systemic transformation. Even after basic questions of state structure have been dealt with, political leaders have opportunities to influence institutional development in individual policy areas by pursuing strategic reforms in an environment where stable patterns of political interaction have not yet emerged.

By the same token, the initial critical juncture presents politicians with challenges that might make it difficult for them to take full advantage of the opportunities for strategic reform. First, the incoherent and unstable decisionmaking environment may make strategic action difficult and unattractive. To the extent that the environment is institutionally incoherent, political leaders might find it hard to locate an overarching normative framework that can guide their actions. Moreover, the very instability that produces unprecedented opportunities for reform also means both that many problems confront political leaders simultaneously, and that the future consequences of various courses of action are unpredictable. In this context, it is easier to engage in short-term decisionmaking than strategic reform. In so far as many political institutions embed norms inherited from the past, such short-term decisionmaking may entrench institutional forms that are incompatible with the emergence of government that performs well.

The rest of this chapter develops the line of argument that I have just presented with specific reference to Prague. It examines the characteristics of the decisionmaking environment after the city's first free elections in November 1990 and the implications of this environment for the behaviour of political leaders. I begin in the next section by introducing the city's new political leaders and party structures. In the early post-communist period, politics in Prague was dominated by the anti-communist Civic Forum movement and its successor, the Civic Democratic Party (Občanská Demokratická Strana, ODS). Like their national counterparts, the Civic Forum and ODS emerged out of the popular protest that accompanied the end of communism. As a result, they were internally organized to embody norms of participatory democracy. Although they were functional for a protest organization, these norms made governing more difficult, because they worked against the development of a coherent policy platform. Prague's post-1990 politicians thus had no partisan policy framework that could guide their responses to the critical decision challenges they faced in individual policy spheres.

In the absence of a partisan governing vision, the character of the broader decisionmaking environment largely shaped the behaviour of Prague's new political elites. In the next two sections, I examine the evolution up to 1990 of institutional structures and norms in each of the two policy spheres that are the focus of this book: transport infrastructure and the preservation and development in Prague's historic core. In each of these spheres, key political institutions present in 1990 had emerged either during the communist period or during the period of mass mobilization against communism in 1989. Administrative bodies and legal frameworks typically retained structures that reflected the communist-era ideals of bureaucratic rationality and comprehensive planning. By contrast, local civic activist groups typically had their roots in the popular protest wave of 1989. They privileged norms of grassroots democracy and were suspicious of positive engagement with the state. In both policy spheres, political leaders confronted a normatively incoherent set of institutions that did not uniformly encourage the pursuit of systematic and open government.

In the final section of this chapter, I synthesize the evidence presented and discuss its implications. The absence of well-established practices in individual policy spheres gave politicians unprecedented opportunity to pursue strategic institutional and policy reforms. The nature of the institutional environment made such longer-range strategic action difficult and unattractive. The organizational underdevelopment of the Civic Forum/ODS, together with the existence of conflicting political norms in key policy spheres, meant that neither the political parties nor the external environment offered political leaders a normative road map that could guide strategic reform. Furthermore, the entire political configuration was new and unstable, which presented a plethora of problems and made prediction of future outcomes very difficult. Together, these factors encouraged political leaders to focus on short-term, simple solutions to policy challenges instead of pursuing strategic reforms. In an environment where many pre-democratic political institutions still existed, the short-term, simple solutions that presented themselves were not always compatible with the longer-term development of systematic and open urban government.

From Protest to Power: Political Elites and
Partisan Institutions, 1990–92

In municipalities across East Central Europe, the fall of communism and the local government reforms of 1990 were accompanied by a sea-change in the composition of local political elites. Both in Prague and in the Czech Republic as a whole, mass protest against the communist regime in November 1989 coalesced around the leadership of a loosely structured anti-communist umbrella movement, the Civic Forum.[2] Dominating the city's interim power-sharing assemblies in 1990, the Civic Forum entered and won the local elections in November of 1990, and subsequently transformed itself into a political party, the Civic Democratic Party (ODS). Throughout this transformation, it retained a highly decentralized internal structure that reflected its origins as a vehicle for popular protest. As a result, it failed to develop a local electoral program in 1990, and remained unable to develop partisan policy positions through most of the city's first post-communist electoral period (1990–94).

In February 1990, after power-sharing negotiations with the communist Party, the Civic Forum replaced 45 per cent of the representatives in Prague's citywide (NVP), district (ONV), and local (MNV) assemblies with its own activists, creating interim assemblies that would last until the elections in November. In choosing interim representatives, the Civic Forum leaders paid a great deal of attention to professional qualifications, since 'the old structures [i.e., the Communist Party hierarchy] took advantage of every opportunity to question the professional quality of Civic Forum candidates' (Interview 41). The interim assembly of the City of Prague (NVP) thus came to be composed of an occupationally diverse group of representatives, including architects, transport engineers, and local government administrators as well as academics, artists, and students (Prague National Committee 1990a). Ideologically, the new Civic Forum delegates embodied the diversity of the movement itself, and shared little other than involvement in the 1989 protests and a lack of political experience (Interview 28).[3] This diversity was reflected in the representatives that the assembly elected to form an interim executive board for the city, headed by Mayor Jaroslav Kořán (Interview 11).

The local electoral system that was to replace the interim assembly with a popularly elected city council was designed to promote two distinct goals: to help develop local political parties and to provide a mechanism for linking individual councillors to voters (Pečínka 1998). Approved by the Czech National Council in September 1990, it took the form of a modified party list system. Contenders – whether political parties or other, less formal groupings of candidates – had to compile ranked lists of candidates corresponding to the number of seats on the city council. Each voter could cast a number of votes that corresponded to the number of seats on the council. Voters could give all of their votes to one list, changing the ranking of candidates if they so desired, or they could select individual candidates from more than one list (ibid.).

Prague's November 1990 elections were contested by twenty political parties, movements, or groups of independents (Lidové Noviny 1990c). At first glance, the elections seemed to provide a strong mandate for the construction of a new governing order in post-communist Prague. Voter turnout was a remarkably high, at 73 per cent (Lidové Noviny 1990d). At both the citywide and borough levels, the Civic Forum achieved a resounding victory. In the city council, the Civic Forum won forty-one of seventy-six seats (54%), with the remaining seats divided among eight other political groupings (Prague City Council 1991). The city council in turn re-elected Jaroslav Kořán as mayor and once again, selected an executive board dominated by Civic Forum activists (Lidové Noviny 1990e).

Although the Civic Forum had a majority of city councillors, many of its interim representatives had declined to stand for office in the November elections. As a result, turnover was extensive, and the city council, once again, had a majority of members without prior experience in office. Of the Civic Forum's forty-one councillors, only nine had sat in the interim assembly (calculated from Prague National Committee 1990a and Prague City Council 1991). While the Civic Forum's interim representatives had been chosen by the movement's leaders, the candidates for the November elections were selected by democratic ballot at the grassroots of the movement. This process brought to the fore candidates from 'high status' backgrounds, such as doctors and teachers, rather than the urban management professionals who had dominated the interim assembly (Interview 28).

The Civic Forum campaigned in the November elections with no electoral program at all at the citywide level. The only policy document with which the citywide Civic Forum entered the race was a brief statement of the 'Goals of the Prague Civic Forum,' adopted by an Assembly of Prague's District Forums on 26 October 1990. This document expressed solidarity with the (extremely broad) goals of the national Civic Forum, emphasized the need to bring communist-era leaders to justice, and called upon supporters of the Civic Forum to vote in the local elections, but made no mention of the urban policy challenges faced by post-communist Prague (Civic Forum 1990).

A vague electoral program would not have been surprising, since across the region the first free elections were typically more about breaking with communism than about charting a political course for the future (Kitschelt et al. 1999: Chapter 3). However, the complete lack of a program in Prague was a result of the Civic Forum's internal structure, which did not mesh well with the centralized metropolitan model of government enshrined in the Law on the Capital City of Prague. Given its origins as a vehicle for anti-communist protest, the Civic Forum was organized in accordance with the ideals of participatory democracy and bottom-up governance, with a highly decentralized internal structure. In Prague, it consisted of local 'forums,' that is, groups of activists organized at the level of the city's ten administrative districts. According to the Civic Forum's statutes, the movement had a 'self-governing structure, based on the autonomy of individual [local] Civic Forums' (cited in Honajzer 1996: 20). Although it also developed a citywide council in Prague, this council was made up of delegates chosen by the district forums and had minimal powers (Interview 41).

As a result, the Civic Forum had no body that could develop a citywide electoral program, and the city's inexperienced post-November councillors entered the early post-communist period with no governing mandate on specific urban issues (Interview 28).[4]

At the national level, too, the Civic Forum was the dominant political force following the first free elections. By the end of 1990, programmatic questions started to tear the ideologically diverse national Civic Forum apart. A deep rift appeared between a majority faction – led by future Prime Minister Václav Klaus – that supported rapid national market reforms and several smaller factions that had a variety of other political leanings (Honajzer 1996: 23–40). Despite efforts by some activists to keep the movement together, centrifugal forces quickly gathered momentum and by April 1991 the Civic Forum had disintegrated entirely (ibid.: 41–6).

The disintegration of the national Civic Forum was paralleled by its split in Prague into several groupings that reflected the emerging national party structure. By far the largest number of Prague's Civic Forum representatives in the seventy-six-member city council joined the newly formed Civic Democratic Party (ODS – twenty-five councillors); smaller numbers went to other new political parties such as the Civic Democratic Alliance (ODA, nine) and the Liberal National Socialist Party (LSNS, three), while several strengthened an already-existing contingent of independents, which now totalled seventeen councillors (Prague City Council 1994). The Civic Forum–dominated council had suddenly disintegrated into one in which no political party had a majority, although the ODS was clearly the strongest.

Since Prague's executive board and mayor are elected by council, this change brought on a period of executive instability in city politics that lasted from 1991 to 1993. As the new parties jockeyed for position in a council where independent candidates often held the balance of power, mayors and executive board members were repeatedly recalled and replaced, although the ODS remained the strongest political force in the executive board and retained a hold on the mayor's post. By the time of the next municipal elections in 1994, only three of the fifteen original executive board members had survived the reshuffling. The city went through three different mayors during this same time. The first, Jaroslav Kořán, was recalled by the city council in September 1991; his successor, Milan Kondr, lasted only twenty months and was replaced in April 1993 by Jan Koukal (Mladá Fronta Dnes 1991; Schreib 1993a).

While executive instability made decisionmaking in Prague more difficult, this might have been tempered had the ODS followed its national counterpart in forging a coherent policy program. This did not happen, however. In November 1992, Mayor Kondr complained publicly: 'The ODS [in Prague] has no municipal political program worked out ... for every decision we have to build another political agreement, another coalition ... In this situation a critical variable is personality. Mine, that of executive board members. Without partisan policy positions we have greater freedom in decisionmaking, but we also face more conflict and struggle ... [These] struggles are a logical reflection of a situation in which every [politician] searches for solutions to problems in his own way' (Schreib 1992: 3).

This inability to develop a program was rooted in the organization of the new party, which inherited the decentralized local structure of the Civic Forum. In early 1991, as the ODS was preparing for its founding congress, Prague party leaders produced a draft document outlining a new local party structure with strong Prague-wide ODS institutions (Kádner and Kašpar 1991). At the founding congress the document ran into opposition. The established district Civic Forum organizations, which had transformed themselves into district ODS associations, strongly opposed the introduction of an autonomous Prague-wide ODS organization. Meanwhile, ODS politicians from outside Prague complained about 'Prague exceptionalism' and argued that the party should have the same local structure throughout the country, regardless of differences in local government structures (Interview 11). The net result was that the ODS's national statutes made no provision for a citywide party organization in Prague (Civic Democratic Party 1991).

The protest-based origins of the Civic Forum/ODS prevented the emergence of a coherent platform in 1990 and continued to stymie the development of a partisan platform in the following years. The potential of the party to function as a vehicle for openness to societal interests and as a framework for developing a systematic governing program remained unfulfilled. As a result, ODS politicians did not have an autonomously developed and publicly legitimated set of governing priorities that they could rely on to guide their decisionmaking. This made the influences of institutional configurations in individual policy spheres all the more important in governing behaviour. In the next two sections, we will look at the structure and normative orientations of the dominant institutions in each of the two policy spheres that this study examines.

State versus Society: The Bureaucrats and Civic Opposition in the Transport Sphere

Meeting the growing need for the modernization of long-neglected physical infrastructure was a key challenge for post-communist urban governments. One of the most difficult infrastructure issues in Prague, and certainly the one that attracted the most public attention immediately after the fall of communism, was the development of transport infrastructure. With the transition to a market economy, post-communist Prague faced the prospect of dealing with rising automobile ownership and use in a city whose physical characteristics were exceptionally ill-suited to dense vehicle traffic. Here we will look at the development before 1991 of two sets of institutions – the bureaucracy and civic groups – that thereafter framed much of the public debate on transport policy and which were the dominant forces producing incentives for political leaders in this issue sphere.

For reasons of both geography and history, Prague – and in particular its older districts – is an exceptionally difficult environment in which to design modern transport systems. The centre of the city, containing the city's historic core, is situated in a deep valley bisected by the Vltava River. Dense nineteenth century residential districts occupy the slopes and tops of the surrounding hills. Together, these areas house more than half of Prague's population on only 17 per cent of its surface area. The combination of hilly terrain and a dense urban fabric with narrow streets means that the expansion of large-scale transport infrastructure must either take place underground or involve significant destruction of the city's historic fabric. The older parts of the city are especially ill-suited to the large spatial demands of automobile transport, whose negative effects are compounded by the tendency of polluted air to get trapped in the central valley.

In the early twentieth century Prague's political and bureaucratic leaders addressed these challenges by developing a dense network of trams to service the city, while plans to push new roads through the city's historic core and residential districts foundered on public opposition. During the communist era, public transit was the main focus of transport policy. A high-capacity subway system was built in the 1970s and 1980s, and it was extended outward to service many of the high-rise housing estates built under communist rule. During this same period automobile ownership in Prague rose from one vehicle per 8.1

inhabitants in 1971 to one per 4.2 inhabitants in 1981, and one per 3.6 in 1990 (Transport Engineering Institute 1998: 10). As the prospect of traffic congestion arose, a network of transport-oriented administrative institutions founded in the 1960s began to pursue construction of a network of freeways for the city.

Structures and Norms in the Administration of Road-Building

The administrative decentralization of the 1960s (see Chapter 2) gave birth in Prague to a massive municipal bureaucratic apparatus, that included strong citywide institutions that dealt with urban development. A transport planning division was established within the city's land use planning body, the Chief Architect's Office (UHA). A separate Transport Engineering Institute (UDI) was also established, and it was charged with providing statistical and technical data and analysis for transport planners. The construction of transport infrastructure was financially managed by the city's General Investment Office (UGI), which was also responsible for securing construction permits from the relevant bodies, while detailed technical plans became the responsibility of a specialized Design Institute for Transport Engineering Works (PUDIS) (Interview 28).

In their basic structure, Prague's communist-era administrative institutions – both in the transport sector and other policy areas – were not all that different from those in many other parts of the world. Personnel management rested on a strict seniority system, and organization was vertically segmented into specialized policy areas that developed complex internal decisionmaking procedures. As is the case elsewhere, these structural characteristics of Prague's municipal institutions encouraged the development of technocratic norms and a strong bias in favour of long-term policy stability. These characteristics were only intensified by the communist context, in which a 'shortage economy' encouraged individual institutions to maximize inputs, while autonomous societal interests were either ignored or suppressed, and comprehensive planning was officially championed as the basis for policymaking.

In the early communist period, the seniority system in local administration was heavily compromised by political appointments. But by the 1970s the KSC's interest in micromanaging the development and administration of Prague had waned. Thereafter, promotion through the ranks was usually based on years of employment, rather than on political criteria (Interview 40). As one pre-1989 transport administrator recalled, 'the communists let people such as myself into top jobs even if they were not members of the party. You just had to be competent and have done your time' (Interview 28).

The strength of the seniority system meant that in 1980s Prague the field of transport planning and administration was dominated by a cohesive group of individuals who had started their professional careers in the 1960s and risen together through the ranks (Interview 16). Having spent their entire careers in one institution, top transport planners and administrators identified very closely with that institution's goals. The perspective of one planner interviewed in June 2000 was typical: 'I've been here for almost forty years, and for that entire time I have been working to develop a modern freeways network for the city. I consider it my life's work' (Interview 1). The seniority system did not reward innovation. Neither top bureaucrats nor their subordinates had much incentive to propose departures from the established policy course – long-term stability was strongly preferred.

Like their counterparts across the region (see Kotchegura 1999), Prague's administrative bodies were strongly vertically segmented. The administration of a single policy area often involved a tight network of organizations that was only poorly integrated with organizations managing other policy areas. In late communist Prague, not only was the transport sector seperated from other urban development sectors, but it was also internally divided into two major organizational networks. The transport planning and administrative bodies had originally been designed as integrated institutions responsible for all aspects of the city's transport infrastructure. In 1967, however, the national government approved the plan to develop a major subway system in Prague (Balcar 1996: 83), and the supposedly integrated transport institutions were sidelined in the process of its implementation.

An autonomous network of institutions was established for the subway planning and construction. It comprised a design office (Metroprojekt), investment company (Investor Dopravních Staveb), and construction company (Metrostav) (Interview 28). As a result, the chief task of the formerly integrated transport institutions became the design and development of a freeways network for Prague.[5] This segmentation produced intense rivalry for centrally allocated resources, rivalry that was intensified by the nature of the communist economy. In his classic work on communist economic systems, Janos Kornai argues that interfirm or interadministrative rivalry in the context of centrally distributed resources and chronic shortages of material inputs led to an 'investment hunger' for which 'there is no saturation ... if a project just finished has appeased this hunger momentarily, it will shortly reappear, and more intensively than ever' (1980: 191–2).

The 'investment hunger' of freeways planning institutions in late communist Prague is clearly evident. The original plans for the freeway system presented in 1968, called for no less than five ring roads – in a city where 94 per cent of trips were made using public transit (Balcar 1996: 83). During the early 1970s these plans were scaled down to feature three ring roads, and were approved in this form by the national government in 1974. Even the scaled-down Basic Communications System (Základní Komunikační Systém, ZKS) was very large, considering Prague's population and the small share of car traffic in its transport system. The ZKS consisted of three ring roads connected by eleven radial roads, totalling 241 kilometres of freeways (Sadílek 1998: 39; Janouškovec 1984). All segments were to be built as six-lane freeways with multilevel intersections (see Figure 4.1).

Around the world, the hierarchical structure and vertical segmentation common in large administrative organizations tends to encourage administrative norms that privilege specialized, technical knowledge in policy processes. Unlike in Western democracies, however, in communist systems this technocratic tendency was not counterbalanced by open political discussion of policy priorities and the autonomous activities of organized societal interests. On the contrary, the official Communist Party ideology claimed that all citizens had a single public interest and that policy development was best conducted through long-term, rational, and comprehensive planning. In line with this doctrine, the involvement of autonomous societal actors in policy processes was deliberately suppressed. As a result, as Charles King notes, communist systems typically had few, if any, feedback mechanisms involving public acceptance of policies, and policies tended to become increasingly divorced from the realities of (forcibly silenced) societal preferences (2000: 159).

Richard Pomahač characterizes top Czech administrators in the late communist era as 'technocrats [who] stress the superiority of technical knowledge ... and believe in social engineering and rationalistic constructivism' (1993: 61). In line with these norms, Prague's late communist transport planners developed a technocratic justification for the merits of the ZKS plans for the city's freeways. They argued that they had at their disposal a sophisticated analytical apparatus which showed that, based on projections of future growth in traffic volumes, the freeways network would serve the public interest. This public interest was defined as the provision of a fast, safe alternative to the current roads system. This would bring 'economic benefits such as savings of gasoline and diesel fuel. Traffic would also be partly diverted from the city centre, limiting noise and emissions caused by this traffic' (Vavírk-ová 1989). The congruence of this vision of the public interest with actual public opinion and the potential reciprocal impact that the ZKS would have on the behaviour of drivers – and thus on traffic volumes – were not considered (Interview 29).

Despite its significant autonomy in matters of personnel and policy development, Prague's urban bureaucracy remained fiscally subordinate to the Communist Party. Although the KSC officially championed long-term rational planning, in the context of a shortage economy it was pressed to make increasingly difficult choices among investment priorities. In Prague's transport sector, the national communist leadership's approval of the ZKS plans in 1974 was followed by fifteen years during which investment priorities were tilted in favour of the development of the subway system (Lukeš 1990). By the end of the communist period only one-quarter of the ZKS had been built, mostly on the southern periphery of the city.

Official political championing of rational planning thus existed in tension with political control of a tight budget. Over time, this produced increasing frustration among Prague's transport planners and administrators. 'We had the [ZKS] plans fully developed, but there was never enough money,' notes one long-time UDI official. 'It was, frankly, a bit ridiculous that these crucial projects were developing at such a slow pace for the sake of lavish spending on the subway system' (Interview 1). Even ten years after the fall of communism, hostility to political involvement in transport policy remained strong among some transport professionals with long records of work under the previous regime. Consider, for example, the following exchange with a senior freeways planner interviewed for this project:

Question: Based on your many years of experience in transport planning under the previous regime and the current one, what role do you think political leaders should play in shaping the city's freeway system?
Response: Frankly, they should play as small a role as possible. Whether it has been the Communist Party or the ODS in power, polit-

ical leaders have done significant harm to the prospects of this city ever managing its car traffic rationally. Transport planning is in its essence entirely apolitical. It's a technical exercise. The key challenge is whether we have the information, expertise, and material resources needed to meet objective transport needs. When it comes right down to it, it doesn't matter whether we have Hitler, [communist-era President Gustav] Husák, or Havel in power; we build roads. (Interview 29)

The technocratic orientation of roads administrators in late communist Prague was reinforced by complex and inwardly focused administrative decisionmaking processes. While complex decision processes exist in administrative bodies around the world, in late communist Prague these largely disregarded actors outside the administration. This phenomenon had deep historical roots in the autocratic administration of the Habsburg Empire (Interview 21), but it was amplified by the massive growth of the state machinery during the communist era. The 1976 Law on Land Use Planning and the Building Code (no. 50/1976), which provided the broad regulatory framework for the planning of transport infrastructure and many other urban development activities, is a case in point.

The communist-era land use plan was a comprehensive document outlining in great detail the physical evolution of the city, including the development of buildings, roads, and other physical infrastructure. The process of preparing the plan involved two steps – the preparation and approval of land use and economic principles for the plan, and the preparation of the draft plan itself. In each step, the planning office in Prague, the Chief Architect's Office (UHA), developed the plan in negotiation with other relevant state bodies at both the national and local levels before passing it on to the municipal assembly for formal political approval (par. 20.3, par. 21.1).[6]

For transport planning in Prague, the relevant administrative bodies numbered in the dozens, making planning a complicated and often conflict-ridden process of negotiation among various parts of the city's vertically segmented bureaucracy (Interview 8). Following such negotiations, the final draft of the plan was publicly presented for comment, during which time administrative bodies, and also enterprises and members of the public could submit suggestions for changes. All parties were granted a thirty-day period in which to submit any objections or suggestions for alterations to the final draft of the plan; these were then either incorporated or rejected by the UHA. In reality, of course, since this public presentation had been preceded by complex and lengthy administrative negotiations the planners rarely incorporated any suggestions from the public realm (Interview 16).

To summarize, Prague's communist-era road-building institutions had several key structural characteristics that encouraged the development of a well-defined set of administrative norms. Top bureaucrats placed a high premium on continuity of policy, were inimical to engaging in a dialogue with societal interests, and believed in the superiority of technical knowledge, which was used to rationalize policies involving maximum public investment. The 1990 Law on the Capital City of Prague transferred the city's communist-era administrative apparatus wholesale into the city's post-communist frame, and its activity was still guided by the communist-era legislation we have just discussed. The structural features and normative orientations of communist administrative institutions in Prague survived the end of communism largely unchanged.

Early post-communist political leaders thus faced in the transport sector an administrative apparatus with substantial technical expertise, one that had long developed and delivered systematic policies largely unchallenged. This apparatus was strongly committed to the completion of a freeways network that had been planned without public input and that was already partly built. On the one hand, this bureaucracy did provide political leaders with the pool of expertise they needed to govern roads development systematically. On the other, these administrative bodies also produced incentives for local politicians leaders to retain closed policy processes. Insofar as it might threaten the completion of the planned freeways network, any political initiative to incorporate dialogue with societal interests into the policy process was bound to encounter resistance from bueaucrats whose expertise and advice the new politicians sorely needed.

The local government reforms of 1990 placed administrative institutions clearly under local political control. Prague's executive board now had the power to decide on the organization, staffing, and internal procedures of administrative institutions in the city. By pursuing a longer-term program of personnel development and structural reform in the civil service, political leaders could open the policy process in the transport sector to greater public input if they so desired. The *incentive* to do so, however, would clearly have to come from somewhere other than the administrative apparatus itself. The most obvious source of incentives to open the policy process was a number of local activist groups that had arisen out of a 1988–89 protest movement against the freeways plans.

The Stromovka Protest Movement and Its Legacies, 1988–90

Dissenting voices regarding the plan to construct a network of urban freeways in Prague emerged well before the communist regime's final days. In the mid-1980s critical articles about the design of the Basic Communications System (ZKS) began to appear in the media, usually authored by architects, environmental scientists, or transport professionals unconnected with Prague's network of road-building institutions. Tapping into a growing public sense of environmental crisis in the country, these early critiques focused on the potential side-effects of the ZKS on the quality of life in the city.

Criticism focused in particular on the western part of the ZKS's 'middle' ring road. This proposed segment involved a six-lane freeway that would lead through the city's densely populated nineteenth century residential districts and would touch at one point on the perimeter of Prague's historic medieval core. Because of the hilly terrain in this part of the city, some of the western middle ring road was to be constructed using covered trenches or tunnels. Nevertheless, building would involve the demolition of dozens of housing units and the destruction of significant expanses of parkland. In 1984 construction began on the first tunnel to be built as part of this segment, the two-kilometre–long Strahov Tunnel. Construction continued through the remainder of the decade, at a slow pace dictated by the disjuncture between the size of the project and the willingness of the national government to fund it.

The most contentious part of the western middle ring road was a proposed two-kilometre segment leading in a covered trench through the historic Stromovka Park, adjacent to a nineteenth century residential district. Many opponents noted that Prague's only existing inner-city freeway, the 1970s North-South Artery, had had a strong negative impact on the quality of life along the eastern perimeter of the city's historic core. They argued that the effects of the Stromovka segment near the northwestern perimeter of the core would be just as harmful. Critics emphasized both the close proximity of the proposed freeway to the city's core and its dense residential districts and the destruction of parkland that would accompany the open-pit construction of the route. One of the earliest officially published critiques of the project put it thus:

Prague is in acute need of new roads. Nevertheless, I cannot help but ask: Was it really necessary to place a six-lane freeway as close to the city centre as the northwest side of Stromovka Park? How many quiet places like that do we have left in Prague? I think they can be counted on one hand. The Chief Architect's Office [UHA] says that construction will lead to the felling of 'only' six hundred and twenty trees; there are many experts, however, who claim that Stromovka will lose more than two thousand trees ... (Janouškovec 1984: 16)

In early 1988 the volume of criticism that appeared in the media increased, sparked by the publication of an open letter in the architectural magazine *Tvorba*, in which a group of architects denounced the Stromovka project (Štursa et al. 1988). A range of publications began giving the issue space in their pages, despite sporadic attempts by the authorities to shut down debate (Lukeš 1990; for examples of articles see Kolářová 1989; Čenovská 1989). Such 'professional' criticisms were joined by the voices of a growing grassroots movement of opposition.

The grassroots movement first found an organizational home in the Prague sections of established, officially tolerated national environmental groups, such as the Czech Union for Nature Protection (Český Svaz Ochránců Přírody) and the 'Brontosaurus' movement. In the summer of 1988 these groups organized a petition campaign that attracted about 800 signatures (Prague City Committee of the Czech Union for Nature Protection 1989). Continued intransigence on the part of transport planners into 1989 sparked public meetings and letter-writing campaigns organized both by official environmental groups and, increasingly, also by ad hoc groups of local citizens (Vavírková 1989). The movement grew rapidly in early 1989 and peaked with a series of six – illegal – rallies in the spring and summer, initiated by an unofficial environmental group, Czech Children (České Děti). The rallies, one of which was violently suppressed by the police, each attracted hundreds of participants (Lukeš 1990; Interview 16; Interview 37).

The emergence of a popular movement against the Stromovka freeway closely mirrored the broader development of environment-related protest in late communist Czechoslovakia. Although the protesters emphasized their specific fears of worsening quality of life if the road were built, the movement was also charged with a much broader symbolic meaning. Communist political leaders saw environmental issues as a 'safer' outlet for broad public frustration with the regime than other areas such as human rights, so they tolerated more criticism in this field. As a result, issues such as Stromovka provided 'a focus for social discontent at the right moment in time' (Fisher 1993: 99). Environmental protest became as much about popular feelings regarding the communist regime's illegitimacy as about the issue at hand.

Throughout this wave of protest, established environmental organizations such as the Czech Union for Nature Protection focused on specific arguments against the construction of the Stromovka segment of the freeway. A draft summary of arguments against the project, developed by the Union's Prague chapter in 1989, provides some examples. In addition to the arguments already noted, this document argued that the middle ring road would 'make driving in the city centre more attractive and thus draw further cars into the city,' while 'across the world the trend in transport planning ... is to try to limit vehicle traffic in the city.' It also pointed out that for all their proclaimed intentions of decreasing traffic in the historic core of the city, the designers of the ZKS proposed no steps to limit traffic in the core through regulatory means such as creating pedestrian zones or regulating parking capacity (Prague City Committee of the Czech Union for Nature Protection 1989).

Such concrete points were increasingly complemented by language that framed the Stromovka issue as a broader symbol of communist disregard for quality-of-life issues and linked this disregard to the dominant technocratic approach to policy development. One June 1989 editorial in an unofficially published anti-communist newspaper summed it up thus:

> Many administrators, planners, investors, and unfortunately even environmental scientists see civic activism as being out of place, in the way, interfering 'unprofessionally' with highly professional decisions and policies ... But we have seen many examples where administrators, planners, and other experts assured citizens that a planned project would have no ill effect on the quality of life, that there was nothing to be afraid of. Examples include the North-South Artery in Prague ... The real impact of such projects upon the environment by no means bore out the assurances of the experts ... [Civic activism] is the only way to prevent arrogant, ill-conceived decisions that later have a negative impact on the environment, health, and quality of life of a country's inhabitants. (Lidové Noviny 1989: 2)

The sense that the protest against the Stromovka freeway was part of a much bigger movement that rejected top-down, technocratic decisionmaking and, indeed, the communist system as a whole, rapidly swelled the ranks of the movement, despite the dangers associated with speaking out in public. The peak of the movement in mid-1989 was at the leading edge of the broad mass mobilization that precipitated the fall of Czechoslovakia's communist leadership a few months later. One participant in the Stromovka demonstrations, who was not involved in post-1989 civic activism, described the meaning of the 1989 events as follows: 'We felt that the power of the communist regime was finally weakening, and here was an important cause and an opportunity to release our frustrations. This gave us all a sort of irrationally strong emotional connection to the Stromovka issue. For all those who went on to work on in local civic groups and protest groups after 1989 this was a formative moment ... it was like their first love, the occasion where they first met and where they felt like they could accomplish something really heroic together' (Interview 28).

Nevertheless, the same broad rejection of the legitimacy of communist rule that swelled the ranks of the Stromovka protesters in 1989 ensured that the peak strength of the movement was short-lived and that its organizational base remained unstable. As the protests against the communist regime reached their apex in November 1989, the Stromovka issue was overshadowed by fundamental changes in national political life. Strongly linked to this broader movement, the Stromovka protest waned after the fall of communism, never to recover its full strength, even though the plans to build a freeway through Stromovka remained operational pending a change in policy by Prague's new political leaders.

Even before elections in November 1990, some of the established environmental groups that had spearheaded the protest against the Stromovka project moved on to address other issues. Furthermore, many of the local ad hoc civic groups[7] that had emerged during the protest wave dissipated. Those that did not, such as the Prague Mothers (Pražské Matky) or those that emerged shortly after the fall of communism, such as the Santoška Citizens' Initiative (Občanská Iniciativa Santoška), attracted a limited number of participants, perhaps a few hundred core activists altogether (Interview 37). As a result, as one former member of Prague's executive board put it, 'after the beginning of 1990 we were left with a small segment of the public that was still actively interested in transport issues and a general public that was inactive' (Interview 9). This decline in activism was by no means an isolated occurrence, but reflected a broad trend across the country. After the fall of communism most citizens soon retreated from political activism, preoccupied with managing the changes in their daily lives brought on by the beginnings of the transition to a market economy.

Despite this decline in activism, the civic groups that remained focused on the Stromovka project and the ZKS initially retained links to some powerful sources of support. First, much of the newly independent media was clearly in their favour. Throughout 1990 and beyond, a steady stream of articles lambasting the 'megalomaniac' and 'grossly insensitive' nature of the ZKS plans appeared in daily and weekly publications (see, e.g., Pokorný 1990; Plicka 1990, 1991). Second, both the interim power-sharing assemblies of 1990, and to a lesser extent in the city and borough councils after the 1990 elections, included local politicians who had been active in 1988–89 in the protest movement against freeways construction. This was most clearly the case in the boroughs immediately surrounding Stromovka, where a number of local mayors and councillors had personally participated in the protests (Interview 28).

Given the broad and powerful support for civic groups in the transport sector, the city's post-November political leaders had a clear incentive to embrace demands for open policy processes and a re-evaluation of the ZKS. The protest-oriented character of civic groups meant, however, that they were of limited use to political leaders as partners in the systematic development of policy alternatives. Oriented towards ad hoc petitions, public meetings, and demonstrations, local civic groups were loosely structured and had no stable leadership, membership, or funding. This instability limited their ability to go beyond the politics of protest to participate in discussing any new policy directions with political and bureacratic elites. Their organizational instability was accompanied by a deep suspicion of state authorities and the structures of state power, a suspicion fostered by prolonged experience of protest against a hostile administration. The continuity in transport administration after the fall of communism only deepened this suspicion. As one activist argued in late 1990, 'the majority of responsible actors among planners and investors [in road-building] are still the same people who ... declared "do not discuss, just build" under the old regime, who lied to the public in the Stromovka case, who still defend the North-South Artery, who looked on silently as police beat up peaceful demonstrators against the destruction of Stromovka' (Škrdlant 1990: 11).

The end of the communist era saw the emergence of a popular protest movement against the development of the ZKS freeways system, and in particular against the Stromovka section near the centre of the city. It was in many ways part of a broader groundswell of opposition to closed, technocratic policy processes and to the communist regime as a whole. But this very fusion with the protests that helped topple the communist regime meant that the movement's strength was unsustainable. The civic groups that remained were relatively small, organizationally unstable, and often deeply suspicious of state authority. While the Stromovka protest movement had given the city's political leaders a strong signal that societal interests demanded policy change and an opening of the policy process in the freeways sector, the actual support that these civic groups could offer the new politicians in pursuit of these ends was limited.

State versus Market: Preservation and Development in the Historic Core to 1992

As a booming post-communist capital city, 1990s Prague shared with other East Central European capitals a second set of key policy challenges in addition to those associated with modernizing the physical infrastructure. These had to do with regulating real estate development in the context of the emerging market economy. In Prague, these challenges were most acute in the historic core, where the interests of a flood of domestic and foreign investors confronted those of historic preservationists and local residents. In this section, we will look at the development up to 1991 of the dominant institutions that shaped incentives for post-communist political leaders in this policy sphere – the administrative bodies and the legal framework governing the relationship between the public and private sectors. Before taking a closer look at them, let us review the rise of the preservationist orientation that dominated communist-era policy towards the historic core.

Prague emerged from the Second World War with less physical damage than any other East Central European capital city. Czechoslovak communist leaders inherited a city whose centre did not easily lend itself to the extensive rebuilding that took place in cities such as Warsaw and East Berlin. While the 1950s did see the emergence on paper of some projects that could change the historic face of the city, none were ever realized except the short-lived (1955–63) giant statue of Stalin gazing across the Vltava River (Maier et al. 1998: 49–50).

Major redevelopment in the historic core was stymied in part by the cost of tearing down existing buildings (Maier, Hexner, and Kibic 1998:

48–9). Furthermore, the mass methods of construction that came to be favoured by the regime were ill-suited to smaller-scale building in the inner-city, which made such development unattractive for the city's large state construction companies. Equally important was the legacy of widespread public and professional mobilization around historic preservation that had emerged during the first decades of the twentieth century. The public reaction against the razing of the medieval Jewish ghetto at the end of the nineteenth century had led to the emergence of a highly active citizens' group, the Club for Old Prague (Klub za Starou Prahu, KZSP), which had been instrumental in mobilizing planners and architects around the cause of historic preservation. Such mobilization had in turn led to the adoption of restrictions on development in the historic core during the 1920s and 1930s (Bečková 2000: 28–70).

Although the Club for Old Prague was co-opted by the Communist Party in the 1950s and its influence on policy declined, it did not disappear entirely. The strong preservationist sentiment that it had embodied during the first decades of the twentieth century survived in the form of a generation of professionals dedicated to the preservation of the city's historic heritage (Bečková 2000: 70–82). Between the 1950s and the 1980s this dominant professional concern was institutionalized in a number of administrative bodies at the municipal level.

Administering Preservation: Structures and Norms in the Communist Era

Just like transport development, real estate development in communist-era Prague was governed at a general level by comprehensive land use plans, produced by the city's planning office, the UHA. Following the initial abortive efforts to redevelop parts of the historic core in the 1950s, however, there were no further efforts at major redevelopment. As a result, the planners at the UHA, so central to the development of the city's freeways network, played a much smaller role in managing changes in the historic core. What role the UHA did have was largely through its Department of Land Use Decisions (Odbor Územního Rozhodovaní, OUR), which was partly responsible for approving the handful of new buildings constructed in the historic core during the communist era.

Prague's construction approvals process in the communist involved a large number of administrative bodies. However, with respect to the historic core, preservationist bodies associated with the city's Department of Culture emerged as the de facto dominant force. In 1960 the Department of Culture established the Prague Centre of State Monument Preservation and Nature Protection (PSSPPOP) as a professional organization dedicated to issuing 'expert opinions' on proposed construction in historic areas (Bečková 2000: 80). The Department of Culture then either approved or rejected proposed construction projects on the basis of these recommendations.

In addition, in 1957 responsibility for managing the Prague branch of the State Institute for the Reconstruction of Historic Sites and Buildings (SURPMO) was handed over to Prague's Department of Culture, giving the city a professional organization dedicated to restoration work (Bečková 2000: 80). The late 1950s also saw the emergence of an informal body, the Prague Monuments Council. This organization, which survived through the rest of the communist era, brought together about forty experts in historic preservation, architecture, and urban planning to advise politicians on questions of preservation and development (Interview 19).

With the exception of the informal Monuments Council, promotion of personnel in institutions dealing with preservation and development in the historic core was governed by the same strict seniority system that prevailed in road-building. Bodies such as PSSPPOP and the Prague branch of SURPMO exhibited what one historic preservation professional called a 'remarkable stability in personnel' (Interview 19) and were dominated in the late communist period by a cohesive cohort of senior bureaucrats who had spent two to three decades in these institutions. Accordingly, these people strongly valued long-range policy continuity and were intimately attached to their organization's core mission. 'Many people don't seem to appreciate today that the base of knowledge that we have in historic preservation institutions took decades of painstaking work to accumulate,' explained one preservation professional interviewed for this project. 'People dedicated their entire careers to mapping and protecting the historic values of very specific, small areas [of the city]' (Interview 32).

Like their counterparts in the transport sector, the preservation-oriented institutions that dominated policy for the city's historic core during the communist era (PSSPPOP, the Prague division of SURPMO, and the Prague Monuments Council) formed a policy network vertically segmented from other institutions. However, the implications of this for the policy orientation of these institutions were quite different than they were in the field of roads construction. Despite a growing need for investment in the upkeep of crumbling old buildings, preservationist institutions lacked the 'investment hunger' exhibited by road-building institutions in the context of a shortage economy.

Throughout the communist era, there was a chronic lack of money for the restoration and upgrading of historic buildings in Prague. As a result, the widespread dilapidation of buildings in the city core, and their ensuing conversion from residences and offices into low-end storage space, was a key inheritance of the communist period. Despite this, preservationist institutions did not focus on seeking to maximize the fiscal resources at their disposal. The primary reason for this appears to be that top personnel viewed their mission as a regulatory one. Thus they concentrated on securing political approval for tight controls on new development in the city centre and the administrative power to enforce them. This regulatory orientation is clear from the words of one pre-1989 administrator interviewed for this project: 'Of course we were unhappy that the regime put so little money into the upkeep of our heritage. But frankly, we were never too keen to draw attention to this, as more money might mean more pressure from interests insensitive to historic values. So actually we were a bit afraid that by pressing for investment we would unleash activity that might undermine the real goal, which was preserving the authenticity of Prague's architectural inheritance' (Interview 19).

In advancing their own interests concerning development policy with respect to the city centre, top personnel in preservationist institutions focused primarily on pressuring political leaders at both the local and national levels to adopt and implement development controls. Over the course of the communist era, a corpus of regulations emerged that strongly restricted development in the historic core. As early as 1951, three of Prague's four historic towns (the Lesser Quarter, the Castle District, and the Old Town) were designated as 'urban historic reserves.' This declaration, however, was largely symbolic and had little substance in terms of concrete development controls.

During the following decades, PSSPPOP and the Prague division of SURPMO devoted much of their energy to systematically documenting the history and architectural value of each building in the city's core, to build a case for comprehensive a preservation policy (Bečková 2000: 80). This effort resulted in the entire historic core being designated the Prague Monument Preserve (PPR) by the Czechoslovak federal government in 1971.[8] The PPR designation ensured that historic preservation institutions were involved in decisions regarding any construction or reconstruction in an area of 8.6 square kilometres that had a resident population of some 90,000 individuals (1971 estimate) and a working-day population of over 200,000 (City Development Authority 1999a: 6–9). In 1985 Prague's political leadership made the terms of this involvement more concrete, passing a by-law that codified guidelines regarding the permissible volume, height, and building materials of new buildings in the PPR. Although the guidelines were aimed at restricting development, they remained quite general, so historic preservation officials continued to have strong discretion in deciding upon the appropriateness of individual proposals for development (Coufalová 1998).

As in the sphere of roads, bureaucratic institutions involved in development of the city centre ultimately depended on the support of the national government to realize their goals. Preservationist institutions in particular shied away from pressing for maximum fiscal resources, to forestall the possibility of inappropriate development in the core. In seeking to protect against such development, they believed in the superiority of their own technical knowledge, as the roads administrators did. The dominant argument in this policy field had to do with claims about the intrinsic value of the historic heritage of the city, claims that were backed by exhaustive documentation on the history and architectural merits of the individual buildings. As in the case of roads, this vision of the public interest was defined within bureaucratic institutions with little reference to any actual public preferences (Lidové Noviny 1988).

In contrast to the transport planning, the dominant challenge to the professionally defined vision about preservation came not from popular protest, but from a change in the political priorities of national leaders of the Communist Party in the 1980s. The 1970s did bring a few new development projects to the historic core – most notably the construction of a new annex to the National Theatre and the razing of the Těšnov railway station and surrounding parkland to make way for the North-South Artery – but preservationist interests remained largely unchallenged until the early 1980s. At this time, however, the national communist leadership decided to begin investing money in the city centre to improve its tourist potential and found support for this policy in the leadership of the city's main planning body, the UHA.

At first, initiatives such as the refurbishment of buildings around the Old Town Square and the restoration of the Royal Way leading from the Old Town Square to Prague Castle were welcomed by preservation professionals (Interview 19). However, a proposal by Prague's political leaders in the late 1980s to develop a number of new hotels in the Lesser Quarter sparked a significant backlash. Taking advantage of the broader climate of protest in 1989, historic preservation professionals began to complain publicly that the politicians planned to 'turn the historic core of Prague into some sort of theme park for foreigners' (Horyna 1990:12). They were supported by the Club for Old Prague, as well as by an emerging residents' group, the Association of Residents and Friends of the Lesser Quarter and the Castle District (SOPMSH) (Horyna 1990; Pešek et al. 1990).

The protest against the planned development of hotels in the Lesser Quarter never approached the movement against the Stromovka tunnel in scale and intensity. Despite the involvement of SOPMSH it was dominated by professional architects and members of the city's historic preservation institutions. The loose alliance between preservation professionals and local residents in this policy area stands in contrast to the sharp animosity between roads administrators and public protesters that existed at exactly the same time.

Communist-era institutions dealing with preservation and development in Prague's historic core had much in common, structurally, with their counterparts in the transport sector, and these commonalities in turn entrenched similar norms: continuity in policy, reliance on professional knowledge, and a reluctance to engage with the broader public. However, the dominant ethos of preservationism gave these institutions a regulatory focus, and they lacked a driving investment project such as the Basic Communications System (ZKS). The absence of conflict with societal actors at the end of the communist era further distinguished their experience from that of transport bureaucrats. Instead of being attacked as dealers in insensitive top-down development, the preservationists who dominated the administration of development in the city centre had the support of active sectors of the public in their struggle against political proposals for new development in 1989.

As in the transport sector, the institutions dealing with preservation and development in the historic core survived the end of the communist era and became components of the new structure of post-communist Prague. Here too, new local politicians faced an administrative apparatus with an entrenched policy orientation, although little pressure had emerged from the public to re-evaluate it. Post-communist political leaders thus faced strong incentives to maintain systematic preservationist policy in the historic core. The emergence of a real estate market in the early 1990s did mean that policy would have to undergo significant reform in order to fulfil the goal of systematic preservation, however, and in a context where regulations regarding conflicts of interest and access to information had not yet been developed, rising investor interest in real estate in the centre soon produced new incentives to pursue development.

Market Pressures and the Public-Private Nexus, 1990–92

During the first two years after the fall of communism, the nature and scope of pressure for development in the historic core of Prague changed radically. Transport infrastructure remained a matter of public investment, but the nationally led transition to a market economy rapidly replaced public with private investment as a dominant force in the real estate sector. This had three key motors, all directed by national legislation: the privatization of real estate; the opening of the real estate market to private investors, both domestic and foreign; and the deregulation of real estate prices. These three factors interacted to generate unprecedented pressure from the private sector for new development in Prague's historic core.

The privatization of real estate (discussed in some detail in Chapter 2) transferred the majority of buildings in the historic core into private hands by early 1992. By far the most important privatization process involved the restitution of apartment blocks to their pre-1948 owners or their heirs, which affected about 70 per cent of all housing stock in the historic core. Although the City of Prague and other state institutions retained control over key non-residential buildings, and the Borough of Prague 1 received most of the housing stock that had not been restored to private owners, the majority of the buildings in the core were transferred into private hands in the space of little more than a year.[8]

Along with the privatization of real estate, national reforms in 1991 and 1992 mandated the privatization and/or liquidation of Prague's large municipal construction companies. Within three years of the fall of communism the city's three mammoth state-owned construction companies – IROP, VIS, and VUS – had been dissolved (Interview 15). Hundreds of private investors, both domestic and foreign, took their place in the rapidly emerging real estate market. During the communist period the lack of a profit motive for state-owned enterprises had helped to keep office and retail development away from the historic core, where buildings were expensive to maintain and were often ill-suited to the needs of modern business and commerce. As soon as private business emerged, however, so did commercial pressure to locate offices and high-end businesses in prestigious historic buildings. As a result, demands for development immediately began to concentrate on the city's historic core.

This change is clearly reflected in the skyrocketing price of real estate in the city centre in the early 1990s. In 1991 the national government lifted restrictions on rent for non-residential premises, as well as for new residential leases in privately owned buildings. In the ensuing state auctions of small business leases in Prague, prices per square metre in the historic core were up to thirty times higher than those in peripheral areas of the city. At the same time, rents for office space in the core jumped to ten times the level in the periphery (Sýkora and Šimoničková 1994: 55–6, Sýkora 1994: 1156). In 1991 the national government also liberalized land prices, and the few lots of vacant land in the historic core, most of which were owned by the City of Prague, suddenly became extremely valuable. In the space of little more than a year interest in commercial property in the historic core rose to a flood.

This new interest in real estate in the core might have offered Prague's new political leaders a chance to harness private money to systematically restore historic buildings or to develop new structures that complemented the historic character of the city centre. However, the commercial investors clamouring to convert old buildings or to construct new ones rarely shared these interests. Most existing buildings were not well suited to commercial needs without extensive alterations (Interview 23), while investors seeking to construct new buildings naturally wanted to maximize available floor space, regardless of a building's fit with its surroundings. As a result, harnessing private money in the service of a preservationist policy for the historic core would have required determined strategic action on the part of the politicians. Two key institutional legacies of the past conspired to weaken the attractiveness of such action.

First, the state-dominated political and economic system of communist-era Czechoslovakia had operated without any regulation separating public from private interests. Although the first post-communist Czechoslovak government rapidly embarked upon a process of market reform, provisions to separate public activity from private interests through conflict-of-interest legislation came later. Even when national conflict-of-interest legislation was introduced, in 1993, it did not apply to the local level (Wollner 1993). Thus, in early post-communist Prague, neither bureaucrats nor politicians faced statutory restrictions on involvement in private enterprises. Elected representatives were officially required to report private for-profit activity, but there were no sanctions for failing to do so (Interview 39). While the new Municipal Law mandated the establishment of a Control Committee to investigate any irregularities in decisionmaking by the executive board (no. 367/1990, par. 56.1), in Prague the Control Committee was appointed and directed by the executive board itself (Interview 39).

Second, decisionmaking in communist-era Prague had been dominated by processes of negotiation that took place behind closed doors, and regulations regarding the release of information on policy processes into the public domain were virtually non-existent. This state of affairs persisted into the early post-communist period. The Municipal Law stipulated that the city's executive board, which had responsibility for negotiating deals with private investors interested in municipal property, was to meet in private (par. 44.6). An intention to sell or lease municipal property had to be publicly announced before being voted on by the city council (par. 36a.4), but the terms of sale or lease were not subject to disclosure (Horský and Schmidt 1991). Likewise, although civic actors were granted some entry points into the development permits process after 1990 (see Chapter 5), civic actors not directly involved in the permits process had no legal means to obtain information about the reasons a development permit was or was not granted (Interview 25).

Together with the transition to the market, the lack of both conflict-of-interest rules and requirements for public disclosure produced a new set of incentives for politicians regarding real estate development in Prague's historic core in the early post-communist period. Given such intense interest by investors, political leaders had the chance to take advantage of these institutional lacunae to pursue private gain by acting as intermediaries. Insofar as municipal property was involved, the members of the executive board and the city council had direct opportunities to enrich themselves by promoting particular investment proposals. Insofar as proposed investments did not involve municipal property, the executive board had indirect levers of control over the administration through its personnel and organizational power. The monetary advantages of pursuing private gain could be great, while the risks appeared negligible. If politicians in Prague responded to these new incentives, they would in turn have good reason to maintain closed decisionmaking processes and to maximize their own discretionary power by resisting the adoption of systematic policies. Administrative and societal pressures to continue pursuing systematic preservation policies in the city's historic core were thus quickly countered by new incentives that encouraged political leaders to pursue private gain through ad hoc, closed-door decisionmaking with regard to real estate development.

Conclusion: Institutions and Strategic Action in Early Post-communist Prague

By the time that Prague's first freely elected council sat down to do business in December 1990, the basic features of a new local government structure were largely in place. Yet the transformation of other state and societal institutions was just beginning. In both of the policy spheres examined in this book, the city's political leaders were faced with a disparate mix of institutions that had emerged at various points in the city's past and that embedded fundamentally conflicting norms of political behaviour. The lack of established patterns of politics and policy meant that local politicians faced critical decision points: They had unprecedented opportunities to shape future outcomes through strategic reform of both institutions and policies. The local government reforms of 1990 had given them the formal powers necessary to effect such reform, including the power to reorganize the administration and to direct urban development policy. But two key features of the early post-communist decisionmaking environment conspired to make strategic institutional and policy reform difficult and unattractive for the city's new leaders.

The first feature was institutional incoherence. The incompatibility of the structure of the Civic Forum/ODS with its post-communist governing role meant that political leaders had no 'road map' of their own to guide reform, and the presence of institutions with conflicting normative orientations in the broader decisionmaking environment meant that this environment did not provide a clear 'road map' either. In designing new state structures in 1990, local and national policymakers had turned to the pre-communist historical experience of local government to guide their choices. Such experience was of limited use at the level of policy, however, where strategic responses had to take account of a context that had been deeply altered by four decades of communist rule. The city's political leaders confronted critical decision points in individual policy areas without any clear guide as to how to deal with them.

Second, Prague's new leaders were inexperienced politicians operating in an unstable political environment that inundated them with complex demands. In addition to facing critical decisions in individual policy spheres, they had to deal with a number of aspects of local state building that had not yet been completed, such as the division of responsibilities between the city and the boroughs. This incompleteness of the institutional architecture contributed to the unpredictability of political outcomes. For example, because the structure of property relations in the historic core was not yet settled in 1991, the possible impact of comprehensive reforms in preservation policy was difficult to gauge.

Together, institutional incoherence and the unstable character of the political system produced a highly disorienting context for decision-making. As one former member of the executive board put it: 'We came into the [November] elections with incredible enthusiasm, a sense that we could participate in history unfolding ... When we found ourselves actually in office, well frankly it was a bit too much for us. The rules were still uncertain, there were a million important decisions to be made and, well, no one knew where to start. We were the new democratically elected politicians and yet we had no idea what to do next' (Interview 28). The combination of institutional incoherence and systemic instability tested the limits of rationality of the individual political leaders. As we will see in the next two chapters, Prague's local politicians began to respond by turning away from longer-range plans and reform proposals and by seeking simple and expedient solutions to the critical decisions that confronted them in various policy spheres. Recalling his experience in the executive board, one former ODS politician noted that 'the November 1990 elections brought in a group of people who were at first strongly committed to making the city work. But we were also inexperienced, and the complexity and difficulty of everything started wearing people down. So there was this overwhelming need to make things simpler, more "primitive," to find a quick and easy way of making sense of things' (Interview 9).

In searching for a way to make sense of their governing possibilities, city councillors began to focus on simple solutions and short-term rewards rather than on strategic reforms that built a foundation for the future. Moreover, in a context where many pre-democratic political institutions remained, the matrix of short-term incentives for political leaders did not always bode well for the development of systematic and open government. In the sphere of roads construction, civic groups offered political leaders the prospect of increased legitimacy if they opened policy processes to public input, but these same groups had little capacity to engage in systematic policy development; the city's bureaucrats, meanwhile, stood at the ready with a long-established plan for freeways construction, but threatened to block any policy processes that involved the public. In the sphere of preservation and development of the city centre, there was strong consensus in favour of preservation; however, the absence of conflict-of-interest rules offered politicians an opportunity for financial gain from ad hoc real estate dealings. How political leaders actually chose among the conflicting incentives in each policy area and what longer-term consequences these early choices had for institutional development and government performance are the questions examined in the next two chapters.

4 Planning and Developing the Main Road Network: The Politics of Mutual Delegitimation

From ZKS to HUS: The Limits of Strategic Reform

At the end of the communist era, public transit was the dominant mode of transport in Prague, accounting for some 80 per cent of total daily trips made in the city (Transport Engineering Institute 2000: 11). Nonetheless, the transport issue that attracted the most attention in 1990 and 1991 was the question of whether and how to continue building the freeways system. About one-third of the ZKS freeways network designed in the late communist era was in place in 1990, and the city's administrative institutions were committed to seeing this project through to completion. Their aspirations were opposed by small but vocal civic groups, remnants of a vigorous 1989 protest movement against freeways development. After the first free elections in November 1990, Prague's new political leaders had to contend with the opposing demands of bureaucrats and civic groups without having a clear policy position of their own, in a turbulent overall context in which decisions had to be made on many complex issues. We will begin this chapter by looking at how these factors shaped the evolution of political action on the freeways issue in Prague in 1990–91.

In February 1990 about a hundred newly appointed Civic Forum deputies took their seats in Prague's communist-era assembly, the NVP, charged with governing the city until the first free elections. Civic Forum deputies had only 45 per cent of the seats, but they had wide public support and faced a contingent of demoralized surviving communist deputies. The NVP elected an energetic new mayor, former theatre director and Civic Forum member Jaroslav Kořán, and a new executive board, and then seized its strong popular mandate to begin taking municipal policy in new directions in advance of the elections. Nowhere did Prague's interim political leadership move to re-evaluate existing policy more quickly than in the sphere of roads development.

The ZKS plans included building a freeway through Stromovka Park, which is just north of the city centre. In 1988–89 Stromovka was the catalyst for a mass protest movement in which a number of the new Civic Forum deputies had been involved. Almost immediately after the interim NVP members were named, civic groups that had led that protest were made voting members of the city's standing committee on transport (Interview 33). Mayor Kořán appointed an Independent Committee for the Evaluation of the ZKS (hereafter IEC), and it was instructed to 'evaluate the conceptual and technical quality of the ZKS, paying special attention to those segments whose construction is in progress or is imminent' (IEC 1990: 1).

The independent evaluation committee was made up of twenty-one members, selected according to two basic criteria: First, to give the IEC credible independent status, only people who had not been extensively involved in the previous ZKS debate were appointed. The committee therefore had no municipal transport administrators or civic activists on it – although at least one transport planner who had spoken out against the ZKS project did make the final cut (Interview 16; IEC 1990: 11). Second, to address criticism that the ZKS had been formulated with only transport needs in mind, committee members were chosen from a variety of professions, among them transport planners, architects, historic preservation professionals, urban ecologists, sociologists, and health professionals (Plicka 1991).

Given the intense public controversy over the ZKS, the IEC deliberations – which were open to observers from transport planning institutions and civic groups – were highly contentious. Some members criticized the committee's terms of reference, claiming they offered insufficient opportunity for alternative proposals for Prague's road infrastructure or for integrating automobile transport with public transit (Interview 35). Seven members resigned over such controversies, leaving only fourteen to draft the committee's final report (Růžička 1991).

Published in September 1990, the IEC's final report was a radical critique of the ZKS plans: 'For [Prague] to achieve equal status with other developed cities, it is imperative to make it once again livable, clean, attractive, and comfortable. One of the conditions for achieving this state is maximum possible protection from the negative impacts of [automobile] transport ... The committee has reached the conclusion that the current ZKS plans do not fulfil these criteria' (IEC 1990: 9–10).

The committee recommended several major changes to the ZKS, aimed at 'sustainably and effectively restricting' automobile transport and thereby 'maintaining a favourable ratio between individual automobile transport and public transit.' Thus, it proposed that (1) priority be given to construction of the city's outer ring road, which would 'provide a bypass for through traffic and heavy vehicles'; (2) the dimensions of the inner ring road be dramatically reduced, downgrading it from a freeway to a boulevard with on-grade intersections and traffic lights; (3) the controversial plan for the western segment of the middle ring road, which included the freeway through Stromovka Park be scrapped, since the 'current development of the city in the northwest provides no rationale for building the middle ring road in this part of the city'; the eastern part of the middle ring road would then be completed by integrating existing roads into the new freeways system, rather than by constructing an entirely new segment of freeway; (4) the radial roads linking the ring roads be reduced in number from eleven to seven and downgraded in status to standard city roads, in the inner city; (5) the ZKS plans be integrated into a more broadly conceived transport policy that would include restricted parking in the city core and the systematic integration of the road and public transit systems; and finally, (6) a standing committee be struck, made up of both professionals and representatives of the public, to 'monitor the development of the ZKS in Prague and its implementation in specific segments' (IEC 1990: 1–11).

The IEC's conclusions amounted to a radical revision of the city's plans for freeways, in line with the political impulse that had driven the Stromovka protest movement. The recommendations called for downgrading or even cancelling plans for most segments of the ZKS that ran through the city's historic core or nineteenth-century residential districts (see Figure 4.1). From a political point of view, the most significant recommendation was to scrap the controversial western middle ring road, which amounted to endorsing the key goal of the 1988–89 protest movement.

Not surprisingly, reaction to the report from critics of the ZKS was overwhelmingly positive (Interview 37). The local newspapers, which had largely sided with the Stromovka protesters, ran articles lauding the IEC's recommendations as a breakthrough in 'the battle for a Prague without nonsensical automobile traffic' (Plicka 1990: 14). Although

Figure 4.1. Basic Communications System (ZKS) 1980s plan (A) vs. recommendations by the Independent Committee for the Evaluation of the ZKS (B)

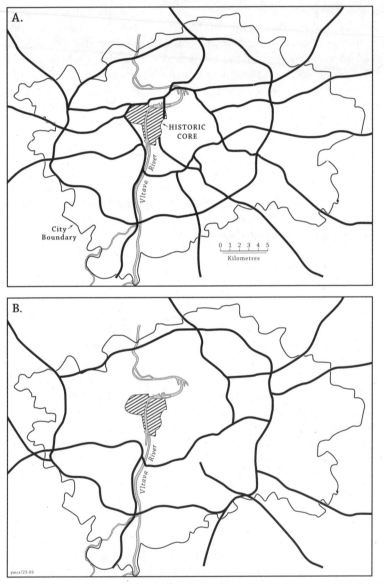

Source: Adapted and redrawn from Transport Engineering Institute 1991, Figs. 1 and 2.

the position of the broader public was not entirely clear, my research found no indication of its active disapproval of the report. On the contrary, the daily media ran many letters to the editor that strongly supported the committee's proposals.

Less than two weeks before the November 1990 municipal elections, Prague's interim assembly passed a resolution endorsing the IEC's conclusions, calling on the city's transport planners to create new detailed plans for the freeways in accordance with the committee's recommendations and to begin immediately to adapt existing roads that would then function as the eastern half of the middle ring road (Prague National Committee 1990b). The city seemed poised to adopt a new comprehensive freeways policy. But the promise of sustained open government, in which civic actors would have substantial input into freeways policy, soon began to fade. A key factor was opposition from transport administrators who were committed to the original ZKS plans.

Even before the independent evaluation committee had issued its final report, other institutions involved in the freeways project had begun to produce documents in defence of the original plans. In June 1990 the Czech Association of Construction Engineers issued a report, in which it is stated: 'The intense public pressure to significantly restrict [automobile] traffic and stop major construction projects ... flows from ignorance, or a misunderstanding or misinterpretation of causal relations. By no means is there a conflict between the functional needs of [automobile] transport and other urban functions' (1990: 1). This report concluded that the ZKS needed to be built as originally planned, and as quickly as possible, because those plans were based on 'transport engineering data that flow from long-term measurement of traffic flows and analyses of the probable future growth of traffic volumes based on the experience of other large cities worldwide.' It also recommended rapid construction of the western sector of the middle ring road, including the Stromovka Park segment (ibid.: 9).

The IEC had reached its conclusions by adopting the overriding aim expressed by the popular protest movement of 1988–89: minimizing the negative impacts of automobile traffic on the quality of urban life. In sharp contrast to this, the construction engineers' report espoused assumptions that growth in traffic volumes is inelastic and that accommodation of this growth is necessary. As such, their report held to the technocratically defined vision of transport development dominant among the city's transport professionals. In late 1990, Prague's transport institutions, including the Department of Transport, the Transport Engineering Institute (UDI), and the Design Institute for Transport Engineering Works (PUDIS) commissioned reports from three foreign consultants, with the aim of further defending this vision. In all cases, the consultants relied solely on interviews with, and data provided by, these transport bureaucrats (Hamburg-Consult 1990; Leutzbach 1990; Mott MacDonald Europe 1991). One report opens with: 'The following observations are based on discussions with members of PUDIS and other associated agencies, and on general inspection. No surveys or analysis have been undertaken ... [This report] is not intended to propose specific policies or remedies to solve the problems. Any specific recommendations should be based on a detailed analysis of the problems and a full estimation of the options' (Mott MacDonald Europe 1991: 1).

An examination of these reports suggests that the consultants were not made aware of the ongoing public debate surrounding Prague's freeways or of the existence of the Independent Committee for the Evaluation of the ZKS. Indeed, some analysts expressed surprise at the apparent absence of such conflict,[1] and all three reports emphasized the importance of having a politically defined vision of transport development. One stated this explicitly: 'A key factor is the definition of goals at the political level. It is necessary to determine the range of variation between demands for a city that accommodates the automobile and a city without automobiles in order to develop specific [freeways] plans in Prague' (Hamburg-Consult 1990: 6).

The institutions that commissioned these reports were interested not in a political redefinition of goals, such as was already taking place under the auspices of the IEC, but in defending the ZKS. Given the data limitations that they worked with, the foreign consultants essentially approved the current ZKS plans, if with some reservations. As a result, in a document produced for the city's executive board at the end of 1990, the Transport Engineering Institute argued that four out of five studies of Prague's freeways system endorse the original plans – which should therefore be retained (cited in Plicka 1991). One transport planner described the value of the foreign consultants' studies as follows: 'The only thing we used the foreign studies for was to try to ensure that civic groups would leave us alone, and the studies helped tremendously by giving us new rationalizations for keeping the current system. Their actual value in terms of analysing what should be built was minimal, since none of the consultants were around long enough to understand much' (Interview 18).

At the moment that Prague's first freely elected political leadership took office in November 1990, a new vision of the city's freeways program, born of the pressure exerted by the protest movement of 1988–89, stood against an old vision that was being vigorously defended by the city's civil service. Prague's new political elites faced this conflict with little or no political experience and with no electoral program of their own on which they could base their policy orientations. Moreover, the broader decisionmaking environment saddled them with the job of managing new and untested municipal political machinery in a context of incipient market reforms. Uncharted waters lay ahead, and a multitude of decisions had to be made. A host of complex issues, such as the return of municipal property, clamoured for their immediate attention. In this context, they ultimately chose what seemed to be the most quick and easy resolution to the controversy over freeways development.

The city council elected a new executive board, and it soon met to discuss options for the future of the freeways system. At its disposal the board had a new vision, endorsed by the outgoing interim municipal assembly and strongly supported by civic groups that continued to campaign for its realization even after the November elections through letters to the press and petitions to the board (see, e.g., Vašků 1990). Media coverage suggests that the new vision had strong popular support, although the Civic Forum's lack of an electoral platform meant that the new city council did not actually have a clear electoral mandate to pursue any particular policy.

On the executive board, the new freeways policy had the support of Mayor Jaroslav Kořán, re-elected to the post by the new city council (Interview 33).[2] Kořán, however was only one of fifteen individuals with equal power on a board comprised largely of newcomers. Collectively, board members quickly realized that pursuing a radically new vision of freeways development would be no easy task. One former board member explained: 'On the one hand, we were nervous about appearing to pander to entrenched interests. On the other, however, we faced an administrative apparatus that was maladapted to the task at hand. They were neither trained, nor in fact willing, to explore multiple policy options' (Interview 28).

The bureaucratic apparatus of the city was 'maladapted to the task at hand' for reasons deeply rooted in its communist-era institutional structure. Ensuring that civil servants would agree to develop a new policy direction in dialogue with civic actors would have implied a restructuring the civil service. The executive board did in fact have the power to do this. It had the power to hire and fire top administrators, reduce the levels of hierarchy and number of sectoral divisions, create and implement a new non-partisan personnel management system based on performance rather than seniority, and put in place new institutional venues for contact between civil servants and citizens. In a context in which they were overwhelmed with competing priorities, however, members of the executive board felt that they had little time for such complex reforms. One former member said: 'To orient ourselves in city politics as newcomers, we had to lean heavily on the existing administrative structures. We never knew where to turn first, there was so much to do, and we needed to simplify things as much as we could. So where the bureaucracy had knowledge and policy proposals to offer, we tended to take advantage of this' (Interview 9).

Prague's new political leaders faced a choice in the freeways sector between a new policy that was apparently popular but whose successful implementation implied complicated institutional reform, and an established policy that faced civic opposition but had strong support within administrative bodies as they currently existed. As boundedly rational actors operating in a context of great uncertainty and overwhelming demands, members of Prague's executive board chose the path that offered the simpler solution and stuck to the familiar ZKS plans.

At a January 1991 meeting the executive board distanced itself from the position adopted by the interim municipal assembly. It resolved that 'there are five expert analyses by individual experts or groups of experts on the future development of the ZKS,' thereby placing the independent evaluation committee's report on an equal footing with the four administration-sponsored reports issued in 1990. The board then instructed the city's transport administrators to come up with a new blueprint for the city's freeways network that took all of these analyses into account (cited in Plicka 1991). This de facto rapprochement between the position of the executive board and the position of the civil service bodies was facilitated by the new deputy mayor for transport, František Polák. A former top administrator in the public transit sector, Polák had a good understanding of the technical issues, and this quickly gained him respect and influence among his colleagues on the executive board (Interview 10).[3] On coming into office, he used his professional connections to establish a strong rapport with roads administrators and took the position that the ZKS offered the most workable solution (Interview 10).

The first draft of a new plan, entitled 'Report on the Development of Transport Infrastructure in Prague,' was completed in May 1991 – and it amounted to a reaffirmation of the ZKS. The introduction asserted: 'The share of individual automobile transport in total urban transport is over 50 per cent across the developed world, and a similar trend is sure to occur in Prague as well. For historical reasons the city is not prepared for such an increase in automobile traffic and faces the real threat of collapse – the death of the transport system ... The situation must be radically altered through the following measures: (1) removal of the acute risk of transport collapse, (2) removal of the discrepancy between transport needs and the current capacity of the road network, (3) completion of the ZKS freeways network' (Prague Executive Board 1991a: 1). The draft noted that the 'ZKS has been subject to a number of expert analyses, of which all – save one – reaffirmed the correctness of the original plans, including the preferential construction of the middle ring road' (ibid.: 5). Having dismissed objections to the ZKS in this manner, it presented a detailed schedule for the completion of the ZKS. It recommended that the city open negotiations with the national government for co-financing construction and that the executive board strike a new standing committee on transport that was to be dominated by administrative personnel (ibid.: Appendices 4, 5, and 8).

Many members of the executive board were inclined simply to adopt this course and close the book on further discussion of the freeways issue (Interview 14). They also knew full well that doing so would bring strong opposition from civic groups, as well as from some city councillors, and that council had to approve the plans. The post-November council had fewer members with links to the Stromovka protest movement than the interim assembly had had; nevertheless, many still saw the ZKS as an odious manifestation of communist disregard for the quality of life (Interview 16). One former member of the executive board summarized the situation like this: 'We felt that we had a workable plan under the circumstances, and that we were in no position to squeeze fundamental innovations out of the administration. But we also knew we had to make some sort of political compromise' (Interview 28).

The executive board took several steps over the summer of 1991 to secure sufficient city council support and deflect public opposition. The draft was sent back several times for revision, with Polák leading the negotiations with administrators. The revisions eventually adopted included renaming the freeways plan the Main Road Network (Hlavní

Uliční Síť', HUS) and cutting four radial roads. The inner ring road was also abolished, in name, although in practice this merely meant cutting plans for a 1.5-kilometre-long new segment in the south of the city.[4] The middle ring road, the most contentious of all the proposed roads, was renamed the 'city ring road' and reduced from six to four lanes. Against the IEC's recommendations, it was retained as a full freeway ring that included the Strahov Tunnel (currently under construction beneath the western edge of the city's historic core), and the controversial northern extension that was to run through Stromovka Park (see Figure 4.2 on p. 151; Prague Executive Board 1991b).

The executive board assured the bureaucrats that actual changes to the ZKS would be fairly minimal. 'Take the city ring road, our most significant concern,' one former board member said: 'Transport professionals *knew* that it had to have six lanes to function well. But *we* knew only four lanes would get through council. So we asked the planners for four lanes, but told them that they should leave enough room for expansion to six once political conditions improved. Another example is the North-South Artery, which everyone loves to hate since it's right in the city centre. In public we announced that once the city ring road was finished it would be closed. But no one actually had any intention of doing so, since its function in the transport system was irreplaceable – and still is irreplaceable' (Interview 28).

To minimize public conflict over the new plan, negotiations involved executive board members and civil servants only. The broader body of city councillors, civic groups, and the general public were neither included in the discussions, nor informed about their content until the new document had been hammered out. Civic groups, which in February 1990 had gained a voice on the city's standing committee on transport, were dropped from the committee, which had passed from council to executive board control under the 1990 Law on Municipalities (Interview 33). According to a board member interviewed for this project, the new plan took shape chiefly in negotiations among four individuals – Deputy Mayor Polák, Chief City Planner Ivo Oberstein, Transport Department Director Jan Fiedler, and General Investment Office Director Jan Macko. Together they formed a 'power centre that connected administrative institutions and the executive board; and [their] collective opinions were of decisive weight in the discussions' (Interview 28).

This closed-door approach to policy development stood in contrast to the more open deliberations of the Independent Committee for the

Evaluation of the ZKS of the previous year. During the summer and early autumn of 1991, widespread debate on freeways policy continued, both in the media and in city council, and civic groups organized rallies and petitions in support of the IEC's recommendations (Polák 1991; Lidové Noviny 1991d). But, given the secrecy of the official negotiations, such debate and protest lacked focus.

In October 1991 the final draft on the future development of the freeways system, now called the Main Road Network (HUS), was put to the city council. To forestall criticism, it emphasized the need to 'slow down the [anticipated] rate of growth in automobile traffic' and asserted that this was to be accomplished primarily by 'further developing and improving the public transit system,' not by revising freeways plans. The environmental impact of automobile transport also addressed, but played down. The HUS was billed as a 'wholesale revision ... based on the criticisms of civic groups [and] a number of expert reports' (Prague Executive Board 1991b: 2, 8).

After fierce debate, city council approved the report, endorsing the HUS (Krásný 1996: 9).[5] The vote was immediately followed by further protests from civic groups and by political leaders in the boroughs affected by the proposed new construction. Nevertheless, a new policy was now in place: a policy that was the result of a compromise between bureaucrats' preferences and the executive board's assessment of what was politically feasible. No analysis of the implications of alternate policy options for traffic distribution or volumes, or for the broader quality of life in Prague, was carried out during the decisionmaking process. To solidify approval for the new policy, the executive board did commission such an analysis ex post facto from the city's Transport Engineering Institute (UDI), a long-time supporter of the ZKS. Completed in December 1991, the UDI's report compared three versions of the freeways network – the ZKS, the IEC's proposal, and the HUS – with regard to the speed and safety of traffic and the impact on air quality (Transport Engineering Institute 1991: 6). The analysis was based on the traditional assumption that traffic volumes are entirely inelastic, that is, the total volume of traffic in a city will grow at a given rate no matter what roads are built (ibid.: 5). Thus, the report concluded that the ZKS plans were best overall, but that: 'the proposed Main Road Network [HUS] solution is a possible and workable compromise regarding the organization and scope of the city's network of arterial roads. Any further reduction in radial roads ... cannot be considered acceptable. Both the city and express [outer] ring roads must be considered basic elements of the HUS, without which the road network cannot comprise a systematic whole that makes possible the development of traffic regulation policies (ibid.: 14).

Over the course of 1990 and 1991, Prague's political leaders thus reversed course on the contentious issue of freeways development: from a radical rethinking and reopening of freeways policy back to a closed policy process and a defence of key elements of the ZKS. This behaviour illustrates the crucial role that the limits of individual rationality play in how leaders make decisions in a time of rapid political change. In early post-communist Prague, the political leadership faced state and civic institutions that offered it conflicting visions of policy development, and it lacked a dominant normative framework that might have guided strategic reform in the freeways sector. Leaders also faced the broader daunting task of governing a rapidly changing metropolis using new and untested instruments of power. Finding an expedient solution to the freeways controversy was of paramount importance, and the most expedient solution appeared to be a closing of the policy process and retrenchment towards the communist-era vision of the freeways network. This choice, made at a critical point in the history of roads policy in the city, had important longer-term consequences for government performance. We now turn our attention to these longer-term consequences in the roads sector in 1990s Prague.

The Politics of Mutual Delegitimation

The adoption, in October 1991, of the HUS plan as the official cornerstone of Prague's automobile transport policy did not give transport administrators all they had wanted. Yet despite political compromise on some issues (most notably, the four radial roads were dropped, out of fear of public opposition) the HUS plan, as well as the closed manner in which it was negotiated, signalled victory for the old technocratic policy orientation over a new policy orientation based on changing civic priorities. This victory did not end the conflict between supporters of the two opposing visions of freeways policy. Rather, it entrenched what I am calling a *dynamic of mutual delegitimation*: a situation in which proponents of each vision rejected not only the substance of their opponents' vision but also their opponents' very ability to act as constructive participants in the policymaking process. This dynamic soon expanded beyond civic groups and administrative bodies and began to involve the city's politicians themselves.

For the vast majority of Prague's inhabitants, the return to closed-door decisionmaking in the roads sector discouraged involvement in municipal transport issues at a time when systemic changes in the economy were already pushing them to focus on securing their own livelihoods, rather than on engaging in sustained political activity. The resulting public demobilization left only a small core of perhaps a dozen active civic groups in the transport sector, totalling no more than about a hundred activists (Interview 2). The approval of the HUS by city council led to widespread disillusionment among these groups. Neither the substance of the new plan, nor the secretive way in which it had been arrived at, reflected their essential demands. The tenuous trust in the city's new political leaders that had emerged in 1990 quickly turned to hostility in 1991. The reintroduction of plans for the western city ring road, so strongly opposed in 1989, was especially resented. Some years later, one community activist recalled:

As I watched the independent committee's recommendations gutted before our eyes, and without public involvement, and saw the city basically turn back to the original ZKS plans, I realized that the [interim] political leadership of 1990 was truly the first and last honest leadership that this city has had. The post-elections leadership was clearly in the pockets of administrators and the associated construction lobbies, and so it has been ever since – the city is led by a bunch of bribed, arrogant, and greedy crooks, 'freely elected' though they may be. It was a bitter disappointment to [civic groups] to have fought so hard and, in the end, achieved so little. (Interview 33)[6]

The protest orientation of civic groups was but reinforced by the way in which the transition from the ZKS to the HUS was achieved, and the category of actors now seen as 'enemies' by civic activists expanded to include the city council. In this manner, a key avenue through which collaboration between civic groups and local government might have been built disappeared.

Civic groups retained an organizational structure designed for the politics of protest. They remained loose, unstable amalgams with a weak organizational base, oriented towards protest actions rather than a systematic articulation of policy alternatives (Interview 2). A handful of local civic groups in the transport sector – such as the Prague Mothers and Optim-Eko – remained active throughout the 1990s, but most such groups sprang up and disappeared rapidly, rising and falling with individual issues rather than adopting any longer-term orientation (Interview 2).

The impact of the developments of 1991 on civic groups was mirrored by the entrenchment of the city's bureaucrats in their old approach to freeways policy. The bureaucratic structures that had encouraged the rise of technocratic norms in the communist period remained essentially unchanged. Furthermore, younger transport professionals were tending to seek work in the better-paying private sector, leaving communist-era personnel dominant in the city's transport bodies (Interview 16). Absent political pressure, these had little motivation to alter their traditional normative orientation. On the contrary, as Prague's new political leaders turned towards their vision of policy process and substance, civil servants felt vindicated. Ten years later, a top transport planner reminisced: '[In 1990–91] every ordinary Joe thought he was suddenly an expert on transport planning, and demanded changes to the long-established plans. Ridiculous and extravagant ideas came at us left, right, and centre and we were hard pressed to defend the essential rationality of what we had proposed. In the end, it was all just a monumental waste of time, since for all of their protesting, laypeople never came up with a single reasonable alternate proposal' (Interview 18).

The city council adopted the bureaucracy's position on freeways policy in an effort to find an expedient solution to a complex problem. In doing so, in the eyes of civic activists, it was now 'part of the problem' in the freeways sphere. At the borough level, many politicians retained their link with civic groups and opposed the HUS. But at the citywide level, where transport policies were developed, politicians were now seen by most civic activists as staunch allies of the civil service apparatus. Facing such hostility, many city councillors, especially those who sat on the executive board, in turn absorbed the norms of the bureaucrats regarding policy processes in the freeways sphere. One former member of the executive board described the lessons learned from his experience of working with civic groups in the early 1990s as follows:

> I very soon discovered that any interaction with civic groups, especially the so-called environmental ones, was intrinsically useless and counterproductive. One day they'd demand one compromise, and you'd give it to them, and they'd turn around and slander you in the media. It became clear to me that these groups are basically made up of three kinds of peo-

ple: there are the fanatics, the dangerous Greenpeace types who are after world domination; then there are the opportunists, who are in it so that their property becomes more valuable; and then there are the rather pathetic foot soldiers, the hangers-on who find their identity in groups like that. So what are you supposed to do other than exclude them from decisions? Broader public meetings don't help either – they're always dominated by fanatics, and people always leave them with their respective opinions reinforced. I don't know a single productive example of public consultation here during the past ten years. (Interview 28)

City councillors had come out against public involvement in policymaking on the freeways issue, and in doing so seem to have quickly internalized the policy orientation of the bureaucrats working in this policy sphere. The views of one former executive board member, who was extensively involved on the transport infrastructure file, are revealing in this respect. In the early 1990s, he said, 'I rapidly began to lose interest in transport alternatives when I took trips abroad to study transport issues. I knew we had the best plans we could have' (Interview 26).

The manner in which Prague's political leadership chose to resolve the 1990–91 critical juncture in the roads policy sphere produced a dynamic of mutual delegitimation between government and civic actors in Prague. After 1991 this dynamic pitted small but vocal civic groups, along with a few dissenting transport professionals and some of the city's news media, against the city's bureaucrats and against its citywide political leaders. In addition to disagreeing about the specific shape of roads policy, each side in this dynamic denied the very possibility that the other could be conctructively involved at all, viewing its opponents instead as illegitimate and morally suspect. Civil servants and most city councillors saw civic groups as misinformed or even malicious, with little to contribute to roads policy, while civic activists saw administrators and politicians as arrogant and/or corrupt individuals driven by a desire for domination or material gain.

Over the years, the dynamic of mutual delegitimation became increasingly entrenched in the political landscape of post-communist Prague. Civic groups remained present and vocal, but they were loose, unstable protest coalitions operating in the context of a demobilized public and without sufficient power to achieve a breakthrough in pursuit of their goals. Transport planners and other civil servants embedded in unreformed institutional structures, and enjoying political support at the citywide level, had little motivation to take the civic activists seriously. Political leaders had the power to break this dynamic. They could have chosen to reform government institutions and decision making processes, but they had little incentive to do so: they were vilified by civic groups as allies of a hostile civil service, and they had no clear signals from the broader public regarding freeways policy.

A key opportunity to break the dynamic of mutual delegitimation came in November 1994, with the second free municipal elections. Electoral processes are crucial to open democratic government, because they represent the public's primary opportunity to exercise its voice. In a situation such as Prague's roads policy controversy, where positions are polarized between government elites and a relatively small but vocal group of civic actors, elections may provide essential cues to politicians regarding broader public opinion. To perform this essential function, electoral contests must be programmatic. In the 1994 elections in Prague, neither the Civic Democratic Party (ODS) nor the smaller challenging parties offered any clear platform, and thus a huge opportunity to overcome the dynamic of mutual delegitimation was missed.

For the ODS, the problem in formulating a clear electoral platform was at least in part organizational. The party had inherited from its predecessor, the Civic Forum movement, a decentralized internal structure that impeded the articulation of citywide partisan positions. This structure was centralized somewhat in 1992, when the party created a citywide ODS assembly with the power to approve the candidate list and policy program for municipal elections. However, the assembly was dominated not by city councillors, but by delegates elected by each of the ten district-level ODS organizations (Civic Democratic Party 1997). In 1993 the party developed working groups to hammer out its electoral platform (Interview 11). But by the time the draft had been vetted by delegates from the ten district organizations with their diverse interests, its substance was heavily watered down. One former top ODS activist explained: 'Developing a program in 1994 was a painful process. Our working groups often produced quite concrete, innovative drafts, but then the district delegates had to put their seal of approval on, and you can imagine that district organizations representing central areas of the city had very different views on many urban issues from peripheral ones. So in the end, the program really lacked concrete proposals that could be used to hold politicians to account' (Interview 11).

The ODS's 1994 electoral platform, once again, endorsed the HUS vision of freeways development, but it did so in a one-sentence statement without specifics: 'We consider the city and outer ring roads to be the backbone of the city's road system, which will relieve the historic core [of traffic] and channel commercial traffic to the edge of the city' (Civic Democratic Party 1994a: 8). The only other promise made regarding freeways was that 'the ODS will strive for the faster completion of the outer ring road,' which is a somewhat misleading statement given that responsibility for financing the outer ring road had been taken over by the national government the previous November (ibid.).

The difficulties of formulating a concrete ODS program may have been partly organizational, but in fact, all parties in the 1994 election tended to focus heavily on personalities. An amendment to the Law on Municipal Elections, passed in August 1994, effectively took independents out of the running in elections in big cities, such as Prague, so the field remained open to major political parties, nearly all of which had their counterparts at the national level. Locally, none of these had worked out clear policy positions on most urban issues in previous years. They therefore assumed that voters would respond best to campaigns that associated parties with personalities and with their national parent parties, rather than with specific policy platforms. The Prague chairman of the small, centre-right Civic Democratic Alliance (ODA) said in a June 1994 newspaper interview, 'I believe that people in Prague will vote more on the basis of their general party preferences than on the specifics of local politics in Prague. Thus, we hope above all to choose as our electoral leader a prominent personality' (Denemark 1994: 2).

The chief ODS personality was Jan Koukal. He was elected mayor in a major executive board reshuffling in April 1993, and was running for re-election. In view of the executive instability of the 1991–93 period, the ascendancy of Koukal to the mayor's chair marked the beginning of a consolidation of stable ODS authority in Prague. Unlike his predecessor, the short-lived mayor Milan Kondr, Koukal projected the public persona of a strong and decisive leader. In 1993 and 1994 he had garnered overwhelmingly positive media coverage for his promises to make government in Prague more systematic, professional, and streamlined (Perknerová 1993; Zemské Noviny 1994). Despite their best efforts, Prague's smaller political parties were unable to present candidates of similar public stature, which placed them at a significant disadvantage in the elections.

Koukal's image as a strong leader was based at least in part on his stated commitment to better-functioning urban government. The ODS campaign itself, however, was largely devoid of specific policy items. Instead, it focused on Koukal's personal qualities, portraying him as a decisive leader who was not afraid to be honest or to challenge the status quo (Civic Democratic Party 1994b). Prague's smaller parties followed suit, capitalizing as best they could on the personal attributes of their leaders. Insofar as specific items did appear in the campaign, they usually pertained to ongoing organizational issues – such as clarifying city–borough relations or council–executive board relations – rather than to specific policy areas (Hrdlička and Táborská 1994; Žaloudek 1994).

The 1994 municipal elections did not give any one party an overall majority. The ODS came out on top with twenty-three out of fifty-five city council seats, and it formed a governing coalition with the centre-right Civic Democratic Alliance (ODA; see Table 4.1 on p. 142 for full results). Koukal was re-elected as mayor, heading an executive board composed of both ODS and ODA members of city council (Večerní Praha 1994a, 1994b). The ODS also captured the mayoralty in the city's fifteen largest boroughs (Doláková and Šárová 1994). The post-election political landscape promised partisan stability at both the citywide and the borough levels. But, because of the lack of focus on policy issues in the campaign, the new city council, once again, took up the reins of power without a clear policy mandate. In the sphere of roads development, politicians again lacked any obvious incentives to reform institutional structures and open up policy processes. They did not win a mandate for policy change of the kind demanded by civic groups, neither did they gain strong public endorsement of the HUS freeways plan.

Roads development policy continued to be dominated in the following years by a dynamic of mutual delegitimation that pitted civic activists against political and bureaucratic elites in the context of a politically demobilized general public. The balance of power between the two sides ensured that closed, technocratic decisionmaking would prevail in the freeways sector. As the sunk costs of continuing HUS construction mounted throughout the 1990s, politicians and civil servants became even less inclined to open decisionmaking processes to public input and to risk major changes.

We will now examine Prague's transport policy record in the 1990s, with a focus on outcomes in the freeways sector. Although in 1996 the city adopted an overall policy that emphasized limiting automobile traffic in the city centre, throughout the 1990s it continued to heavily fund HUS construction, especially for the controversial western segment of the inner city ring road. To explain this inconsistent policy orientation, in subsequent sections we will direct our attention to how the dynamic of mutual delegitimation affected urban planning processes.

Meeting the Challenge of the Car in 1990s Prague

Throughout the 1990s, the challenge of coping with automobile traffic in Prague grew more difficult. As the city prospered, and consumer goods became more widely available, car ownership increased rapidly. Between 1990 and 1999 the ownership rate rose from one vehicle per 3.6 inhabitants to one per 1.9 inhabitants (Transport Engineering Institute 2000: 8). Actual traffic volumes rose even faster, more than doubling between 1990 and 1999, while the proportion of commuters using public transit declined from 80 per cent to 60 per cent (ibid.: 11). This situation had significant negative effects on the quality of life in the city. Roads of all sizes increasingly suffered from gridlock; the number of traffic accidents went up by 150 per cent, and despite national measures to phase out leaded gas and improve engine quality, air pollution associated with vehicles became significantly worse (ibid.: 35; Novotný 1997; Zavoral 1996; Prague City Information Institute 1999: 52–7).

Decades of suffering the negative effects of automobile traffic in Western cities have produced a wide range of approaches to mitigating them. One is based on simply accommodating the automobile, as typified by some large U.S. cities; the idea is that the growth of vehicle traffic is inevitable and that the negative effects of this growth can be dampened in part through the construction of freeways to concentrate the bulk of the traffic away from residential areas. At the other end of the spectrum is an integrated approach that seeks to limit the growth of traffic, as typified by many West European cities; the goal here is to shift travel patterns away from the use of automobiles towards other modes of transport using a combination of measures such as low-cost public transit and user fees or administrative restrictions on driving and parking (Pucher and Lefevre 1998).

Prague's landscape and built environment are exceptionally ill-suited to the accommodation approach to traffic management, especially in the older parts of the city (see Chapter 3). During the 1990s the city council consistently recognized the significance of these physical limitations and in its policy pronouncements endorsed an integrated approach to traffic management. In April 1993, for example, Mayor Kondr defended the need for high subsidies for Prague's public transit system, arguing that only continued operational subsidies and a large-scale program of subway and tram route construction could keep public transit competitive with automobiles (Hrubý and Studnička 1993).

Following the 1994 elections, the city council decided to enshrine the integrated policy approach in a document entitled 'Principles of Transport Policy for the Capital City of Prague.' The document, developed by the Transport Engineering Institute (UDI), was approved by a strong council majority in January 1996 (Interview 18). It stated that the city would pursue an integrated transport policy, in which various forms of transport 'complement each other and cooperate in a rational manner' with the overarching goal of providing an effective working transport system, while limiting its negative effects on the quality of life, especially in the city's older central districts (Prague City Council 1996: 2). It emphasized the need to further expand the public transit system and to integrate transit in communities surrounding the city with the city's own transit system (ibid.: 4). Moreover, it asserted the need strictly to limit automobile traffic and parking in the city's historic core and to implement an extensive park-and-ride system, such that 'the definitive share of demand for transport [in the city centre] be satisfied by public transit' (ibid.: 2). Finally, the document endorsed the plan to build a network of freeways that would channel traffic away from the densely populated central area of the city, but without specifying routing or dimensions.

The city's record on implementing these declared principles in the second half of the 1990s was highly uneven. Its strongest accomplishments were in the sphere of public transit, although at great cost in terms of the municipal budget. The city had inherited an extensive public transit system consisting of three subway lines and a network of supporting tram and bus routes, which at the beginning of the 1990s carried approximately 80 per cent of Prague's daily commuters. During the 1991–92 fiscal crunch political leaders, concerned that operating subsidies for public transit were consuming nearly a quarter of the city's entire budget (City of Prague, Department of Finance 1995), considered the possibility of radically raising fares and even privatizing public transit (Adamková 1992; Večerní Praha 1992).

By the time that the Transport Engineering Institute's principles were passed, however, the city's financial position had improved greatly, and these options had been ruled out. Prague's public transit was city-owned and fares remained heavily subsidized (in 1997 fares contributed only 23% to transit operating costs; Prague Transit Company 1998: 11). In June 1996, after three years of preparation, the city began operating ROPID, a regional transit management system that connected public transit in Prague with transit in surrounding communities using a unified fare and ticketing system (Mladá Fronta Dnes 1996a). The city continued to invest extensively in the development of its subway system, adding 11.3 kilometres of track between 1991 and 1999 to bring the system up to a total of 49.8 kilometres (Transport Engineering Institute 2000: 21). Smaller organizational measures aimed at improving the performance of public transit, such as designated bus and tram lanes, were also introduced (ibid.: 32–3).

With respect to policies aimed directly at automobile traffic, the city's record on implementing the transport policy principles was not as good. The goal of minimizing automobile traffic in the city centre, stated in the document, stood in tension with the officially endorsed HUS freeways system. To help minimize car traffic in the city centre, the planned city ring road either would have to be moved sufficiently far away from the centre so as to not draw in additional traffic or complemented by regulatory measures such as restrictions on driving and parking in the historic core together with an extensive park-and-ride system in the city's peripheral areas. For reasons to be explored below, moving the city ring road outwards was not considered to be an option.

Traffic restrictions in the core and a park-and-ride system were both explicitly endorsed in the Transport Engineering Institute's principles. Nevertheless, progress towards implementing them was weak. In 1996 the city's executive board voted to construct 11,000 park-and-ride spaces adjacent to subway stations in peripheral areas of the city by the year 2000. Sufficient funding to meet this goal was not set aside, however, and by October 1999 only 1,108 spaces were in place (Interview 31; Transport Engineering Institute 2000: 41). The city's record with respect to implementing the council's goals of restricting driving and parking in the historic core was also poor. Throughout the 1990s there was little progress either in making streets pedestrian-friendly or introducing one-way traffic flows in the historic core, although tour buses were banned from the area in 1994 (Mladá Fronta Dnes 1994). In 1996 a new paid parking system was introduced that raised the price of parking in the city centre for visitors and employees of businesses. The new arrangements actually increased the total number of parking spaces available in the historic core, (from 22,600 to 27,339) as well as the number of short-term spaces (Interview 18; City Development Authority 1999a: 5; 2000: 76).[7]

Given the relative lack of progress on measures such as park and ride and on restrictions on driving and parking in the historic core, the construction of the western and northwestern segments of the city ring road, along the edge of the historic core, was likely to worsen, rather than improve, traffic conditions in the central area of the city. But the administrative and political supporters of the HUS argued that a comprehensive freeways system was a necessary precondition for such traffic restrictions, even though the 'Principles of Transport Policy' counted on simultaneous implementation of these measures. One public service announcement explained the official line in 1997 like this: 'The creativity of Prague drivers in finding shortcuts, advantageous detours, and ways to circumvent regulations is incredibly high. Thus, we have no choice but to first provide a sufficient supply of road space on the main communications network, that is, on ring roads and radial roads. Only after this can we adopt measures – restrictions or closures – that clearly signal to drivers that driving through the centre is disadvantageous' (City of Prague 1997a: 6).

These assertions had little basis in actual evidence. Indeed, the behaviour of commuters during a major campaign of road repairs, launched in the mid-1990s, suggested that limiting through traffic in the city core might have accomplished the goal of traffic calming even without the city ring road, since the historic core was already densely serviced by public transit. When half of the North-South Artery – Prague's major existing inner-city freeway (it runs along the eastern edge of the city core, as shown on Figure 4.2) – was closed for repairs in 1994, traffic delays did not increase significantly. This led the borough mayor of Prague 2, unsuccessfully, to call for a permanent narrowing of the North-South Artery (Dvořák 1994). A year later, when further road closures worsened traffic conditions in the city core, commuters responded by reverting to public transit, and ridership went up significantly (Červenka 1995).[8]

The city's own projections suggested that the impact of the freeways system on traffic levels in the city centre would be mixed at best. In 1996 more than 170,000 vehicles passed through the city's historic core daily in a north-south direction, using the five busiest through roads (annex to City Development Authority 1999b).[9] Projections suggested that after the completion of the city's freeways system, set for the year 2010, the volume of through traffic on these five roads would decrease by about 38 per cent. The western city ring road however, included the Strahov Tunnel and a yet-to-be-built segment through Stromovka Park, both of which would pass along the borders of the historic core, well inside the densely built-up inner city. If the western city ring road is included in the calculations, the total volume of daily through traffic in the central area of Prague was projected to *increase* by about 20 per cent (to almost 210,000 vehicles) after the completion of the freeways system (ibid.).

The benefits of the existing plan were questionable in terms of Prague's transport policy. Nevertheless, the city invested huge resources in the construction of freeways both before and after the adoption of the 'Principles.' Paradoxically, these resources were especially concentrated on the segment of freeway that had ignited the major protest in 1989, the one most problematic from the point of view of traffic reduction in the city centre: the western city ring road.[10] Between 1991 and 2000 the city invested a total of Kc 32.8 billion (about U.S. $1.2 billion) in the construction and repair of subway lines, tram lines, and roads (calculated from City of Prague, Department of Finance 2001). Of this, 39.7 per cent was directed towards freeways.[11] In 1994 the national government took over financing of the outer ring road (Balcar 1996: 84), and as a result, after that the bulk of the city's freeways money went towards the city ring road, and in particular its western segment. By 1991 about Kc 1.8 billion had been spent on the western city ring road, and its first phase – the Strahov Tunnel – was about one-third complete. By 2000 the city had spent another Kc 8.5 billion to complete this tunnel and on the next phase of the western ring road (calculated from Handl 1992; City of Prague 1997a; Janík 1999).[12]

In the 1990s, Prague's political leaders spent more than one-quarter of the city's total transport infrastructure investments on a project that had been the object of a major public protest movement in 1989 and whose benefits were questionable in terms of the officially stated goals of the city's transport policy. Perhaps even more surprising, the project was carried forward in the absence of any organized civic voices calling for its completion. A detailed analysis of media coverage of Prague transport issues between 1990 and 2000 indicates virtually no evidence of lobbying activity by groups such as automobile clubs, commuter groups, or the Prague Chamber of Commerce (Horak 2000). By contrast, opposition to the construction of the western city ring continued throughout the 1990s and indeed increased as the decade drew to a close.

Among opponents of the western city ring road, a widespread assumption emerged during the 1990s that the continued emphasis by Prague's political leadership on the construction of this project was the result of lobbying by the three large design and construction firms – PUDIS, SubTerra, and Metrostav – that dominated freeways development in Prague (Interview 26; Interview 33). Research for this project, however has found little evidence to support this claim. These three firms, which were privatized in the 1990s, obviously had an interest in maximizing the volume of freeways construction. Yet personal links to the city's political leaders, and thus opportunities for direct ad hoc lobbying, remained weak. While a few politicians did have such connections,[13] in general political links to the design and construction firms were few and far between.

The transport design and construction companies had stronger personal links to civil servants, many of whom had either worked for these firms in the past or had moved into them in the 1990s (Interview 29; Interview 31). Some civil servants might have functioned as indirect channels for lobbying. However, as public-sector employees with a strong technocratic orientation, these bureaucrats tended to guard their autonomy jealously. One veteran transport planner asserted, for example, that 'design and construction companies will always pursue the most expensive schemes possible. In the early 1990s, we sometimes made the mistake of relying on them too much for input regarding design parameters, and we quickly learned that this was an excellent way to waste money' (Interview 29).[14]

An entrenched dynamic of mutual delegitimation provides another explanation for the continued attachment of Prague's political leadership to a freeways project that was of questionable value in terms of the city's stated policy goals. This dynamic entered into land use planning, as well as strategic planning decisions regarding freeways. By frustrating any attempts to initiate dialogue between the city's governing elites and civic groups, mutual delegitimation helped to prevent the rise of open planning processes that might have defused state–society conflict in the freeways sphere. Instead, conflict mounted in the late 1990s, and culminated with a 1999 protest movement against the city's new overall land use plan, which was strikingly reminiscent of the movement against the Stromovka freeway ten years earlier.

HUS and the Development of Prague's Land Use Plan

At the beginning of the 1990s, the practice of land use planning was discredited in Prague. Politicians associated land use planning with the inflexible, bureaucratic policy practices of the communist regime and thus saw it as incompatible with a market-led approach to urban development. However, the problems of pursuing such an approach in the *absence* of a land use plan quickly became apparent enough. As foreign investors crowded into Prague, and in particular into its historic core, ad hoc decisions generated a series of controversies that threatened the legitimacy of the process of decisionmaking on development and preservation issues in the city (Večerní Praha 1991; see also Chapter 5).

The practice of land use planning made a gradual comeback, engineered initially not by the politicians but by the city's planners themselves. In the early 1990s, the last communist-era land use plan for Prague, approved in 1985, was still in force. However, having been designed for a state-dominated setting, its provisions were routinely overridden on the grounds that they were outdated (Drasnářová 1992). The city's main planning body, the Chief Architect's Office (UHA), took the initiative in 1991 to create a new planning apparatus that would take into account private property rights through greater flexibility in zoning and construction regulations (Interview 8). Recognizing that producing a land use plan for all of Prague would take a long time, the city's planners next turned their attention to producing guidelines for the city's 'stabilized zones' – areas that were fully built up and deemed unsuitable for further large-scale development. Led by bureaucratic bodies, this process included consultations with both citywide and borough-level politicians, but excluded civic actors (Interview 8). The geographical extent of the Prague's stabilized zones was a source of some debate between the politicians and bureaucrats, but the guidelines themselves were very general and did not generate much discussion (Interview 8). In the end, the city council quietly passed the 'Plan for the Stabilized Zones' in 1994.

A new land use plan for the whole city, including areas open for major development, was a much more complex and lengthy undertaking, one that might have offered a key opportunity to defuse controversy surrounding the HUS by reopening public discussion about the future shape of the city's freeways. Although the country's communist-era Law on Land Use Planning and the Building Code (discussed in Chapter 3) remained the basis for planning processes, in the early 1990s the law was amended to facilitate more public input. Following the adoption of basic principles, and prior to the drafting of a full plan, the city was now required to prepare a conceptual draft that would include alternative solutions for resolving controversial issues. As with the final draft of the full plan, the conceptual draft was to be shepherded through a 'public commentary' phase – during which administrative bodies, boroughs, individual members of the public, and civic groups could voice their objections and suggestions – prior to being approved by city council (Tůnka and Sklenář 1999: 41–4).

These national regulations stipulated the minimum level of public involvement, but the executive board could choose to include civic actors in the planning process above and beyond that level (Interview 8). In hammering out the new land use plan, the board chose instead to minimize the transparency of the process. Far from defusing controversy about the freeways, the resulting process of preparing Prague's new land use plan helped to intensify it. How and why did this happen?

In 1992–93, at the same time that the 'Plan for the Stabilized Zones' was being formulated, UHA began work on the first stage towards a new overall land use plan for the city, and produced a document entitled 'Land Use and Economic Principles.' It was to constitute the strategic basis for the plan. Like other planning activities in the early 1990s, this was undertaken in the face of widespread indifference among political leaders. One top planner explained: 'The "Land Use and Economic Principles" were still prepared in a political atmosphere that rejected the idea of land use planning. We prepared it internally, within the UHA itself. So in the end, the resulting document was an administrative, not a political thing, although it was approved by city council. It did provide some basis for the plan, but it was vague, and the hard issues – such as the HUS question – hadn't really been addressed yet' (Interview 8).

Adopted by city council in November 1993, the 'Land Use and Economic Principles' endorsed a broad vision of transport development not unlike the one approved by council some two years later in the 'Principles of Transport Policy.' The emphasis was on improving the attractiveness of public transit and on strictly regulating automobile traffic in the city centre (Prague City Council 1993: 61–2). Here the vision was presented in very general terms only, and offered little guidance on implementation, in particular regarding the shape of the city's freeways network. The UHA document recommended the construction of a 'supply of radial and ring roads in the intermediate to outer belt of the city [in order to] decrease the pressure of through traffic in the central area' (ibid.: 62), but did not specify any further.

The task of specifying a more concrete vision of the freeways network was thus deferred to the second stage of planning: the conceptual draft, mandated under the revised national planning law to allow for broader input into the planning process, especially where controversial issues were concerned. However, the law did not mandate any specific mechanisms for gathering such input, only that interest groups and individual citizens were entitled to participate in a public commentary phase that must precede city council's approval of the conceptual draft (Tůnka and Sklenář 1999: 41–4).

In developing the conceptual draft for the new land use plan, Prague's second post-communist government (1994–98) chose to keep the opportunities for public input at the lowest levels required by national law and to narrow as much as possible the range of options presented on any contentious issues. Preparation of the conceptual draft in 1994 and 1995 was led by the newly renamed City Development Authority (URM, formerly the Chief Architect's Office), and it consisted primarily of consultations among citywide politicians and local and national administrative bodies, with but the limited involvement of borough politicians. Civic actors, whether interest groups or individuals, were not involved at all (Interview 8). Furthermore, despite its nominal purpose, the conceptual draft did not offer alternative solutions to controversial issues. The only exception was with regard to the freeways, where for one southeastern segment of the outer ring road the draft offered three routing options. Otherwise, the draft simply reproduced the HUS vision of freeways development, introduced in 1991, including the controversial plans for the western city ring.[15]

The decision not to include civic actors in the process, and to submit only one possible solution in most issue areas, was at least partly a product of the dynamic of mutual delegitimation. The freeways controversy was a key issue sphere in which Prague's civil servants and politicians had interacted with organized civic interests in the early 1990s. The outcome of this controversy contributed to the political demobilization of the broader public and led to the entrenchment of mutual distrust and hostility between bureaucrats and politicians, on the one hand, and civic activists, on the other. Although it was present mainly in the roads sphere, this dynamic directly influenced the decision to limit public input into the conceptual draft of the overall land use plan for the city as a whole.

Following the 1994 municipal elections, political responsibility for overseeing land use planning was given to ODS executive board member Zdeněk Kovařík. With the support of Mayor Jan Koukal, as well as most other executive board members, Kovařík 'used all available leeway in the law [on Land Use Planning and the Building Code] to insulate the development of the land use plan from public discussion' (Interview 20). One executive board member later explained that the board's consensus in favour of this approach was linked directly to the members' experiences with civic groups in the freeways sphere:

> We [the executive board] made a clear decision in the early stages of developing the new land use plan to adopt a minimalist approach to public consultation. And given our previous experience with public input, I think this was the only way to go. The broad public is never that interested in urban politics, and interest groups, particularly these so-called civic initiatives focusing on transport and environment issues, were and still are very immature here. I mean all they know how to do is make a big stink when they don't like something and slander [city government] in the media for alleged corruption. They don't know how to discuss things seriously. Land use planning here is complicated enough as it is, with all of the administrative bodies and boroughs involved. If we involved the public in all stages of the process as well, we'd never get it done. (Interview 20)

The belief among civil servants and politicians that organized civic interests had little to contribute to the land use plan was reinforced by the experience of public consultation over the conceptual draft. As required by national law, the draft went through a public commentary phase in the autumn of 1995. Submissions were taken from individuals and organized civic groups, boroughs, and national, citywide, and borough-level administrative institutions. In total, the city received about 1,000 submissions; of these, about a hundred dealt with various aspects of plans for the freeways (Interview 8; Interview 37). However, the civic groups opposed to the city's plans for the freeways made but a handful of submissions and the nature of these was strongly shaped by the protest orientation of these groups and their experience of being excluded from developing the draft that was presented to them. One long-time freeways activist noted: 'In 1995 we and some other civic groups made submissions criticizing the transport section of the conceptual draft, and the inclusion of the city ring road plans in particular.

But frankly, our hopes weren't very high in the first place, since it was clear that the planners preferred the old freeways development vision and had excluded groups such as ours in the preparation of the draft because of that. Anyway, we hardly had the resources to put together a proper response to a huge, complicated document that was thrust at the public as a fait accompli' (Interview 37).

Submissions regarding the conceptual draft of the land use plan were assessed by the URM, the institution that had prepared it. Submissions made by municipal institutions carried considerable weight, since disputes that arose over them had to go to the relevant national ministry for resolution. Submissions made by borough politicians, civic groups, and individuals could be incorporated or rejected at will by the URM alone (Tůnka and Sklenář 1999: 28–32). With only a handful of submissions from protest-oriented civic groups, the URM's planners felt confirmed in their suspicion that such groups did not have much to contribute, and they rejected their submissions out of hand. One transport planner said: 'There was really very little of use in the submissions made by civic initiatives. They were usually poorly written, uninformed, and, frankly, mainly aimed at attacking our credentials as professionals. They were clearly expressions of some sort of general hostility, rather than serious efforts to develop alternative solutions' (Interview 27). As a result, the impact of submissions by civic groups on the shape of the final conceptual plan was minimal. Approved by the city council in October 1996, it contained no significant changes as a result of public input, except with regard to one controversial segment of the city's outer ring road (Prague City Council 1999: Appendix 1, 1; see also note 15 for this chapter).

Planners then began work on the final draft of the new overall land use plan for Prague, a process that took over two years and that, once again, was closed to civic actors (Interview 21). As with the conceptual draft, preparations involved administrative actors first and foremost, although this time around politicians took part in the process in a more structured manner. Prague's executive board set up a committee of politicians, headed by their member responsible for land use planning, Zdeněk Kovařík, to steer negotiations. This committee coordinated and had input into internal discussions among the staff of various municipal administrative bodies, as well as discussions between these institutions and the city's fifty-seven borough councils (Interview 8).

Once again, the plans for the freeways went unchanged into the final draft. They were dominated by the Main Road Network (HUS) model of seven radial roads and two ring roads, including the city ring skirting the edge of the historic core on the western side. In May 1998, the final draft was made available for comments from civic actors, borough councils, and administrative bodies, as mandated by national law. The URM received 4,005 submissions regarding the draft land use plan between 4 May and 17 June (the closing date for submissions); of these, 473 came from government institutions, 897 from borough councils, 2,357 from individual citizens and private-sector corporate bodies, and 227 from sixty-five different civic groups (City of Prague 1999: Appendix 1, 7).

The large number of civic group submissions, about half of which dealt, once again, with some aspect of plans for the the city's freeways (calculated from City of Prague 1999: Appendix 4), reflected the resurgence of the freeways debate in public discourse in Prague during the previous year. In 1997 and early 1998, the freeways issue had received increasing media attention, as traffic conditions in the city continued to worsen and as controversy continued regarding the routing of various segments of the freeways under construction or scheduled for construction (see below). This attention was accompanied by an upsurge of activity among civic groups. By 1998 some thirty groups involving several hundred core activists operated in the area of transport policy, and they mounted a concerted effort to deliver submissions regarding the land use plan during the public consultation phase (Interview 33). Once again, both planners and politicians tended to see public input as a necessary but bothersome exercise, and put little stock in its real value. One transport planner observed: 'We were constantly attacked in the media as being "antidemocratic" in the way we developed the land use plan, so we extended the process of public consultation beyond its regular thirty-day limit. But to be honest, 90 per cent of the suggestions we got from individuals or groups in society reflected uninformed opinions or the narrow material self-interests of property owners. The rest were from crazies such as these so-called civic associations' (Interview 29).

Despite the objections by civic groups, Prague's new land use plan was headed for political approval in late 1998 without any significant changes to the plans for the freeways. But the civic groups had one important new resource that enabled them to stall the process. Before it could be approved by the city council, the land use plan had to be checked by several national ministries to ensure that it conformed with national laws. In the June 1998 Czech national election, the Civic Democratic Party (ODS) was defeated by the Social Democratic Party (CSSD), which then formed a minority government. The new minister of the environment had personal connections to Prague's civic activists and shared their objections to the city's plans for its freeways. On their urging, in the summer of 1998, the Ministry of the Environment refused to approve the draft land use plan for the City of Prague, on the grounds that it contradicted national environmental standards (Interview 22).

At the same time, the attention drawn to transport issues by the controversy over the land use plan ensured that the city's freeways policy became a major focus of the campaign for the city's third free municipal elections, in November 1998. In July 1998 the Prague ODS, whose popularity had been waning, pushed through a proposal to divide Prague into ten multimember electoral districts – in an effort to bolster the ODS's chances in the election that was coming (Konečný 1998). To maximize their chances of defeating the ODS, four small local parties – the Freedom Union (US)[16], the Civic Democratic Alliance (ODA),[17] the Christian Democratic Union – Czechoslovak People's Party (KDU–CSL), and the Democratic Union (DEU) – formed coalition and called it the Union for Prague (UPP) (Janík and Konečný 1998a).

The Union for Prague selected Martin Bursík as its leader and mayoral candidate for the elections. A city councillor since 1994 and minister of the environment in an interim national government between February and July of 1998,[18] Bursík had strong views on urban policy issues and used his personal prestige to lead the process of developing a UPP electoral platform in a centralized manner (Interview 4). As a result, the UPP's platform was for more specific than any seen in the 1994 municipal campaign. One UPP candidate explained:

> We felt that the Prague public was at a point of maturity where certain concrete issues would resonate strongly. We didn't have opinion polling data available, but we picked issues that we thought would be of most public interest ... We ultimately chose to highlight two issues above all others. First, there was transport. Transport is clearly the most important development issue that the city faces; and with the passing of the new land use plan drawing near, it was very much in the public eye. Second, and this was a more general point, we emphasized the vital need of city hall to make decisionmaking more open in order to give citizens confidence and to clamp down on corruption. (Interview 4)

Table 4.1. Citywide results of municipal elections, 1994 and 1998

	1994		1998	
	Vote (%)	Seats (n)	Vote (%)	Seats (n)
Civic Democratic Party (ODS)	41.2	23	36.9	21
Social Democratic Party (CSSD)	8.6	5	17.6	10
Communist Party (KSCM)[a]	10.7	6	10.0	8
Union for Prague (UPP) (ODA + DEU + KDU–CSL + US)	n/a	n/a	28.1	16
Civic Democratic Alliance (ODA)	9.4	5	n/a	n/a
Democratic Union (DEU)	5.2	3	n/a	n/a
Free Democrats (SD)	4.9	3	n/a	n/a
Other parties / independents	20.0	10	7.4	2

Sources: Šprunková and Kovářová 1998, Schreib 1998b, Dobrý Večer 1994.
[a]The KSC had changed its full name to the Communist Party of Bohemia and Moravia (KSCM) in 1990.

In the UPP's electoral program, transport issues got top billing. In terms of freeways policy, the coalition pledged among other things to stop the construction of the western city ring road and to transfer the funds for it to further public transit development (Union for Prague 1998). The UPP's position on freeways policy was clearly distinguishable from that of the ODS, which endorsed the completion of the HUS freeways system, including the western city ring road (Civic Democratic Party 1998). For the first time since the fall of communism, urban development policy had a prominent place in a municipal electoral campaign in Prague, and in the transport sphere, the campaign offered voters a clear choice among alternative platforms.

Like in 1994, the 1998 municipal elections focused strongly on personalities – in this case, the personal qualities of Mayor Jan Koukal, who was running for re-election, and his main challenger, Martin Bursík. In addition, however, specific development issues, most notably freeways and the overall land use plan, also received a lot of attention (see, e.g., Nachtigall 1998b; Schreib 1998a). In the end, the ODS got 4 per cent less of the popular vote than in 1994 (Table 4.1). It remained the single largest party on city council, but with twenty-one of fifty-five seats it did not have a majority. The UPP came second, winning sixteen seats, while the Social Democratic Party, which had just won the national election, came third, with ten seats (Schreib 1998b).

With its erstwhile governing partner the ODA now in the UPP coalition, the ODS had no obvious coalition partner. But after lengthy negotiations, the ODS formed a governing coalition with the Social Democrats, leaving the UPP in opposition. Under pressure from national ODS leaders, the Prague ODS dropped its mayoral candidate, Jan Koukal, to seal the deal with the Social Democrats (Interview 13). The city council then elected ODS councillor (and 1993–94 executive board member) Jan Kasl as mayor, ushering in the first change to the post in five years (Právo 1998a).

Although the electoral challenge mounted by the UPP on transport issues did not remove the ODS from power in Prague, the emergence of programmatic competition in the electoral race did inject energy into the conflict over the plans for the freeways as laid out in the draft overall land use plan. The ODS, which in its electoral campaign had clearly stated its support of the HUS, interpreted the election results to mean that the public had given it a mandate to complete construction of the proposed network (Interview 14). From the point of view of many UPP members of the city council and members of civic groups, however, the 1998 election results suggested that the undercurrent of public opposition to the HUS was strong, since focusing on the issue had helped a new and untested political force win nearly 30 per cent of the popular vote (Interview 4).

In early 1999, both the new municipal government and civic groups went on the offensive regarding freeways policy and the overall land use plan. Prague's executive board members mounted a media campaign of interviews and advertising, arguing that the absence of an approved land use plan was hindering investment in Prague and that it was far too late to reconsider the merits the HUS, given the amount of money that had already been spent on its construction (see, e.g., Hospodářské Noviny 1999). The city continued to negotiate with the Ministry of the Environment over getting the ministry to withdraw its opposition to the overall land use plan. Moreover, the new mayor, Jan Kasl, decided to try a new approach to dealing with civic groups. In February 1999 he met with representatives of several civic groups opposed to various aspects of the land use plan, with the intention of introducing a regular schedule of meetings with them that could contribute to negotiating compromise positions on freeways policy and other contentious issues (Interview 37).

The dynamic of mutual delegitimation was too entrenched to be broken by an ad hoc, if high-level meeting. Both sides judged the meeting to have been of little value, and the schedule of regular meetings was subsequently cancelled. From the politicians' point of view, the civic groups were entrenched in unyielding opposition to long-established policy positions. Furthermore, huge sums of money had been invested already in the construction of freeway segments such as the western city ring road, making a change to those plans all the more unattractive to them. One executive board member, who had initially been sympathetic to the position of civic groups on the freeways issue, noted: 'It was evident when [Kasl] met with civic groups that they had become radicalized by years of closed decisionmaking at city hall. I don't think that unreasonable demands and mistrust of us [political leaders] were necessarily in their nature, but this is what they came with anyway. They could hardly expect us to throw away things such as the city's freeways plans, that we had already spent years developing and building' (Interview 14). Among civic activists, the perspective on the meeting initiated by Mayor Kasl was equally negative. One long-time civic activist explained: 'We came to the meeting well prepared, our objections to the city ring road in hand. However, we came out with a realization that it had all been part of a cynical public relations plan on the part of the political leadership. Our objections were brushed aside as "unrealistic," and that was the end of it' (Interview 33).

Instead of pursuing what they saw as fruitless efforts at dialogue, civic groups developed new strategies for making their voices heard on land use planning issues. In March 1999, thirty-one groups active in transport and other urban development issues established a coalition, SOS Praha, to mobilize opposition against the overall land use plan (Interview 37; SOS Praha 1999). During the following months, SOS Praha organized a major campaign of petitions, letter writing, and demonstrations in front of city hall protesting various aspects of the plan, most notably the provisions for freeways. Their rhetoric, which labelled city officials as corrupt, arrogant, and insensitive to the wishes of citizens, was strikingly reminiscent of the rhetoric used by the Stromovka protesters some ten years earlier (Šnajdr 1999). In terms of mobilization and visibility, SOS Praha was quite successful. Its petitions got thousands of signatures, its demonstrations drew hundreds to city hall, and the media covered their activity heavily (Slonek 1999b; Zemanová-Kopecká and Kubátová 1999; Šálek 1999). In late summer 1999, SOS Praha added legal means to its tactics: it launched a lawsuit against several key city bureaucrats for 'knowingly threatening the environment' in Prague by approving the construction of the western city ring road (Mladá Fronta Dnes 1999a).

The SOS Praha initiative nonetheless failed in its objectives to change the freeways plan and any other elements in the overall land use plan. Throughout spring 1999, Prague's political leaders negotiated intensively with the Ministry of the Environment. In May, under pressure from the national government, the ministry agreed to approve the land use plan on condition that one controversial segment of the outer ring road (see footnote 15, this chapter) be scheduled for construction *after* 2010 (Prague City Council 1999: 1). The environment minister, however, continued to voice his objections to the western inner ring road even after this agreement was reached (Schreib 1999). The final draft of the overall land use plan at last received approval by city council in September 1999. The vote was, once again, accompanied by demonstrations both outside and inside city hall. Yet little in the final plan reflected the demands of civic groups (Šnajdr 1999), and the HUS plan for Prague's freeways system remained intact.

HUS and the Development of Prague's Strategic Plan

Over the past couple of decades, the practice of strategic planning, that is, articulating an overall vision of future physical, social, and economic development, has become an increasingly common way for cities to forge consensus around urban development through dialogue with civic actors. Unlike land use planning, strategic planning had no historical tradition in the city of Prague prior to the 1990s. During the communist era, economic and social planning was done in a comprehensive but highly sectoral fashion, and it did not involve dialogue with civic actors (Interview 18). Even after the fall of communism, strategic planning had no standing in the national laws of the Czech Republic (Fišer 1995b). As a result, Czech municipal politicians who were interested in strategic planning had no template to guide them, and so had to devise their own methods for coming up with a strategic plan. In Prague, the dynamic of mutual delegitimation in the roads sector helped to ensure that the strategic planning process remained closed to civic opponents of plans for the city's freeways, and did not ease conflict over these plans.

The first two attempts to initiate strategic planning in Prague had few concrete results with regard to the city's freeways. The idea of developing a strategic plan for Prague first came to the fore at the initiative of Deputy Mayor Jiří Exner in early 1992. Following a visit to Barcelona, where he had learned about the success of a strategic plan in mobilizing consensus around urban development goals in that city, Exner prepared a document entitled 'What Is Prague? Draft Ideological Concept of Socioeconomic Development of Prague, the Capital City' (Fišer 1995a; Exner 1992). Intended as a basis for discussion, it was formally adopted by city council in May 1992; however, given the still prevalent rejection of planning by the city's politicians, discussion about the city's strategic goals did not follow (Interview 9).

A second and larger-scale attempt to get strategic planning off the ground was made in 1994 under the leadership of executive board member (and mayor from 1998) Jan Kasl. The city hired a local private-sector foundation, EcoTerra, to prepare a comprehensive document, which would be entitled 'Prague 2010,' that would lay out options for the future strategic direction of the city based on detailed analysis of its current problems. EcoTerra organized a series of discussions with some hundred experts from various professions (including architects, urban planners, ecologists, sociologists, and others), who identified a large number of problems that the city faced, and proposed a wide variety of solutions (Blažek 1994: 3). The result was some 2,400 pages of text, which was then condensed into two reports issued in September 1994. The first identified five key problem areas in contemporary Prague: infrastructure, local institutions, environment, social tensions, and planning. The second proposed ten key goals that the city should work towards in order to alleviate those problems (Blažek 1994: 15; Blažek, Kasl, and Turba 1994: 14).

The initiators of 'Prague 2010' envisioned that, in the short term, the city's political leadership would discuss the document, while in the longer term, it would form the basis for a full strategic planning process that would involve discussions with organized civic groups and the broader public (Blažek, Kasl, and Turba 1994: 2). In preparing the document, EcoTerra did not work closely with the city's political and administrative elites and, as a result, the contents of 'Prague 2010' did not fit well with their opinions. The work was criticized by political elites for lacking a single concrete vision, for overemphasizing public participation in decisionmaking processes, and for not suggesting implementation mechanisms for its proposed strategic goals. One land use planner observed: 'The EcoTerra documents basically irritated many political leaders and planners, as they contained many elements for which the time was not yet ripe' (Interview 36). 'Prague 2010' ended up on the shelf and was never seriously discussed by the city's leadership (Fišer 1995b).

The third exercise towards strategic planning in post-communist Prague was more successful. Learning from the failure of the 'Prague 2010' project, shortly before the November 1994 municipal elections the city council created a new Strategic Planning Section (USK) under the auspices of the City Development Authority (URM). Milan Turba was appointed to head it. Turba was a planner by profession, and – unlike most of his colleagues – he had been pressing for a strategic plan for Prague since 1990 (Interview 36). The USK relied largely on current URM employees for personnel, since other qualified individuals usually preferred employment in the better-paying private sector (Interview 36). Beginning in 1995 the USK, in conjuction with consultants from the Know-How Fund, a British government aid agency, organized a series of nine three-day workshops to discuss key challenges for Prague's future development. The aim of the workshops, according to one of the organizers, was to 'bring together politicians, professionals, business groups, and civic groups to search for common ground and realizable strategic goals' (Interview 36). Workshop participants were selected by the USK, in consultation with the city's executive board.

The strategic planning workshops might have offered a key opportunity to move beyond confrontational politics in the transport sector. Just as in the land use planning process, however, political and administrative leaders tended to see civic groups opposed to the city's freeway plans as illegitimate, while these groups remained oriented towards protest and put little stock in the value of the strategic planning process. According to one of the organizers of the workshops, 'it soon became clear to us that involving civic groups would be of limited utility, since they had trouble thinking conceptually about issues, but rather remained very narrowly focused on their individual causes' (Interview 36). 'Neither we nor other civic groups were invited to participate in developing the strategic plan,' noted one civic activist, 'but frankly, it was never that much of a priority for us. I personally was convinced that it was another opportunity for the city to legitimize plans that it was going ahead with anyway' (Interview 33).

Civic groups did not participate at all in the key transport planning workshop hosted by the USK in January 1996. Participants in the automobile transport section of the workshop included five URM/USK employees, eight senior city administrators, one representative of a construction company, four representatives from national ministries, four borough politicians, one city executive board member, and two observers from the British Know-How Fund (City Development Authority 1996a: 9). Given this roster of participants, it is not surprising that the workshop supported the HUS plans that had been approved five years earlier and that it prioritized in particular the need to build the western city ring road as a means of relieving pressure on existing streets in this area (ibid.: 11).

Following the workshop process, the strategic plan draft went through a public consultation phase, similar to that conducted with the overall land use plan. However, the strategic plan had a much lower public profile than the land use plan, since it did not directly affect the interests of individual property owners. The general public paid little attention to the consultation process, and the limited civic involvement was dominated by groups active in the transport sector and other policy spheres (Interview 36). Once again, as in the land use planning process, these often strident voices were dismissed by planners and politicians alike as illegitimate, and the impact of public consultation on the parts of the strategic plan that pertained to freeways was negligible. The strategic plan supported building the western city ring road, although – unlike the draft land use plan – it emphasized that 'in view of the limited availability of land on the perimeter of the city centre, the road must be planned to a size that limits its damaging impact' (CDA 1998b: 122). In July 1998 the draft version of the strategic plan was approved by the city's executive board without controversy. Only the formulation of implementation mechanisms now stood in the way of finalizing the overall strategic plan (City of Prague 2000a: 10).

Following the November 1998 municipal elections, Jan Kasl (originator of the 'Prague 2010' project) became mayor of Prague. Kasl was strongly committed to the completion of the strategic plan and was ready to expend considerable energy on seeing the project through (Interview 36). During his first year as mayor, the city's administrative and political leaders devised implementation mechanisms for the first seven years of the strategic plan (1999–2006). A 'reliable, functioning transport system that is kind to the environment' was billed as the top priority among six priority areas identified in the plan (City Development Authority 1999c: 1). The specific projects endorsed within this priority area involved the expansion and optimization of the public transit system and the completion of the full HUS network, including the western city ring road (City of Prague 2000a: 89–91).

Preoccupied with the controversy surrounding the draft land use plan, Prague's media and civic groups paid little attention to the strategic planning process. The draft plan, including the implementation mechanisms, was passed quietly by city council in June 1999, and the final document was approved virtually unnoticed the following May. In the meantime, in 1999 the draft strategic plan was used to prepare a submission to the European Union for funding to support the city's strategic development priorities. The HUS freeways network was given clear priority in this submission, accounting for 30 per cent of the estimated cost of the city's entire development strategy (calculated from City Development Authority 1999d: 57–9).

Far from serving as an instrument for achieving social consensus regarding freeways policy, Prague's strategic planning process in the end served mainly as a tool for securing increased external funding for the completion of a freeways network whose shape had been determined long before the strategic planning process had begun. The dynamic of mutual delegitimation, born in the early 1990s and embedded in the very structure of technocratic administrative bodies and protest-oriented civic groups, once again reinforced a closed, state-dominated mode of decisionmaking. The persistence of closed planning processes ultimately contributed to a resurgence of widespread conflict over freeways policy at the end of the 1990s. In addition, it had significant implications in terms of the city's ability to implement the HUS scheme on schedule and on budget. We now turn to these implementation problems.

Implementing HUS: The Western City Ring Road

The closed character of transport planning had a significant influence on the city's ability to implement the HUS scheme consistently and on budget. Although excluded from the policy planning processes, civic groups had a significant presence during the implementation stage. In the early 1990s this was mainly because of the political support at the borough level, but after 1992 a national law that gave civic groups a right to appeal construction approvals played a key role. The involvement of civic groups in the implementation stage of freeways policy ensured that the construction of the western city ring road in particular was marked by chronic delays and cost overruns.

Local government reforms in 1990 gave Prague's politicians strong control over road construction on municipal territory. The local bureaucracy that administered road construction underwent little change in the 1990s. Coordinating the design of major roads remained the responsibility of the Chief Architect's Office (UHA, renamed URM in 1994), and the management of city investments in transport infrastructure stayed with a centralized city investment office (Interview 28). In the early 1990s the large publicly owned design and construction firms that dominated freeway construction in Prague (such as PUDIS and Metrostav) were privatized; however, they retained their oligopolistic position in road construction (Interview 16).

The most significant changes to the process of city freeway construction in the 1990s related to the actors involved, by law, in the process of obtaining development permits. In the Czech Republic this process involves two steps (see Chapter 2): (1) obtaining a planning permit that certifies conformity with existing land use planning documentation and then (2) obtaining a construction permit that approves the details of a project. For roads in Prague, this process was managed at the city-wide level – planning permits were issued by the Department of Land Use Decisions (OUR), and construction permits by the Department of Transport (Kylářová 1999: 110). Although the permits process was officially a 'transferred' function of state administration, the executive board retained strong control over the way in which this function was exercised in the roads sphere, both through its control over the planning process and through its personnel and organizational powers vis-à-vis local administrative bodies.

After 1990 the city's fifty-seven boroughs gained status as self-governing bodies that by definition had a say regarding the issuing of planning and construction permits for major transport arteries, and they could appeal the issuing of a permit to the relevant national ministry.[19] The national Law on Nature and Landscape Protection, passed in 1992, gave civic groups the same right, provided that these groups had an environmental focus and that the project in question was deemed, according to national guidelines, to have environmental implications (Interview 15; Interview 22). Both the boroughs and some civic groups, then, had opportunities to influence freeways development at the construction stage – opportunities that they did not have at the planning stage.

Throughout the 1990s the City of Prague invested a large proportion of its transport infrastructure budget into the construction of the western city ring road. This freeway included the Stromovka Park section,

Figure 4.2. The western city ring road, schematic showing its three segments

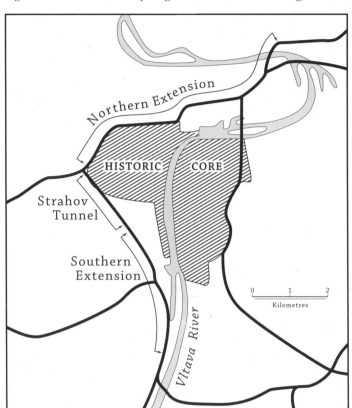

Source: Adapted and redrawn from Transport Engineering Institute 1991.
The Stromovka Park section is part of the northern extension to the western city ring road.

which had been the object of mass public protest in 1989. The adoption of the HUS in 1991 effectively closed off further discussion about the future shape of Prague's freeways and produced a dynamic of mutual delegitimation that helped to maintain closed planning processes through the 1990s. The inclusion of the boroughs and, later, of civic groups in construction approvals transferred the conflict over the western city ring road to the implementation stage.

According to the pre-1989 ZKS plans, the western city ring road was to run in a north-south direction along the perimeter of the city core (see Figure 4.2). Construction of the road was divided into three main segments, whose specific design and routing was independently negotiated. As of 1990 the central segment, the 2-kilometre-long Strahov Tunnel, was about one-third completed. Its construction was to be followed by a 3.5-kilometre-long southern extension linking it to the already-built southern part of the city ring road on the outskirts of Prague and then by a 5- to 6-kilometre-long northern extension (which included the Stromovka section) connecting to the eastern half of the city ring road in the north of the city. As of 1990 both of these extensions were still in the planning stage.

The new HUS plans, adopted in 1991, decreased the dimensions of the western city ring road from six to four lanes, but otherwise retained its basic location and design. In implementating the plans for the western city ring road, city administrators and politicians ran into opposition from borough politicians who had strong connections to local civic movements. Such opposition did not have a significant effect in the case of the Strahov Tunnel. Since the tunnel was already under construction, borough politicians could not appeal its construction. The utility of completing the project was widely called into question in 1990–91, and ideas such as using the tunnel for public transit were floated by borough politicians (Večerní Praha 1990a, 1990b). With the approval of HUS, the dimensions of the tunnel were simply reduced from six to four lanes, with provisions for the eventual expansion back up to six lanes; otherwise construction continued as planned (Interview 28).

In the case of the freeways' southern and northern segments, however, the threat of the boroughs appealing planning or construction permits had a significant impact on their design. The southern segment, which was originally supposed to run along the edge of the nineteenth-century city district of Smíchov, was strongly opposed in 1990 by local residents who had mobilized against it in conjunction with the Stromovka protest movement (Santoška Citizens' Initiative 1991). On the basis of this opposition, the newly elected political leaders in the local Borough of Prague 5 told city council that they would appeal any move to implement the original proposal, and they commissioned studies for alternate routings (ibid.: 3). After lengthy negotiations, Prague's executive board buckled to borough pressure and decided for a new routing in May 1992. The first kilometre of the southern segment was rerouted from the surface into another tunnel, to be built through a hill adjacent to the Smíchov district, in order to minimize impacts on the quality of life in Smíchov (Večerní Praha 1992). In return, city administrators and politicians secured the widening of the planned extension from four lanes (as proposed in the HUS plans) back up to the original six lanes envisioned by communist-era designers of the ZKS (Interview 28).

A similar process of revision took place in the case of the northern segment of the western city ring road. This was the segment that had originally included the much-discussed covered trench through Stromovka Park. After the November 1990 elections, local politicians in the boroughs of Prague 6, Prague 7, Prague 8, and Troja all had strong connections to civic groups in the area, and they demanded that this segment of freeway be dropped from the city's plans, in accordance with the recommendations of the Independent Committee for the Evaluation of the ZKS (Interview 37). After the acceptance of the HUS by city council, however, city council refused to entertain this option, producing a lengthy stalemate between the city and the boroughs.

To break the stalemate, the city and the boroughs established a committee in late 1992, composed of the borough mayors and Prague's Deputy Mayor for Construction (Brno Technical University 1994: 5). This committee was to consider the relative merits of five alternate routings of the city ring road in this sector, four proposed by the boroughs involved and one proposed by the city's administration. In response to fears that the original ring road plans would severely degrade the environment in this part of the city, all of the proposals moved to put much of the road in tunnels, instead of in covered trenches or on the surface. In accordance with the HUS plan, all routings counted on a four-lane freeway with off-grade intersections. The committee was to develop a set of criteria for evaluating the competing routings and then hire two independent firms to evaluate the routings on the basis of these criteria (ibid.). The committee, however, had no mandate to consider the option of *not* building this segment of the ring road at all.[20]

The work of the committee was contentious from the start, with members taking several months to agree on the criteria for evaluation. Halfway through the evaluation process the city introduced another potential routing. In its report on the various routings, one of the two firms hired by the committee strongly criticized the scope of the evaluation process itself and suggested that the committee revisit ideas similar to those put forth in 1990 by the independent committee evaluating the ZKS (Brno Technical University 1994: 60–4). Nonetheless, in 1994 the committee selected three of the proposed routings for further study. After two more years of deliberation and reports, the city and the boroughs finally settled on a routing that placed about 5 kilometres of the 5.9-kilometre segment in tunnels running just north of the city's medieval Castle District, and then under the Stromovka Park and the Vltava River (Interview 26; CDA 1994; City of Prague 2000b).

In the case of both the northern and southern extensions to the western city ring road, pressure by borough politicians, who had strong links to local civic groups, resulted in major changes in the design of the city's freeways that were outside the city's planning processes. Given the commitment of citywide political leaders and administrators to the HUS vision, these changes did not ultimately involve a fundamental re-evaluation of the utility of the western city ring road. Instead, large segments of the road were placed in tunnels – dramatically raising the costs of construction. In the case of the southern extension, the cost of the new plans was about twice that of the old ones; while in the case of the northern extension, the anticipated costs nearly tripled (Interview 28). As a result, the pace of construction slowed dramatically. In 1997 the city estimated that at the current rate of investment, the HUS system would not be complete before 2025 (City of Prague 1997b). In the late 1990s the city increasingly turned to loans and bonds to boost its finances for transport infrastructure and to speed up construction (City of Prague 1997a, 2000b).

Prague's political and administrative elites were thus willing to significantly raise the costs of constructing the western inner ring road in an effort to overcome opposition by boroughs and civic groups. However, these measures did not effectively defuse opposition either. The completion of the draft land use plan and the 1998 elections threw the freeways issue back into the public spotlight, and civic groups redoubled their efforts to block the construction of the western city ring. In doing so, they took advantage of the 1992 national Law on Nature and Landscape Protection which allowed them to appeal planning and construction permits.

By the time that this new wave of civic protest had emerged, the Strahov Tunnel was already finished and in operation. Its completion had not proceeded smoothly, but ultimately the project had been too far advanced for it to be seriously derailed. Arguing that it would provide relief from through traffic to residents of the nearby historic Lesser Quarter, the tunnel's political and administrative supporters assured a steady pace of construction through to the mid-1990s (Kubieláš 1992; City of Prague 1997b). In 1994 civic groups did successfully press borough politicians in Prague 5 to oppose a construction permit for the southern off-ramps to the tunnel, arguing that the project would channel additional traffic into an already overburdened part of the city (Linková 1994).

The following year, after a study reported high rates of asthma among children in Prague 5, this argument was also taken up by the city's chief medical officer, whose consent was necessary for the opening of the tunnel (Volejník 1995; Šubrt 1997). As a result of this opposition, construction stopped for about six months in 1995. After negotiations, Prague 5 and the chief medical officer agreed to drop their opposition to opening the tunnel in return for funding for the installation of new apartment windows and air quality monitoring devices in parts of Prague 5 (Frýšarová 1995; Šubrt 1997). The tunnel was then completed, and it was fully operational in early 1998.

Despite the claims of its supporters, the Strahov Tunnel did little to decrease through traffic in the historic core, as quickly became clear, because the low capacity of existing streets at the tunnel's southern entrance made it an unattractive option for most drivers (Lochmanová and Sysel 1998). City officials adjusted their stance regarding the tunnel's benefits, now arguing that its positive impact would be felt only when the section of the city ring road leading south from the Strahov Tunnel was complete (Kolomazniková and Janík 1997; Málek 1997; Lochmanová and Sysel 1998).

By 1998 the detailed plans were ready, the planning permits had been obtained, and construction was set to begin on the southern extension to the city ring road. As the final stage of the permits process drew near, however, several civic groups began a petition, letter, and media campaign objecting to both the location of this segment near the city centre and its six–lane volume (Janík 1998a, 1998b). When this approach was unsuccessful, and a construction permit (for the first phase) was granted, civic groups used their power under the 1992 Law on Nature and Landscape Protection to appeal the decision to the Ministry of Transport, which resulted in a six-month delay in the construction start date. The appeal was ultimately rejected, but they subsequently took their case to Prague's high court, and from there to the Supreme Court (Slonek 1999a; Interview 22). Throughout 1999 and into 2000, civic groups continued this tactic, appealing construction permits for the various phases of the project (Janík 1999; Šárová 2000). Although as of summer 2000 none of the appeals had been successful, the delays in construction mounted, and the original opening date of 2002 was pushed back (Šárová 2000).[21]

In 1999 the construction of the northern extension of the western city ring road, which had been the object of the mass protest movement of 1989, was still a rather distant prospect, since the city's funds were committed to the section leading south from the Strahov Tunnel. Nevertheless, the resurgence of civic group activity regarding Prague's freeways also began to affect the prospects for this project. In 2000 the SOS Praha coalition, which had been formed to fight the city's overall land use plan, launched a campaign of letters and petitions opposing work on the northern extension, once again arguing that extending it would draw additional traffic into the heart of the city (see, e.g., SOS Praha 2000). The campaign included a public information fair held in Letná Park in Prague 7 that November, as well as threats that SOS Praha would appeal any planning or construction permits, unless an environmental impact assessment was carried out (Mladá Fronta Dnes 2000).[22]

Conclusion

By the end of the 1990s, the politics of freeways development in Prague had come full circle. Largely excluded from planning processes in the early 1990s, civic groups re-emerged as a significant force opposing elements of the city's freeways network, using new channels of influence open to them in the broader democratic context, but also returning to protest tactics strikingly similar to those used in the 1989 anti-freeways mobilization. Ten years of democratic rule had not succeeded in fundamentally opening closed policy processes or in helping to forge a clear social consensus around Prague's automobile transport policy. Prague's post-communist government had maintained a long-range strategy of freeways development, but this strategy stood in tension with the broader goals of the city's transport policy and faced significant opposition from organized civic groups.

In this chapter, we have linked these outcomes to the character of the decisionmaking environment in Prague in 1990–91. During the fluid critical juncture that followed the collapse of communism, civic groups and administrative institutions presented politicians with fundamentally conflicting normative visions of the process and substance of freeways policy. In a broader context of rapid institutional change and uncertainty, politicians chose the apparently simpler option of allying themselves with administrators over the option of pursuing a new policy direction and confronting the complex attendant task of institutional reform.

Once this choice was made, further administrative or policy reform became increasingly difficult and unattractive over time, due to the emergence of what Paul Pierson calls 'increasing returns' processes – processes that strengthen over time the incentives to retain an existing institutional configuration (2000a). The increasing returns process that we have focused on the most in this chapter is the emergence of an institutionally embedded dynamic of mutual delegitimation. After 1991 the city's administrative bodies retained their old structural characteristics and the accompanying normative orientation towards technocratic policy development, an orientation that was soon internalized by political leaders as well. Civic groups, for their part, retained their ad hoc, protest-based character. The normative incoherence of the early post-communist period thus remained institutionally embedded with regard to the freeways sector, and it congealed into a deep mutual suspicion, in which each side in the debate denied the very legitimacy of the other. In the years that followed, the dynamic of mutual delegitimation repeatedly frustrated the emergence of more open patterns of decisionmaking that might have begun to build a state–society consensus on the city's transport policy. Over time, a second increasing returns process emerged as well: As the sunk costs of developing the freeways network mounted, the prospect of a policy shift became even less attractive.

Despite these continuities, the political system that civic groups operated within at the end of the 1990s was, of course, very different from that within which the Stromovka protest movement had arisen a decade earlier. Prague had a functioning democratic system of government, incorporated within a stable democratic state structure that gave a number of important legal rights to civic organizations. In Prague, this meant that civic groups in the 1990s could find political allies, whether at the borough level (primarily in the early 1990s) or at the citywide level (in the 1998 elections). It also meant that important new avenues of recourse, such as appeals of development permits and legal protests and petitions, were now open to them.

As of 2000, however, these differences had not been sufficient to overcome the power of the processes that early decisions had set in motion. Instead, they only ensured that the city's political and administrative leaders had a difficult time implementing their chosen policy initiative in the transport sector. Over the course of the 1990s construction of the HUS project, and in particular the western city ring road, became extremely expensive as a result of design changes forced through by borough politicians allied with civic groups. As civic groups learned to take advantage of opportunities to appeal construction permits for various segments of the HUS, an additional source of expense and delays to construction emerged.

The net result of the dynamics of policy and politics in Prague's transport sector in the 1990s was weak government performance as measured by our two key criteria. Throughout the decade, politicians and administrators worked to minimize openness to civic preferences in the roads sphere, opening policy processes only insofar as national legislation mandated it. While the 1998 municipal elections saw the emergence of programmatic competition around the freeways issue, an important development in terms of open government, the return to power of the Civic Democratic Party in coalition with the Social Democrats meant that the elections were not followed by a significant shift in policy substance or policy process. Furthermore, while Prague's politicians and bureaucrats were obviously committed to a systematic long-range strategy of freeways development, by the mid-1990s this strategy stood in tension with the broader official policy of integrated transport management, and by the late 1990s renewed conflict with civic actors was leading to significant implementation problems for the HUS project.

A decade after the fall of communism, the politics of freeways development in Prague was still shaped by incompatible normative visions of the process and substance of policy. Decisions made by political leaders in the early 1990s had entrenched institutional incoherence for the longer term, and had frustrated the development of systematic and open democratic rule. In the next chapter, we turn to the politics of preservation and development in the historic core, where we will find distinct but parallel processes at work.

5 Preservation and Development in Prague's Historic Core: The Politics of Profit

Regulating Development in the Historic Core: New Opportunities and Constraints

At the end of the communist era, Prague had perhaps the best preserved historic city centre of any large city in East Central Europe. The historic core had experienced some rebuilding between the world wars, but the early rise of a preservationist movement (see Chapter 3) had prevented wholesale redevelopment. During the communist period the continued strength of preservationist sentiment and a lack of new construction ensured that the city's core retained its historic character, however, it entered the post-communist era with a large number of buildings in acute need of repair.

As defined by the boundaries of the Prague Monument Preserve, established by the Czechoslovak federal government in 1971, Prague's historic core had an area of 8.6 square kilometres. Administratively, about three-quarters of this area constituted the Borough of Prague 1, with the southern end of the New Town under the jurisdiction of the Borough of Prague 2. Throughout the communist era the historic core had remained the city's commercial heart, and in 1990 about 200,000 people, or one-third of the city's total workforce, were employed there (Hrůza 1992: 79). The number of people who lived in the historic core had declined steadily in the twentieth century, from a peak of about 170,000 around 1900, due to pressures for commercial and government building uses and the evolution of higher housing standards. Nevertheless, in 1990 it still housed over 60,000 people or about 5 per cent of the city's population (City Development Authority 2000: 11).

Prague's new political elites faced the challenge of governing devel-

opment and preservation in this large and functionally mixed area. As
we saw in Chapter 3, the city inherited from the previous period an
administrative apparatus that was committed to a policy of comprehensive preservation in the Prague Monument Preserve, a policy supported in 1990 by a number of newly formed civic groups. National
market reforms, however, began to produce new pressures for commercial development in the historic core. In the context of underdeveloped
regulations separating public from private activity, these pressures generated opportunities for politicians to profit from acting as intermediaries for development interests. This chapter begins with an examination
of the policy levers that Prague's political leadership had at its disposal
in responding to these conflicting incentives. We will then look at how
they actually did respond and what the longer-term implications were
for the quality of government in the sphere of preservation and development in Prague's historic core.

With regard to transport policy Prague's post-communist politicians
had at their disposal a comprehensive apparatus of state institutions
responsible for the construction of roads and supporting infrastructure
– from the planning to the implementation stages. The city's control
over real estate development was less comprehensive. In the 1990s the
primary role of municipal government regarding development in the
city centre quickly changed from monopolistic developer to regulator of
private-sector real estate activity. Nonetheless, Prague's elected political
leaders retained strong levers to control the process of real estate development in the historic core even after the fall of communism.

The national privatization program placed most city centre real
estate in private hands during 1991 and 1992. However, the city
received title to about 150 key historic buildings or vacant lots in the
historic core, real estate that it had owned before 1948. Furthermore,
most housing that was not returned to private owners, amounting to
about 20 per cent of the total in the historic core, passed into city ownership, and was thereafter managed by the boroughs of Prague 1 and
Prague 2. As the owner of these properties, the city had a right to dispose of them as it wished, subject to its own development regulations
and, in the housing sphere, to national laws with respect to tenants'
rights and rent regulations.

In addition to directly owning buildings and land, the city got extensive control over the administrative institutions involved in the development of the city centre. Of the communist-era bodies described in
Chapter 3, most survived and were incorporated into the city's new

governing structure.[1] These bodies included the Department of Land Use Decisions (OUR), which issued the planning permits; the Prague Centre of State Monument Preservation and Nature Protection (PSSP-POP), which issued expert opinions for the city's Department of Culture with regard to the appropriateness of development projects in the area of the Prague Monument Preserve; and the Prague Monuments Council, an informal advisory body of preservation professionals that met at the behest of the city's Department of Culture. In 1990 the PSSP-POP was renamed the Prague Institute for Monument Preservation (PUPP), but its mandate remained the same (Interview 19).

The local government reforms in 1990 made the OUR and the PUPP components of state administration, managed the city by using its transferred powers. In formal terms, this meant that politicians could not directly intervene in the individual decisions made by these institutions. However, they had a number of other important levers with which to exert control over them. First, just as with the freeways, they could make use of aspects of the land use planning process to direct development in the historic core. Although Prague's overall land use plan was drawn up at a scale too large to allow for detailed regulation in the historic core, the city could produce more detailed plans for smaller areas of the city,[2] and the could issue regulations specifying height, density, design, and other requirements for buildings in certain areas of the city (Tůnka and Sklenář 1999: 15). In 1990 there was in existence an old set of building regulations for the historic core that was part of the city's overall land use plan of 1985.

The planning process offered the political leadership a comprehensive way of limiting the discretion of bureaucrats. In addition, over and above detailed planning regulations, policians had a second means of influencing the municipal institutions involved with development and preservation issues. As was the case with all government institutions at the municipal level, the city's executive board had the power to change the organizational structure and to name the heads of the OUR and the PUPP. This gave the board considerable leverage to pressure bureaucrats to adopt positions on individual development projects – or indeed to adopt a general orientation and decisionmaking procedures – consistent with the board's political preferences.

Although Prague's political leaders did not have the comprehensive control over real estate development issues that they had over municipal infrastructure projects such as freeways, a number of strong mechanisms were available to them with which they could control the institutions that administered development in the city's historic core. As we shall see, they used some of these powers extensively – in particular their power to reorganize and name the heads of the OUR and the PUPP. This reformist activity stands in sharp contrast to the behaviour of political leaders in the freeways sphere, where administrative reform was shunned. Let us look at how and why this occurred.

From Comprehensive Preservation to ad hoc Development

As in the freeways sphere, when it came to the preservation and development of Prague's historic core politicians in the early post-communist period faced an incoherent set of state and civic institutions that produced conflicting incentives regarding the process and substance of policy. The municipal civil service was committed to out-and-out preservation. Unlike transport policy officials, preservation officials did not face a strong challenge from the local citizenry in the late 1980s; instead, organized community interests generally supported the goal of systematic preservation. The new political leaders, however, were soon under intense pressure, primarily from foreign investors, to commercially develop the historic core. In the context of weak regulations regarding conflict of interest and access to information, this pressure soon produced incentives for politicians to use public office for private gain. In this section, we will examine how these conflicting incentives shaped the decisionmaking behaviour of Prague's politicians in the early post-communist period.

During the communist era the dominant policy orientation of administrative institutions with respect to the historic core was one of systematic preservation. Over the course of several decades, historic preservation institutions had built up a strong position in the city's civil service system and had successfully pressed for regulation that restricted development in the historic core, while enjoying broad decisionmaking discretion in individual cases. As in the freeways sphere, policy was developed in a professionalized, technocratic manner, without significant civic input. But, unlike in the roads sphere, the resulting policy seemed to have broad public approval. Indeed, as we saw in Chapter 3, when this policy was challenged in the late 1980s by a new Communist Party focus on developing the centre's tourist potential, preservation professionals found themselves allied with the Association of Residents and Friends of the Lesser Quarter and the Castle District (SOPMSH) in opposing hotel development in the historic core.

When members of Prague's interim municipal assembly (NVP) took their seats in February 1990, they came face to face with protests against development in the historic core of the city from both preservation professionals and local residents. Such protest was not confined to the historic core alone. Throughout late 1989 and into 1990, a number of new civic groups composed largely of architects, professional preservationists, and art historians – such as Zlatí Orli (Golden Eagles) and Společnost Praha (the Prague Society) – organized petitions and demonstrations against the proposed demolition of parts of some nineteenth-century residential districts such as Smíchov and Vysočany (Váchová 1990). Although this opposition was never of a scale equal to the movement against the Stromovka freeway, it did put significant pressure on the interim assembly to put a halt to development projects that were under way in older parts of the city.

Arising as it had out of the mass anti-communist protests of 1989, Prague's interim assembly supported the campaign against what was seen as insensitive urban renewal. Like with the freeways issue, this offered politicians chance to both symbolically and concretely disassociate themselves from the previous regime. One interim assembly member recalled: 'We felt strongly that we needed to change the way that development was done in older parts of the city, and to brake the influence of those planning and construction bodies that had colluded with Communist Party officials, and had promoted the destruction of our city's historic values' (Interview 33).

Putting a halt to communist-era redevelopment initiatives was not always simple. Some redevelopment, especially outside the historic core, continued to have support among the city's planning bureaucrats (Peterka 1990). However, with respect to the historic core itself, the dominant administrative policy orientation favoured comprehensive preservation, and the institutions that supported large-scale development – most notably, some sections of the Chief Architect's Office (UHA) – were isolated from the mainstream consensus. As a result, between February and November 1990 the interim assembly and the city's executive board successfully stopped plans for the construction of hotels in the historic centre and took steps to arrest the redevelopment of some of the city's nineteenth-century residential areas (Vlček 1990; Interview 19).

New private-sector development pressures began to arise, however, primarily from foreign investors seeking to enter the emerging market economy. By June 1990 foreign investors had proposed some U.S. $5 billion worth of development projects for the city (Kordovský 1990). Most of their proposals involved commercial development in or near the historic core. The Cunard Hotel Group, for example, wanted to convert a series of historic buildings in the Lesser Quarter into a hotel; several foreign investors favoured transforming the city's main market into a high-end retail and administrative centre; others expressed interest in constructing an office complex that would cover the rail sorting yards behind Prague's main train station (Kordovský 1990; Tichý 1991).

During the November 1990 municipal election campaign, the dominant Civic Forum had no stated position on how to deal with this flood of foreign interest in commercial development, and thus the newly elected city councillors took up office with no clear mandate on this issue. The new executive board set up a Foreign Investment Section (Sekce Zahraničních Investic – SZI), headed by board member Michal Hvížď'ala, with instructions to cooperate with investors in developing individual projects. At first the SZI could do little to see any proposed development projects through, as privatization was ongoing and property relations were very unclear. As a result, virtually none of the proposals submitted by foreign investors in 1990 and 1991, whether they involved the historic core or elsewhere, got off the ground (Interview 15). However, privatization was largely complete by the end of 1991, while foreign interest in commercial development of Prague's historic core continued to gain strength throughout the first half of the 1990s.

Interest in large-scale commercial development in the historic core was driven primarily by foreign firms seeking space for office headquarters or seeking high-end retail space (Sýkora 1995: 330). The number of foreign tourists visiting Prague increased rapidly from about 500,000 per year in the late 1980s to more than five times that by 1996 (Czech Statistical Office 1999: 97), and correspondingly, pressure to develop tourist facilities such as hotels also increased. The strength of investor interest was reflected in the rapid rise in commercial rent and the accompanying demand for conversion of residential into commercial property. The national government deregulated commercial rents in 1991, and in the historic core they soon skyrocketed to ten or even (in the case of office space) fifty times the rent levels in peripheral parts of the city (Sýkora 1995: 328). Residential rents for tenants with pre-existing leases remained strictly regulated, however, and often they were too low to cover even the upkeep of dilapidated historic residential units (see Eskinasi 1995). Most housing in the core was returned to private owners in 1991, and owners had strong incentives to convert their units to commercial uses, either by removing their tenants themselves or (more commonly) by selling their properties to real estate agencies that would remove the tenants and convert the properties to commercial uses (Sýkora 1995).[3]

As property relations began to stabilize, city councillors were presented with real opportunities to exploit the demand for commercial development in Prague's historic core for their own gain. In the early 1990s, city councillors had no statutory restrictions with regard to their private-sector business activity, and there were no regulations to compel them to publicly declare such activity. Decisions on the terms of sale or rental of municipally owned property were made behind closed doors, as were the administrative decisions regarding private-sector development proposals. As a result, opportunities emerged for city councillors, especially those with positions on the executive board, to profit personally from their public positions by acting as intermediaries for development interests.

Prague's post-November 1990 political leaders thus faced a critical decision point with regard to development of the city's centre. Preservationist administrators and civic groups pressed for a systematic preservation strategy, yet city councillors also had opportunities to profit from responding favourably to the strong interest in the historic core expressed by developers. How city councillors chose to respond to these conflicting incentives would have far-reaching implications for the emergence of systematic and transparent policymaking in this issue area. Once again, the bounded rationality of political leaders came to play a crucial role in determining how they acted. Confronted by conflicting normative visions of policy and embedded in a disorienting context of rapid change, they took what appeared to be the simplest and most immediately rewarding course of action, and ultimately, for many this course of action proved to be one of pursuing opportunities for private gain through public office.

There was broad consensus among the civil service and active segments of the general public that development in Prague's historic core should be guided by a systematic focus on historic preservation. Yet putting this into practice was by no means straightforward. The guidelines on construction in the historic core, part of the city's 1985 overall land use plan, did not constitute a full strategy for preservation, but only presented standardized limits on some aspects of construction, such as the height of buildings and some specifics regarding materials (Interview 24). Given that the historic core is a large area with a highly diversified character – from the very well-preserved medieval parts of the Old Town to the business district of the New Town, with its substantial concentration of nineteenth- and early twentieth-century buildings – the 1985 guidelines were a poor reflection of the actual development potential and preservation requirements of various areas of the core. As a result, they tended to be interpreted loosely by historic preservationists its in the PUPP, who maintained strong de facto discretionary power in deciding on the appropriateness of development in different parts of the Prague Monument Preserve (PPR; Interview 19).

A fuller strategy for preservation and development in the historic core would require different regulations for distinct parts of the Prague Monument Preserve. It would also need to grapple with some other key issues. First, as we have seen, the residential function of the historic core had been in decline since at least 1900. There was broad consensus among the city's planners and preservation professionals, as well as local residents' groups such as SOPMSH, that the historic core should remain a major residential centre (Interview 35). The city council could support this goal by setting restrictions on the conversion of buildings to non-residential uses, as part of a detailed land use plan for the city's core; however, this would mean directly resisting the pressure for commercial development. Second, many of the historic buildings were in acute disrepair, and massive injections of funds would be needed to remedy this situation. If harnessed through development charges or other linkage mechanisms, the flood of investor interest might have provided a possible source of such funds. However, the interests of investors rarely coincided with those of historic preservation professionals, so efforts to tap investor capital to cover major renovation costs would likely run up against resistance.

Shortly after taking office in 1990, Prague's new political leaders tried to engage officials at the PUPP in the idea of preparing a comprehensive strategy for development and preservation in the historic core that would address these issues. They quickly encountered opposition. In the wake of the controversial tourist development proposals of the late 1980s, the PUPP was wary of political input into preservation and development policy. It jealously guarded its professional decisionmaking discretion and was reluctant to provide the necessary expert background information for formulating a comprehensive set of guidelines for real estate investment, for fear that any such guidelines might be misinterpreted or misused (Interview 10).

Faced with PUPP resistance, politicians tried a different route towards a comprehensive preservation strategy. The 1987 Law on State Historic Preservation (no. 20/1987) gave the city's executive board the right to set up a Department of Historic Preservation (OPP), which it did in 1992. According to the law, the OPP was to act as a legal body that issues binding opinions on the appropriateness of individual development proposals on the basis of professional recommendations submitted to it by the PUPP (par. 28). Because of the PUPP's uncooperativeness, however, the executive board gave the OPP both the power to issue binding decisions on individual cases of development *and* its own professional preservationist staff (Interview 19).

In building the OPP, the executive board ran into problems regarding a lack of qualified personnel. The relatively low salaries of public-sector employees, as well as an emerging boom in private restoration work across the country, made it very difficult to recruit adequately trained professionals. During the initial period of its existence, therefore, the OPP was severely understaffed and thus unable to carry out the functions that the executive board had hoped it would (Schreib 1992; Interview 10). However, councillors had yet another institution at their disposal that could be of help in coming up with a comprehensive preservation strategy: the Chief Architect's Office (UHA).

The top brass at the UHA had supported the previous regime's push for hotel development in the historic core in the late 1980s, but the UHA also had a Prague Monument Preserve Studio (Atelier Pražské Pamatkové Rezervace), a small professional unit expressly dedicated to the creation of a comprehensive preservation policy for the historic core. After the fall of communism and the rejection of the hotel development plans, this special unit had, of its own accord, begun work on a detailed study of the Prague Monument Preserve that could be used as a basis for a comprehensive preservation strategy. In 1991 city council officially sanctioned this study, but it would not be completed before another two years had passed (Interview 3).

Pressure to develop the historic core kept growing. Civic groups such as SOPMSH and Společnost Praha continued to lobby for guidelines that might harness this pressure in the service of preserving historic sites (see, e.g., Horský and Schmidt 1991). But the prospect of private gain through public office presented city councillors with more immediate and tangible rewards than did the complex and frustrating efforts required to hammer out a comprehensive preservation strategy. Indeed, for politicians disoriented and wearied by the demands of the early post-communist period, the alternative of pursuing private gain offered a broader opportunity to redefine for themselves their purpose in holding public office. One former executive board member explained:

> As the city got its own property, many of us started realizing just how much money these elected positions could be worth. So the initial enthusiasm with which we came into office turned into enthusiasm for personal gain. Executive board members started to use their power over the bureaucracy in pursuit of their own narrow self-interest, and as property relations became clearer city councillors got in on the game as well and started to using their personal contacts with executive board members and administrators to press for particular development proposals. I'd say that by 1993, what we could call the 'crude pragmatist' faction had become dominant both in the council [as a whole] and on the executive board. (Interview 9)

Rapid growth in the number of city councillors who were personally involved in real estate dealings provides some evidence of this shift in approach. The precise number of councillors, including executive board members, who were personally involved in real estate developments in Prague in the early 1990s is impossible to ascertain, since there were at the time no requirements to report such activity and most of it remained strictly informal. In interviews conducted for this project, municipal politicians pegged the proportion in 1992–93 at between one- and two-thirds of their entire contingent (Interview 28; Interview 9; Interview 20). By November 1992 Mayor Milan Kondr publicly complained that 'the social and personal situation of most councillors has changed [since 1990]. They have changed employment, many of them are in the development business, and this is reflected in the positions that they take in city council' (Schreib 1992: 3).

More city councillors involved in real estate dealings for personal gain meant that more councillors had a vested interest in maintaining an ad hoc, closed-door style of decisionmaking with regard to development in the historic core. To maximize their potential for personal benefit, it was necessary to maximize the discretion that they had in deciding how to develop city property. These councillors' personal interests would not be well served by a comprehensive preservation strategy for the historic core. However, neither would they be served by a comprehensive strategy that favoured major new developments, since *any* clear strategy, no matter what its substantive orientation, would limit the councillors' discretionary influence. To forestall objections to their pursuit of private gain, political leaders also needed to maintain the closed nature of the development approvals process and to keep to a minimum public participation and public access to information.[4] Prague's political leaders institutionally entrenched the politics of profit. How did they do this, and what is the evidence regarding the extent to which public office was used for private gain in 1990s Prague?

Entrenching the Politics of Profit

As some of Prague's political leaders began to act as intermediaries for development interests, they also began to take steps to adapt institutions and policy to serve their personal interests. They did this in two main ways: (1) by halting the process of systematic policymaking and striving to reorient the institutions charged with historic preservation towards a more development-friendly approach and (2) by maintaining closed policy processes in the real estate development field. In pursuing these initiatives, city councillors contributed to a transformation within the historic preservation institutions, whose front-line employees also began to exploit opportunities for personal profit from their role in the development process. The net result was that throughout much of the 1990s conditions remained very good in Prague for the pursuit of private gain through public office.

As we have seen, in 1992 the executive board established a Department of Historic Preservation (OPP), under its direct control, originally with a view to having a professional resource to aid it in devising systematic preservation policy. Although building the OPP was a slow process, because of the lack of qualified personnel, by the end of that year a small core of employees, including both legal specialists and historic preservation specialists, was in place. Since the department was designed as an institution that not only executed the recommendations submitted by the Prague Institute for Monument Preservation (PUPP) but also had its own professional preservationist staff, the city now had two competing historic preservation institutions.

In late 1992, the city's executive board appointed Pavel Pirkl, known for being relatively development-friendly, to head the new department (Interview 10). Conflict soon developed between Pirkl and Věra Müllerová, the director of the PUPP, since the OPP started to reject the institute's preservation-oriented recommendations (Marvan 1993). To bolster the PUPP's position in this conflict, Müllerová tried to recruit the support of non-governmental preservationist groups such as Zlatí Orli and Společnost Praha. She asked them to participate in reviving the moribund Monuments Council, an informal body of professionals founded in the communist era to provide counsel to the city's preservationist bodies. However, this initiative was opposed by the OPP, which was responsible for actually calling meetings of the council. No such meetings were called, and the effort to revive the Monuments Council failed (Marvan 1993; Štětka 1992).

Conflict between the OPP and the PUPP erupted to the media in February 1993. The trigger was the case of one nineteenth-century building in the city's historic core. The OPP had granted a permit for its demolition to make room for a new office building, despite PUPP opposition (Lukeš 1993; Kvačková 1993). This highly publicized controversy caused the city's executive board to recall both Pirkl and Müllerová. However, the board then immediately appointed Pirkl to head the PUPP, raising further protests from preservation professionals (Bečková 1993; Marvan 1993).

Making Pirkl director of the PUPP did ease tensions between the PUPP and the OPP, but at the expense of creating considerable conflict within the institute itself. The PUPP now found itself under the leadership of its former nemesis, and its internal cohesion seriously weakened. Throughout the following years Pirkl repeatedly overturned the recommendations of his subordinates, ruling in favour of development interests (Coufalová 1998). Conflict within the organization boiled over into the media again early in 1998, when eight PUPP employees went public with their criticism of Pirkl's leadership (see, e.g., Kovářová and Janderová 1998). On the instructions of the city's executive board, all eight were fired, despite objections from the national Ministry of Culture. Furthermore, they were not replaced, and thus PUPP's total staff complement went down from seventy-six to sixty-eight (Klapalová 1998a; City of Prague Department of Historic Preservation 2000: 19).

At around the same time that the first OPP–PUPP conflict was coming to a head, in early 1993, the Chief Architect's Office (UHA) completed its detailed study of the Prague Monument Preserve and presented it to city council. The original purpose of the study was to provide a basis for a comprehensive strategy for the preservation and development of the city's historic core, including differentiated guidelines for different areas and regulations that limit would the conversion of buildings from residential use to non-residential uses. The completion of the city's interim 'Plan for the Stabilized Zones,' such as the historic core, was imminent (see Chapter 4), and the UHA envisioned that its study would provide the basis for a detailed addendum to it that would codify preservation and development policy for the historic core (Interview 3).

When the UHA's study of the Prague Monument Preserve was presented to city council for debate in 1993, however, council rejected it as premature, and no further work on it was commissioned. Officially, the study was rejected on the ground that the broader context of transport infrastructure in and around the historic core had not yet been settled, but the reasoning behind this claim was never explained (Interview 3). The 'Plan for the Stabilized Zones,' adopted by city council in early 1994, was therefore not accompanied by detailed guidelines for the preservation and development of historic core. On the contrary, its adoption automatically invalidated even such general guidelines as had been in place since 1985. As of 1994, therefore, the City of Prague had no official development and preservation guidelines whatsoever for the Prague Monument Preserve (Interview 32).[5]

The executive board's intervention in the functioning of historic preservation bodies, and the city council's concomitant scuttling of plans for systematic policymaking, contributed to the overloading of historic preservation bodies and the emergence of administrative corruption in the early 1990s. In the absence of overall guidelines, the PUPP and the OPP each produced case-by-case evaluations of every development proposal within the Prague Monument Preserve, right down to minor interior renovations. As investor interest in the historic core grew, the number of cases that the PUPP and the OPP had to process skyrocketed. In 1993 the executive board extended the designation 'historic' to other areas of Prague, thus further increasing the case load (Schreib 1993b).[6]

In the late 1980s the PUPP had assessed some five hundred submissions per year (Interview 42). After 1990 this number began to rise dramatically: in 1995 the PUPP and the OPP each dealt with about 4,200 cases, and by 1999 that number had gone up to 6,500 (City of Prague, Department of Historic Preservation 2000: 24, 37). During this time the number of PUPP employees did not increase, but as we saw above, actually dropped significantly in 1998. The number of OPP employees did increase, gradually, although it remained at fewer than thirty (ibid.). With no official policy guidelines that could have provided detailed regulations for different kinds of development and thus streamlined the decisionmaking processes, the PUPP and the OPP found themselves severely understaffed. This compromised the quality of their work on individual cases (Interview 24; Interview 42). One PUPP official lamented: 'We simply haven't been able to keep up with the number of cases that we have to deal with. Last year [1999] we had six and a half thousand cases of development, and we had twenty-two employees who dealt with them. That works out to five administrative proceedings per employee each week, which is ridiculous given that we are supposed to conduct a site visit and a full investigation for each case. Needless to say we can't always do this, our records are a mess, people get stressed and leave the institute for better work' (Interview 42).

The lack of an official historic preservation policy also intensified the appeal of the opportunities for private gain that emerged for OPP and PUPP employees in the early 1990s. In the communist era, there was no reason to minimize contact between public-sector investors and other public-sector administrators. The development permits process had thus involved developers negotiating directly with all of the relevant administrative bodies, and then taking their collected approvals to the Department of Land Use Decisions (OUR) and, later on, to the appropriate building permits office (Interview 15).

Prague's political leaders made no move to reform the permits process after 1990. As a result, private developers negotiated individually with all the institutions involved in the process – at least twenty-eight of them, including the OPP and the PUPP, in the case of larger projects (Interview 23). In the absence of national access to information legislation, proceedings remained closed, and individual decisions did not have to be publicly justified. Furthermore, throughout 1990s the Czech Republic had no legislation that restricted the private-sector activities of civil servants (Interview 40; Interview 15). In this broader context, some overworked and poorly paid OPP and PUPP employees took advantage of their positions for private gain, either by granting permits in exchange for bribes or by going into the development business themselves and taking advantage of public office to push their particular projects.

The use of public office for private gain became a significant problem in the OPP, which faced particularly strong pressure from developers since its decisions were binding. After Pavel Pirkl was transferred to the PUPP, in 1993, the city's executive board appointed lawyer Jiřina Knížková to head the OPP (Interview 10). She had no specialized training in historic preservation, and she kept in place the wide-ranging discretion of the preservation professionals in her organization. Although this research has not uncovered irrefutable evidence of corruption in the OPP under Knížková's leadership, in the second half of the 1990s the department developed the reputation among many professionals, politicians, and investors that it had become corrupt. For example, one OPP insider interviewed for this project in 2000 stated:

> This institution has basically been turned into a business run by [one long-time preservation professional in the OPP]. He's the one who is in charge, who decides which investors will have to pay for the privilege of getting their way. Of course, he's not the only one who profits – a number of our people are in on it. But what can anyone else do? If we spoke out, we would be called liars and fired on the spot, and we would have no concrete evidence to show for our claims, since there are no guidelines that we could point to that have been contravened in individual cases. So the rest of us in the OPP basically live in a climate of fear and try to do the best we can. (Interview 32)[7]

This view of the OPP was shared by a number of people interviewed for this project. One ODS city councillor claimed that 'everyone knows that OPP officials routinely take bribes and have done so for years, that there is a set schedule of payments to employees for permitting various kinds of development interventions in the Prague Monument Preserve, and this kicks in unless some politician favours the project' (Interview 5). A developer with several years of experience working for foreign investors in Prague asserted that 'outlays in the permits process ... can be huge, since some administrative bodies ask for pretty major sums to grease the wheels. I'm thinking of the preservationists, though they're not the only ones' (Interview 23).

In the absence of a systematic policy with respect to the historic core, the door of opportunity for personal gain thus swung wide open for historic preservation professionals in early post-communist Prague. It apparently did not take long for the pursuit of private gain to become entrenched in their institutions, most notably in the OPP. An administrative apparatus that had been in favour of systematic preservation policy during the communist era was now fragmented on the basis of the position of individual civil servants in the system of contact with investors.

Through intervention in personnel appointments and the scuttling of plans for systematic policy, city councillors in early post-communist

Prague contributed to the weakening of and internal division within the city's preservationist institutions, a situation that prevailed throughout the rest of the 1990s. This situation in turn enhanced possibilities for councillors to profit personally from their access to the levers of decisionmaking with regard to real estate development, especially in Prague's historic core. To avoid public scrutiny and criticism, councillors, in turn needed to keep political and administrative decisionmaking processes as closed as possible.

Insofar as municipal property was concerned, Prague's executive board had the right to negotiate the terms of sale or lease with individual buyers or tenants before putting the contracts to a vote by the entire city council. Board meetings took place behind closed doors, and the minutes of these meetings were not available to the public. Furthermore, the Control Committee, whose job it was to monitor any irregularities in the activities of the executive board was appointed by, and responsible to, the board itself. The contracts signed by the executive board and private parties were accessible to city council members, but they in turn were prohibited from sharing the information these contracts contained. This was the system throughout the 1990s despite protests from the media and from opposition councillors (Interview 14; Bartoníček 1999). Also throughout the 1990s, Prague also maintained a system of collective responsibility for decisions made by the executive board.[8] While individual board members typically had responsibility for particular policy areas, how they cast their votes on any particular issue was never made public. In this manner, as one of them put it, 'executive board members have hidden behind a veil of collective responsibility. Since the mayor cannot direct an executive board member to release information about his own positions on issues, there is no way to hold an individual to account in the city council or in the broader public arena' (Interview 14).

Where the city did not own the property in question, the executive board still had influence over development decisions, since it could threaten to use its personnel and organizational power over and within the city's institutions to achieve the desired result. To use this power without facing public scrutiny, members of the executive board had an interest, shared with those civil servants who were taking advantage of their own positions for private gain, in maintaining a closed-door system of development approvals. Throughout the 1990s, executive board and, indeed, the majority of all city councillors defended a development approvals system that kept a tight lid on information regarding the proceedings, and did not make public the grounds on which individual development approvals were granted or denied (Interview 14).

How the Civic Democratic Party (ODS) evolved also fostered the entrenchment of the politics of profit. After the 1994 municipal elections, when the party successfully formed a stable governing coalition with the Civic Democratic Alliance (ODA), the ODS had strong partisan control over real estate development in the city. As the number of councillors involved in pursuing private gain in real estate development grew, so did the function of the ODS as an umbrella under which they could find protection. One long-time ODS member said: 'Our party should have defence mechanisms that punish those who use public office for their own private goals, but the reverse is true – the ODS protects its individual members at all costs ... everyone [in the party] knows what someone else is doing to make a quick buck, but no one says anything for fear of opening up the Pandora's box' (Interview 9).

Conditions that facilitated the use of public office for private gain in real estate development thus quickly became institutionally embedded. After 1992 the executive board moved to weaken the cohesion of preservationist institutions and council halted the development of systematic policy for the city's historic core. These moves maximized the discretion of political and administrative decisionmakers and contributed to case overload and corruption in preservationist bodies. Throughout the 1990s the city's elected leaders supported the maintenance of closed decisionmaking in real estate development in both the political and the administrative spheres. Together, these elements ensured that conditions remained favourable for the pursuit of private gain through public office in Prague.

The precise extent to which city councillors used their positions for private gain is impossible to ascertain, since they were not compelled to report any such activities and most of them remained informal. One post-1998 executive board member noted: 'As a rule, executive board members and councillors don't report a conflict of interest unless it's really obvious. I think we all know that a significant minority, at least, are involved in pursuing their own interests, but no one except a trusted few ever find out about 99 per cent of these cases' (Interview 14). Nevertheless, the indirect evidence of such activity is quite strong. In 1999, among a total number of fifty-five city councillors, forty-four were formally involved in private enterprises, most often as members of boards of directors, and of these, twenty were involved in real estate companies operating in the city (Zelený Kruh 1999).[9] Given that city councilors are part-time public servants who receive only a modest monthly stipend for their council work, their involvement in private enterprise might be expected; nevertheless, the concentration of councillors in the real estate sector was notably high. Executive board members however, are full-time municipal employees, and in the 1990s their monthly salaries were more than twice the national average wage. Yet, in 1999, nine of the twelve executive board members were also involved in private enterprise (Janderová and Brych 1999; Zelený Kruh 1999).

The available evidence suggests that the undeclared and untraceable use of public office for private gain was common among city councillors and executive board members, and likely involved some of the most powerful from among them. Several people interviewed for this project – including political leaders and real estate developers – alleged that two of the city's most powerful politicians in the 1990s were extensively involved in pursuing private gain in real estate development (Interview 11; Interview 14; Interview 32; Interview 23). One developer, who works primarily for foreign investors, claimed that 'between 1993 and 1998 we often had a difficult time getting projects approved, since [one executive board member] had his own private bank account and if you weren't willing to pay into it, getting anything built in this city was tough' (Interview 23). And as we will see below, while conclusive evidence of the pursuit of private gain by politicians and civil servants did not emerge in any cases of major commercial development in the historic core, in the context of nonexistent development guidelines and closed-door decision making processes, just about every major development project fell under a shadow of suspicion and controversy. Before we turn to some specifics, however, let us review the overall policy record in preservation and development in the historic core in 1990s Prague.

Governing Development in Prague's Historic Core: The Policy Record to 1999

While Prague's post-communist political leaders quickly shifted towards pursuing ad hoc, closed-door decisionmaking regarding real estate development in the historic core, this shift certainly did not reflect any wider consensus. On the contrary, throughout the 1990s civic voices calling for systematic preservation policy grew ever stronger. Some of the preservationist groups that emerged in 1990, such as Zlatí Orli and Společnost Praha, faded away, but other new ones arose to take their place. The venerable Club for Old Prague (KZSP), founded in 1900, revitalized its activity, and in the historic core's Lesser Quarter, SOPMSH continued to lobby for preservation and residents' concerns. The activity of such groups ensured that preservation issues remained in the media spotlight, albeit to a lesser degree than the transport issues discussed in Chapter 4. In January 1993, the public legitimacy of the preservationist position was strengthened when the U.N. Educational, Scientific, and Cultural Organization (UNESCO) accepted a national government application to make Prague's historic core a world heritage site (Kuncová 1993a).

Faced with continued public pressure, Prague's political leaders maintained a consistent focus on preservation and protection of residents interests in their official pronouncements regarding the historic core. In May 1993, when Jan Koukal (ODS) replaced Milan Kondr as mayor, he strongly criticized the lack of a systematic policy. He welcomed the existence of preservationist groups, and pledged to work closely with them in developing a systematic strategy for preservation and development (Brdečková 1995). In a June interview published in a Prague daily newspaper, Koukal responded to a question regarding historic preservation in the core as follows: 'I think that – and I don't want to point fingers here – the city has lacked a systematic approach to questions of urban design and construction. Individual problems have been dealt with as they have come up. For this reason, issues that appeared minor ... did not get serious treatment. Emphasis was placed on maximizing financial gain; but this is not a viable strategy' (Schmidt 1993: 3).

Under Koukal's leadership, the dominant ODS entered the 1994 elections with a policy platform favoring systematic preservation of the historic core. As we saw in the previous chapter, however, specific urban development issues received little attention in the 1994 election campaign, and the policy platforms of all of the political parties tended to be vague. The issue of preservation and development in the historic core was no exception. Nevertheless, insofar as the issue was featured in the electoral platform of the ODS, the emphasis was clearly on preservation. The ODS's platform stated that the party supported the 'preservation of the unique atmosphere and relatively untouched nature of the Prague Monument Preserve,' viewed as 'undesirable' the 'depopulation of the centre to meet the demand for office space,' and would 'definitively give preference to historic preservation in the renewal of the city centre' (Civic Democratic Party 1994a: 5, 7, 14). In order to

achieve these goals, the ODS pledged to increase funding for the renovation of historic monuments, channel commercial investment outside
the historic core, and put in place regulations regarding the conversion
of buildings to non-residential uses (ibid.).

Throughout the 1990s there was a wide gap between preservationist
rhetoric and action on establishing mechanisms that could make systematic preservation a reality. As we saw, late in 1993 city council
rejected UHA's study of the Prague Monument Preserve and did not
incorporate it in the Plan for the Stabilized Zones. Soon after the elections, the new executive board declared its commitment to working out
detailed planning guidelines for the Monument Preserve in conjunction with the new overall land use plan that was due to be approved in
1998 (Mejstřík 1995); however, this declaration did not come to anything.

In 1993 the city council had approved a document that was to provide the preliminary foundation for a new overall land use plan for Prague, with emphasis on the importance of systematic preservation
policies for the historic core. Prepared by planners at the Chief Architect's Office, the 'Land Use and Economic Principles' stated, among
other things, that 'The area of the Prague Monument Preserve is of
exceptional, world-class historic value, and is composed of a set of elements that are subject to protection. The land use plan must fully
respect these elements. They include not only architectural and urban
elements and spaces and visual panoramas, but also a multi-use character, including a significant residential function. Given the current full
capacity of the Prague Monument Preserve, it is not possible to develop
new local commercial centres here' (Prague City Council 1993: 67). The
document further declared that 'binding regulations in historically pro-
tected areas or parts thereof will be developed in a special plan ("Plan
for Preservation and Development"), worked out on the basis of
detailed analysis of these areas' (ibid.: 68). Finally, it introduced the idea
of expanding the area defined as the 'central business district' beyond
the boundaries of the historic core to encompass the surrounding nineteenth-century districts, in order to take advantage of vacant land in
these areas and to relieve development pressure on the core (ibid.: 67).

The promise of comprehensive policy did not materialize. Between
1993 and 1996, the city council commissioned no further work towards
a detailed plan for the historic core. In 1996 the city council approved
the conceptual draft for the new overall land use plan, stipulating that
'detailed documentation for the Prague Monument Preserve will be

worked out in conjunction with the draft of the land use plan, and will subsequently be worked into the land use plan ... as an addendum' (cited in Prague Executive Board 1999). Once again, this declaration was not followed by any instructions to city planners to work on such documentation. In a 1997 debate in city council, a proposal to commission a detailed plan for the historic core was voted down on the grounds that the overall land use plan should be developed and approved before working out detailed regulations for the historic core (Interview 3; Interview 17).[10]

Prague's new overall land use plan was approved in September 1999, and it contained no detailed guidelines for the historic core. The plan did lay out general zoning instructions for the historic core, but only on the scale of entire city blocks (see City Development Authority 1998a). On the urging of the Borough of Prague 1, the plan also stipulated the minimum proportion of housing space that had to be retained in various specific parts of the historic core. This too was specified on the scale of city blocks, and thus it left open the key question of which buildings in those blocks were to remain residential and to what extent (Interview 38).[11] The overall land use plan contained no specific guidelines on the physical form that development could or could not take in various parts of the historic core.

One pillar of the 1993 'Land Use and Economic Principles' for Prague's new overall land use plan was the expansion of the central business district into areas adjacent to the historic core, so as to relieve development pressure on the core itself. This point did find its way into the land use plan that was finally approved, and several areas near the historic core were zoned for major development (City Development Authority 1998a; Právo 1998b). The plan thus promised at least an indirect form of protection against development pressure on the historic core. Ironically, however, prior to the adoption of the overall land use plan, major development was in some respects actually simpler in the historic core than on adjacent vacant land.

We should recall that while the Prague Monument Preserve (PPR) was classified as a stabilized zone, covered by the interim land use plan of 1994, major vacant lots outside the historic core were not. As a result, until 1999 Prague had what Luděk Sýkora calls a condition of 'double governance' in development approvals (1995: 335): The few vacant lots in the historic core could be individually developed, because they were covered by the 'Plan for the Stabilized Zones.' Development of the more abundant vacant lands *outside* the core required that investors prepare an 'urban study' of the area, at their own expense, and that the study be approved by the Chief Architect's Office (Blažek 1994: 14). In this manner, the absence of an approved land use plan for areas outside the historic core actually intensified development pressure within the core, by making development outside the core more costly and time-consuming (Interview 21).

This situation was made all the more difficult by the fact that while most vacant lots in the historic core were owned by the city, ownership of undeveloped land outside the core was usually fragmented. Developing the latter thus required investors or the city to negotiate extensively with various public and/or private owners (City of Prague 1998). Not surprisingly therefore there was little major development of the vacant lots adjacent to the historic core. The one exception was the central area of Smíchov, in Prague 5, for which the city, the borough, and investors had successfully prepared a detailed urban study and developed a public-private partnership. As a result, Smíchov experienced a boom in office and commercial construction in the late 1990s (Nachtigall 1998a).

During the second half of the 1990s, the city was also trying to work out a strategic plan for itself (as discussed in detail in Chapter 4). In contrast to what happened regarding transport infrastructure, the strategic planning process in the historic preservation sphere was quite open to civic actors. In April 1996 the City Development Authority's Strategic Planning Section (USK), held a workshop on preservation and development in which representatives of civic preservationist groups and of the city's preservationist institutions participated (City Development Authority 1996b: 1). The workshop produced a set of recommendations for a comprehensive preservation strategy for the historic core that would articulate a clear conception of preservation, differentiated by locality, and a clear policy of what is and is not welcome in that locality. In addition to some 'at least basic, simple regulations,' workshop participants called for detailed plans that would 'harmonize the use of historic building stock with its potential without significant alterations [to the building stock]' and for the 'priority protection of historic buildings with housing, and the maintenance of the current concentration of the housing function' (ibid.: 12–13).

The final version of the city's overall strategic plan incorporated these goals and added some others, such as minimizing traffic in the historic core and relieving commercial development pressure by providing development zones outside the historic core (City of Prague

2000a: 53). However, establishing the mechanisms to implement these goals was beyond the scope of the plan itself, but a matter for the land use planning process. The strategic plan did contain some suggestions for coordinating the work of the relevant public institutions involved with the preservation and development of the city's centre (see ibid.: 83, 97–98). As in the roads sphere, the plan was used in 1999 to request European Union funding for historic preservation, although the amount requested was not very large – about 6 per cent of the total EU funding requested that year by the city (City Development Authority 1999d: 57–9). But the work of putting together specific regulations for preservation and development in the historic core remained to be done.

In the absence of any concrete, systematic policy on to real estate development in the historic core, the way in which Prague's historic core actually was developed in the 1990s diverged significantly from that described in the official political pronouncements. In terms of the mix of uses in the core, the city failed in its goal of restricting commercialization and maintaining residential capacity: Between 1991 and 1999 total retail space in the Prague Monument Preserve increased by 65 per cent (from about 152,000 m^2 to about 250,000 m^2), commercial office space increased by about 40 per cent (to 1 million m^2), and the number of hotel beds increased several-fold to 8,000 (City Development Authority 2000: 15, 21).

Of all the new office space of 'international standard' developed in Prague between 1993 and 1996, 70 per cent was in the core boroughs of Prague 1 and Prague 2 (Sýkora 1999: 85).[12] By contrast, between 1991 and 1998 the number of residents living in the Prague Monument Preserve decreased by 16 per cent (from 61,000 to 51,400; City Development Authority 2000: 11–12).

The record in terms of historic preservation itself was mixed. By no means did the historic core undergo massive redevelopment, and only a few historic buildings were torn down to make way for new ones (for a list of them, see Bečková 2000: 83). The city undertook some major renovation projects of municipally owned historic landmarks, most notably the municipal library and the Obecní Dům concert hall. It also dispensed a total of Kc358 million (U.S. $9.5 million) – about 0.2 per cent of its overall budget – to support the private restoration of 350 buildings between 1993 and 1999, most of them in the historic core (City of Prague Department of Historic Preservation 2000: 30).

Decisionmaking, however, with regard to individual cases of development in the historic core was highly inconsistent. Overworked preservation administrators, working without guidelines and subject to both political pressure and the temptation of bribery, were alternately strict and lenient when dealing with ostensibly similar applications regarding the reconstruction of historic buildings. In some cases they would approve substantial alterations to – or even the wholesale gutting of – historic buildings (see, e.g., Holub 1994, Mejstřík 1995), while in others they ruled in favour of very strict historic preservation. One PUPP employee offered this example: 'I think it was around 1994, I was working on a case where a new owner wanted to reconstruct a baroque house in the Lesser Quarter and add skylights. Of course I recommended against it, since the roof-scape is an integral part of what makes the centre historically authentic. That went fine, but a few months later we had an almost identical case; we ruled the same way, but this time we were overridden by our director – evidently the owner had good connections. So then the first owner caught wind of it and came back to us and complained, and justifiably so. So this is how we have lost a lot of credibility in recent years' (Interview 42). Furthermore, some city councillors and board members consistently pushed for large-scale commercial development on the historic core's few remaining vacant lots. As we will see in the next section, even in face of opposition from preservation administrators, civic groups, and the media, by the end of the 1990s virtually all vacant land in the historic core had been filled with offices, hotels, or high-end retail establishments.

The combination of inconsistent decisionmaking regarding the renovation of existing buildings and the commercial development of open land invoked national and international criticism. For example, although Prague's record in historic preservation had been praised by UNESCO in 1992 when the city's core was added to the list of world heritage sites, by 1995 the institution monitoring the sites, the International Council on Monuments and Sites (ICOMOS) issued a damning assessment. In its report, ICOMOS noted that 'the theoretical and practical principles of historic preservation are not pursued and respected in Prague' and cited examples of what it considered to be inappropriate development (see Mejstřík 1995). In 1997 the World Monuments Fund, a U.S.-based non-governmental organization, placed Prague's historic core on its list of 'most threatened heritage sites' worldwide, once again citing some of the most egregious violations (Kuncová 1997). In 1998 the Czech Republic's Ministry of Culture overturned fifty-two of the sixty-three decisions regarding development in Prague's historic core that municipal institutions responsible for preservation had submitted for review – and the minister, Pavel Dostál, publicly expressed 'grave concern' for the city's historic heritage (Biegel 1999). What was it about the processes of real estate development in the historic core that sparked such criticism? Much of the criticism focused on the commercial development of the city centre's few remaining lots of open land, which we will now look at in some detail.

Developing City Property in the Historic Core

At the beginning of the 1990s within Prague's historic core there were about a dozen vacant lots. When the city regained title to its pre-1948 properties in 1992, most of these passed into municipal ownership, and by the end of the decade, virtually all of them had been developed by foreign investors for commercial purposes. In the absence of regulatory guidelines, and with no requirements to disclose information regarding real estate development in the historic core, nearly every case was highly controversial and evolved under a cloud of public suspicion, even though no hard evidence emerged of officials using their public positions for private gain.

An account of what happened to vacant lots cannot provide a full picture of the dynamics of preservation and development in Prague's historic core. It does, however, illustrate the difficulties associated with pursuing development in the context of a closed, ad hoc system of regulation that in turn fed a widespread perception of pervasive corruption. In general, the approvals process followed a clearly discernible pattern: starting with confidential negotiations between the developer and the city's executive board or the relevant municipal offices, which engendered public controversy over the project, and ending with a lengthy process of revision. We will first review the emergence of this pattern and then examine one concrete example.

Negotiating with property investors regarding the terms of development for individual sites was primarily the responsibility of administrative bodies in post-communist Prague. Acquiring approval to develop a site involved two steps: (1) obtaining a planning permit from the city's Department of Land Use Decisions (OUR) that set out the overall dimensions and proposed function of the building, and then (2) obtaining a construction permit in which the technical parameters of the building were detailed. In the case of the historic core, the latter were issued by the Building Permits Offices located in the boroughs of Prague 1 or Prague 2 (Interview 15).

If the property or site in question belonged to the city, however, the executive board had the right to first sign a contract that set the terms of development. This contract was subject to approval by the city council, and subsequent review through the two-step development permits process just described. In formal terms, the development process thus varied depending on who owned the property in question. In reality, however, it appears that whether city property was involved or not, decisionmaking about foreign investment in the historic core was strongly centralized in the hands of a few political leaders.

We should recall that in 1991 the executive board established a Foreign Investment Section, headed by one of its members, Michal Hvížd'ala. As the city regained ownership of its pre-1948 properties, it also established a Department of Municipal Property that was made formally responsible for managing the city's holdings (Dušková 1997: 12–15). Between 1991 and 1993 Hvížd'ala remained the main overseer of foreign investment in the historic core, regardless of who owned the property. It was through his Foreign Investment Section that investors typically made their first contact with city officials and through his office that preliminary development deals regarding city property were negotiated before they were taken to the executive board or to the OUR (Interview 20).

In February 1993 the executive board took advantage of Hvížd'ala's absence at one of its meetings to disband the Foreign Investment Section, in a deliberate effort to weaken his control over negotiations with foreign investors (Kuncová 1993b; Interview 20). While Hvížd'ala continued to be an influential figure on the executive board until 1998, it was not long before a second dominant figure in negotiations with foreign investors emerged. According to people interviewed for this project (Interview 11; Interview 21), from the early days of his five and a half years as the mayor of Prague (April 1993 to December 1998), Jan Koukal had quickly developed a pivotal role in managing foreign investment in real estate development. One former member of the executive board said: 'I'd call this period one of "Koukal's centralism." He was a strong personality, in fact a brilliant man, perhaps the only one who could actually understand what was really going on in municipal politics. He could negotiate the labyrinth of bureaucratic regulations and personal connections better than anyone else, and he took full advantage of this to concentrate decisions in his own hands – although of course in public everyone talked about "collective" decisionmaking and consensus. Decisionmaking slowed down during his tenure, less got decided – but what did get decided, especially with respect to property development and foreign investment, often had his stamp on it' (Interview 11).

Hvížd'ala and Koukal had key roles in bringing before the municipal regulatory bodies (and, in the case of city-owned property, to the executive board and city council) a series of proposals for commercial development of vacant land in the historic core. Typically, the initial agreements attempted to secure the maximum commercial floor space, be it for office, retail, or hotel purposes (see, e.g., Klapalová 1998b).

Officially, in the case of city-owned property, the politicians aimed to maximize the commercial space in order to secure maximum revenue for the city. Overall, as it turned out, the city did not receive any substantial revenues from such deals. But since contracts signed by the executive board with developers were confidential unless politicians decided otherwise, what amount of money the city made from individual projects remains impossible to ascertain.[13] More generally, however, revenues from all sale or lease activities (including real estate outside the historic core and privatized municipal enterprises) peaked at 7.4 per cent of total city revenues in 1993, and thereafter stabilized in the range of 1 per cent to 3 per cent range (Bosáková 1999; Czech Statistical Office 1999: 47).[14]

To some extent this inability to secure significant revenues from property development stemmed from the political leaders' lack of experience in dealing with developers. One developer interviewed for this project observed that 'when we started working here in the early 1990s, it was a bit of a disaster zone. Politicians didn't even know how to draw up a contract' (Interview 23). In a newspaper interview published in July 1993, the deputy mayor responsible for city-owned property, Tomáš Kaiser, explained that in the early 1990s, Prague's city councillors believed that 'we are good businessmen and we can measure up to the best firms that come to Prague ... [but] they showed us very quickly that we are wrong if we think that our business skills match theirs' (Schreib 1993c: 5).

There is also evidence however, that some city councillors used public office to pursue private gain by acting as intermediaries for property developers. We cannot ascertain the true extent of such activity with respect to development of vacant land in the historic core. Nonetheless, among politicians, bureaucrats, civic groups, and the media there certainly was widespread suspicion that such activity was endemic. That political leaders pressed for the interests of developers and did not secure substantial revenues for the city, even after they had gained considerable experience in negotiating with development interests, only deepened this suspicion. One former member of the executive board asserted: 'I wouldn't say that most major development deals in the centre have been tied to the particular interests of individual politicians. But certainly some of them have, to the detriment of the interests of the city. You've asked me to give examples, and frankly, I'd rather not ... but you just need to look at the quality of the contracts signed with developers on city land, and the kinds of buildings that have gone up, and I think it speaks volumes' (Interview 26). In pressing for development that maximized the commercial use of the historic core's remaining open land, city councillors often faced stiff administrative resistance during the development approvals process, a process that involved harmonizing the interests of a multitude of institutions. In the historic core, preservationist institutions were a key force. They often mounted significant resistance to commercial developments that had the support of the city council, typically objecting to both the function and the dimensions of a proposed project (Interview 19).

The city council could use a couple of different strategies to deal with such resistance. If the particular development was on city land, it was in a stronger position. Councillors who supported the development could, and usually did, argue that the terms for the project had already been set in an initial contract signed with the developer and that change to them would open the city to the charge of negotiating in bad faith (Interview 15). If the project did not involve city property, the executive board could apply pressure on administrators through its discretionary powers regarding personnel and other organizational matters. One developer described the process like this: 'If the politicians come to bat for you, it can help a lot [in getting a development project approved], even though it's the administrators that are supposed to have the final say. Some executive board member can go to the preservation people or the land use permits people and say, 'look, we really want this approved – and by the way, remember you owe us your jobs.' That's the sort of thing you have to do from time to time to get things done' (Interview 43). The development approvals process typically became a lengthy, conflictual ordeal of negotiations between politicians and developers, on the one hand, and preservation administrators, on the other, often involving successive revisions to the original proposal, pressure on employees in the city's administrative bodies from the executive board, and the increasingly widespread suspicion that the personal interests of politicians and civil servants were involved (Interview 15). On occasion such conflicts spilled over into the media, further complicating the development process.

Preservationist activists in 1990s Prague made development approvals even more conflictual. The issue of preservation and development in the city's historic core did not, in general, have as high a public profile as the issue of freeways construction. Nevertheless, lobbying by preservationist groups ensured that it resurfaced repeatedly in the media spotlight. Two groups were particularly active. Freed from communist-era restrictions on its activities, the Club for Old Prague grew substantially in membership and profile over the course of the decade (Bečková 2000). Also very active was the Prague Panel, which was founded by architects and art historians in 1993 as a body of professionals who would issue independent opinions on preservation and development in the city (Interview 19).

Preservationist groups had no way to access or influence the development approvals process directly, since access to the development permits process itself was limited to civic groups that defended environmental concerns, as defined in the 1992 national Law on Nature and Landscape Protection. In the absence of such access, they turned instead to criticizing development initiatives in the media, using such information as was publicly available or information leaked by sympathetic government sources. One member of the Prague Panel said: 'At first, we had envisioned ourselves as a sort of independent consultative group that political leaders could turn to resolve controversial development issues. But we soon found that they would turn to us only opportunistically, if at all, and that we had to fight for access to the most basic information about what was going on. But then we found that if we brought issues to the media instead – and the media in Prague have been very sympathetic to heritage preservation issues – we got better results. Politicians and administrators had to take our positions seriously, or else they'd be raked over the coals in the media. So this is what we've been focusing on, and I must say that we've had some success' (Interview 19).

Thus, the Club for Old Prague and the Prague Panel pursued a media-based strategy of revealing leaked information about development proposals or criticizing controversial proposals that were already in the public realm. In dealing with this challenge, the executive board at first tightened its control over information on development proposals for the historic core. Later in the 1990s, however, it shifted to a new strategy, and began to present development proposals through public exhibitions in an attempt to forestall as much criticism as possible (Interview 15). Even so, however, the proposals were usually not presented until after a contract with a developer had been signed, and the public was not offered any meaningful opportunity for input (Solař 1999). As a result, such moves did little to defuse the chronic controversy over commercial development projects in the Prague's historic core. While the final version of a project often differed from what had initially been proposed, it usually took a long period of acrimonious negotiation and public conflict to reach a resolution.

Let us now briefly examine one case of commercial development in the historic core. Given the closed nature of development decisionmaking in Prague, it is difficult to compile information on a representative sample of cases. The single case described below is therefore simply illustrative of the dynamics discussed above, and it was selected partly because of the availability of information about it. The case had its genesis in the early 1990s, but its evolution was a complex process that reached through much of the rest of the decade.

As part of the national government's undertaking to return 'historic property' to Prague, in 1991 the city got title to a partly vacant parcel of land on the Alšovo Embankment by the Vltava River in the middle of the Old Town, about 200 metres from the landmark Charles Bridge which was built in the fourteenth century. The parcel included three small historic buildings – a house from the baroque period, a classicist building erected at the beginning of the nineteenth century, and a neo-renaissance apartment building from the 1880s (Solař 1999). Two of these were owned by the city, while the third had been returned to private owners (Interview 14).

In 1992 the executive board organized a competition for the commercial development of a vacant city-owned lot in the New Town (Kvačková 1991b). The investors who lost out in this competition were offered a chance to bid on the Alšovo Embankment land. Two international hotel firms, the Ritz-Carlton and the Four Seasons Hotels, took up this offer and began negotiating with executive board member Michal Hvížd'ala, even though the land in question had been zoned for higher education in the still valid 1985 overall land use plan (Kostlan 1993; Imrych 1994).

At first, the city's political representatives promised Four Seasons and the Ritz-Carlton a public competition. A few months later, however, the competition was abruptly cancelled, without explanation, and – much to the consternation of Ritz-Carlton representatives – the land was offered to Four Seasons Hotels, which had in the meantime signed a long-term lease with the owners of the private building that sat on the parcel of land (Kostlan 1993; Kvačková 1994). In February 1994 the executive board signed a confidential contract with Four Seasons for lease of the land held by the city. The executive board released partial information on the contract, which stipulated that the property had been independently valued at between Kc196 and Kc245 million (U.S. $5.4 to U.S. $6.8 million). Four Seasons was given approval to construct a 180–room hotel on the site, which was to include retail shops, a fitness centre, and underground parking. The company agreed to organize an architectural competition for the design of the hotel and to pay the city Kc14 million (U.S. $400,000) during construction, as well as an additional, but undisclosed annual sum after the hotel's opening, scheduled for 1996 (Turková 1994).

The release of this information produced a strong reaction from the Prague Panel and the Club for Old Prague. They argued that 180 rooms was far too large a number for this site, as it would necessitate the construction of an eight-storey building that would overshadow surrounding historic structures, and they also expressed concern about the fate of the three small historic buildings on the site (Imrych 1994). In November 1994 the Prague Panel published a statement to this effect, signed by about 600 prominent individuals, including architects, writers, and national politicians (Mejstřík 1996). The chorus of protest was joined by President Václav Havel, and by a number of historic preservation professionals, who claimed that they had been pressured by political leaders into approving the 180-room hotel project (Taborská and Hrdlička 1995; Interview 32).

In the wake of this protest, the competition for the site design of the hotel produced no winner. Instead, the nine-member jury, comprised predominantly of architects selected by the Czech Architects Association, recommended that the hotel be made at least 10 per cent smaller and that any future competition for its design be organized by the city – rather than by Four Seasons (Krejčí 1994; Svobodné Slovo 1995). In the meantime, opposition city councillor Martin Bursík provided reporters with the full text of the original contract with Four Seasons, which revealed that the city was to have received between U.S. $400,000 and U.S. $700,000 a year (on a sliding scale over time) from the company once the hotel was built, but that these amounts would decrease by U.S. $10,000 per year per room if the total number of rooms approved in the end turned out to be lower than 180. The contract thus placed strong pressure on city officials to stick to the original size of the hotel so that the city could make money from the deal (Lidové Noviny 1995).

Throughout 1995 and into 1996, the city's executive board negotiated with Four Seasons on a new contract for a smaller hotel, and tried to keep the terms of the new contract strictly confidential. Nevertheless, some details were leaked to the media – including that the executive board had agreed to waive the first five years of rent for Four Seasons in return for reducing the room capacity from 180 to 165 (Konečný and Šprunková 1997). Once a new contract had been hammered out, a new architectural competition (this time run by the city) was successfully concluded in November 1996, and the hotel project was finally ready for the development approvals process (Mladá Fronta Dnes 1996a).

The approval of the winning architectural design for the hotel brought on another wave of public criticism from groups such as the Prague Panel, the Club for Old Prague, and also the Czech Institute for Monument Preservation. For the next three years they criticized plans to gut the interior of two of the three historic buildings on the site during the hotel's construction (Hušek 1999; Mladá Fronta Dnes 1999b). Nevertheless, the tightly closed development approvals process slowly but surely ground on. Construction finally started in early 1999, and the hotel opened in February 2001, to an enthusiastic reception from wealthy travellers and continued criticism from preservationists and the local media (Solař 1999; Klapalová 2001).

In the absence of a comprehensive policy regarding the historic core, and in the context of closed-door negotiations between developers and city officials, commercial development in Prague's city centre thus became a lengthy, unpredictable, and controversial affair.

Although the precise extent to which public office was used for private gain by political leaders in Prague impossible to determine, there was strong consensus among civic actors, politicians, developers, and administrators alike that the phenomenon was endemic. Indeed, as we have seen, indirect evidence of the widespread nature of this phenomenon is substantial, and there has appeared no plausible alternative explanation for the vigour with which political leaders defended investor priorities and resisted establishing systematic, transparent governing processes in this policy area.

The 1998 Elections and Beyond: Towards Better Government Performance?

By the end of the 1990s, a number of factors began to reduce the attractiveness for political leaders of ad hoc, closed-door policymaking with respect to central Prague's real estate. The historic core's potential to absorb further commercial development without major demolitions of existing buildings had been exhausted, and thus opportunities for city councillors and civil servants alike to benefit from acting as intermediaries for developers decreased. The near-simultaneous approval of a new overall land use plan and a strategic plan for the city formally enshrined the city's official policy of preservation in the historic core, challenging political leaders to finally put their declared priorities into practice. Closed-door real estate dealings and allegations of corruption became a major issue in the 1998 municipal elections, and a new national Law on Free Access to Information, passed in 1999, put a damper on the previously ideal conditions for the pursuit of private gain through public office. In this context, the new mayor, Jan Kasl, was able to spearhead efforts to make development policy with respect Prague's historic core more systematic and open.

By the end of the decade, the development boom in the historic core had used up virtually all of the commercially attractive open land and historic buildings in the area. As opportunities for further development grew thin, investors began to lose interest in the historic core. In 1999, 40,000 square metres of retail space and 100,000 square metres of office space were still under development in the historic core as a result of projects approved earlier in the decade, but there was relatively little investor interest in further projects (City Development Authority 2000: 15). Pressure to convert residential buildings to non-residential uses was also declining. While in 1991 historic preservation bodies had received about twenty requests to permit such conversion each month, by early 1997 they were getting virtually none (Kvačková 1997). As investors lost interest in the historic core, the very high real estate prices of the earlier 1990s began to decline (Interview 38), and so did the opportunity for both political leaders and administrators personally to benefit from acting as intermediaries for development interests.

As we saw in Chapter 4, the city council approved a new overall land use plan and a strategic plan for Prague in 1999. The land use plan promised to further decrease investor pressure on the historic core by finally opening up adjacent lands for commercial development.

Although neither of these documents contain a detailed strategy for preservation and development in the historic core, both endorse the goal of developing such a strategy. Long proclaimed but not actually pursued by the city council, this goal was now institutionalized in two key policy documents. As a result, the city council began to experience mounting demands from the media and civic preservationist groups to live up to these declarations and to put a systematic policy into practice by developing detailed regulations (see, e.g., Solař 1999; Biegel 1999).

The issue of preservation and development in the historic core did not, in itself, play a major role in the municipal election campaign of 1998, although the two strongest political groups in the running – the ruling Civic Democratic Party (ODS) and the Union for Prague (UPP) – both promised to implement systematic policies without delay (Civic Democratic Party 1998: 6; Union for Prague 1998). However, the broader issue of transparent decisionmaking, which was conspicuously absent in the real estate development sector, was a dominant theme of that campaign.

Seizing on the widespread perception that the closed decisionmaking style of ODS politicians and city administrators hid corruption in the real estate sector, the UPP highlighted its intention to take steps to minimize opportunities for corruption and maximize the openness of policy processes. In its platform, it proposed a number of measures to meet these ends, including rotating administrators among different posts, making city contracts with investors public, posting all information regarding policy decisions that was not legally subject to confidentiality, and involving the general public and civic groups more extensively in decisionmaking processes in individual issue areas (Union for Prague 1998). Although the UPP came second and was relegated to opposition status by an ODS–Social Democrat coalition, its campaign raised the public profile of these issues. After the elections, UPP leaders continued to press the new governing coalition on these issues, challenging its members to address such concerns (see, e.g., Bartoníček 1999).

The pressure to make Prague's property development system more transparent was reinforced by the new national Free Access to Information Law (no.106/1999), which was passed in May 1999 and came into force at the beginning of 2000. Driven by a desire to regain public confidence in the wake of national corruption scandals, as well as by pressure from the European Union in the context of the Czech Republic's ongoing accession talks, the national government mandated that all government information that was not explicitly confidential by law must be made accessible to the public on request and for a nominal fee (par. 14, par. 17). As such, the new law promised to undermine one of the key institutional legacies of the communist period that had helped to produce conditions encouraging the pursuit of private gain in the real estate development sector.

All of these factors came together to create an environment in which Prague's post-November 1998 mayor, Jan Kasl, began to pursue efforts aimed at making municipal policy with respect to the historic core – and with respect to preservation and development more generally – more systematic and open. An architect by profession, Kasl first became involved in municipal politics as an activist in the protests against hotel development in the Lesser Quarter in 1989 and 1990. In November 1990 he was elected to city council, and he served on the executive board in 1993–94, where he was responsible for urban planning. He returned to municipal politics in 1998 after four years in private practice as an architect.

Although he had not been active in preservationist groups during his period out of politics, Kasl retained a strong interest in historic preservation, and upon being elected mayor took on the issue as one of his areas of responsibility. From the outset, he declared developing systematic policies for the historic core to be one of his priorities. In a media interview in December 1998 he stated: 'I support the idea that there should be hard and fast rules for all listed heritage buildings and for those that are a significant component of the Prague Monument Preserve, that clearly say what is permitted, and what is not. Although architects and investors have wanted these rules, they have never been set. I actually think that there was no interest in setting them because then the rules of the game would be clear and everyone, even historic preservationists, would have limited discretion' (Schreib 1998a).

Taking advantage of the fact that approval of both the overall land use plan and the strategic plan was imminent, Kasl successfully pressed the executive board in early 1999 to commission the City Development Authority (URM) to update the urban study of the Prague Monument Preserve that had been produced by the Chief Architect's Office in the early 1990s. The intention was to turn the study into the basis for a detailed plan that could guide preservation and development in the historic core. In the spring of 1999, the URM conducted a series of workshops involving city councillors, administrators, independent professionals, and representatives of civic groups such as the

Club for Old Prague, aimed at developing consensus regarding the planning aims for the historic core (see CD Authority 1999b, 1999e).

In the workshop process, the URM initially faced some resistance from the city's Department of Historic Preservation (OPP) to the idea of adopting differentiated rules for different parts of the Prague Monument Preserve (Interview 3). However, faced with decreasing opportunities to profit from their decisionmaking discretion, as well as personal pressure from Mayor Kasl, the OPP relented. In November 1999 a document entitled 'Assignment for the Updated Urban Study of the Prague Monument Preserve' was completed and approved by city council, giving the URM the go-ahead to develop an actual draft land use plan for the centre of the city.

By September 2000, the draft was complete, and it was presented to the public for comments.[15] This plan, once again, laid out basic goals for the development of the Prague Monument Preserve, including halting the further spread of commercial development, maintaining the current level of residential population, decreasing traffic pressure, and developing individual buildings with reference to specific historic preservation guidelines (City Development Authority 2000: 21, 40, 49). For the first time, however, the goals were accompanied by recommendations for concrete regulatory measures. In terms of historic preservation, the plan divided the Prague Monument Preserve into five distinct zones with different degrees of heritage protection, ranging from zones of 'comprehensive conservation' to zones of 'regulated development' (ibid.: 49). Furthermore, for each of the 1320 individually listed heritage buildings in the historic core,[16] the document contained specific preservation guidelines (ibid.: 44).

The plan introduced targets for the proportion of floor space in each building in the Prague Monument Preserve that was to be devoted to housing, with the aim of ensuring that any future development either maintained or increased housing space in the historic core (City Development Authority 2000: 11–17). In terms of commercial space and parking, the plan's provisions for meeting the broad goals were somewhat weaker. Despite its declared aims, it allowed, for example, for the development of another 123,000 square metres of office space, some of which was already under construction (ibid.: 21). It also allowed for another 10 per cent increase in parking spaces (from 27,399 spaces to 30,688; ibid.: 76).

Nevertheless, if the plan were successfully adopted, Prague would finally have a detailed document that laid down the conditions for preservation and development in the Prague Monument Preserve.[17] Along with restarting the planning process with respect to the core in early 1999, Mayor Kasl put pressure on the city's Department of Historic Preservation (OPP) to develop a preservation policy to guide its own and the PUPP's activity. This policy was to encompass the whole city, but would include the guidelines being developed as part of the historic core land use plan.

At first, in pushing for such guidelines Kasl encountered considerable resistance from the OPP. As one executive board member explained in an interview conducted for this project, 'we really had to force the Department of Historic Preservation into developing a clear policy. They were strongly against it since they wanted to keep their discretion and their money-making opportunities, and we basically had to threaten them with drastic reorganization to get them to work on it' (Interview 14). After a few months, however, the OPP gave in and began working on a framework document outlining systematic principles of historic preservation. By the end of 2000 this framework document had been approved, and the OPP began working on detailed policy guidelines and methodological documents that would codify preservation policy. The city appeared to be finally on its way to systematizing the practice of preservation and development in the historic core (City of Prague Department of Historic Preservation 2000; Interview 14).

In addition to pressing for systematic guidelines with respect to development and preservation in the historic core, Kasl launched a broader campaign to increase the openness of urban development decisionmaking in Prague. Shortly before the November 1998 municipal elections, in an effort to head off criticism of the city's record on historic preservation, Kasl's predecessor Jan Koukal had re-established the Monuments Council, the consultative body of independent professionals that had been disbanded in 1992 (Klapalová 1998c). However, the council was little used during the last days of the Koukal administration. At the beginning of the year 2000, Kasl broadened the council's mandate and strengthened its position, renaming it the 'Mayor's Advisory Council on Architecture, Urban Planning, and Historic Preservation.' Composed of about thirty independent professionals, it started meeting monthly with Kasl to discuss a wide range of preservation and development issues (Schreib 2000).

Kasl's push for more inclusive and transparent government reached beyond the real estate development sphere. While some of the initiatives in this broader push were successful, many met with strong political and administrative resistance. Shortly after the 1998 elections, Kasl began to press members of the executive board to publicly declare their positions on individual decisions made in executive board meetings. Here he ran into fierce resistance, especially from individuals who had already served on the executive board during the Koukal era, and Kasl's efforts in this respect did not bear fruit. One of his political allies said: 'The mayor has faced implacable opposition to any suggestions that executive board members take individual responsibility for the way that they vote on the executive board. To my mind, it highlights the simple fact that many of them have taken advantage of their positions in rather unscrupulous ways in the past, so they have a lot to hide' (Interview 13).

Kasl had more success in pressing the executive board to create a separate Department of Public Relations (OSV) to provide more resources for the public provision of information. The OSV was created in February 1999 to replace the former municipal information office. However, the OSV encountered major difficulties in actually fulfilling its mandate. When it tried to arrange to second one employee from each of the city's other departments to act as an information officer for the public, the initiative was rebuffed by the city's chief administrative officer on the grounds that the city did not have sufficient staff to comply with the request (Interview 13).

In addition to such personnel problems, the OSV faced a civil service and an executive board that strongly resisted any efforts to actually develop a new system of rules that would facilitate the public dissemination of information on municipal decisionmaking. After the 1998 elections, opposition UPP councillors mounted a campaign in city council and the local media to compel the executive board to provide more information about the city's dealings with private actors. Citing the upcoming national legislation on Free Access to Information, UPP councillors pushed through a resolution in March 1999 that called on the executive board to make the full text of contracts signed between the city and private actors accessible to the public – effective retroactively to 1990 (Bartoníček 1999). In response, the executive board introduced a new system in September. According to this system members of the public were still not allowed to see the text of contracts directly; rather, they were to petition a city councillor to request access to a contract through the city's Legal Affairs department. This department then had the right to either grant or deny the request; if access was granted, the councillor could then view the contract and take notes, but could not photocopy the text on behalf of the petitioner (ibid.).

The introduction of this new system raised an uproar in the local media, as it appeared to contravene the provisions of the Free Access to Information Law that was soon to come into force. The controversy was heightened when in January 2000 the city's chief administrative officer, Zdeněk Zajíček, released a document detailing the loopholes in the law that might allow administrators to withhold information from the public (Lidové Noviny 2000a). Faced with allegations that the document contravened at least the spirit, if not the letter of the new national law, Zajíček said that the city intended to proceed as it saw fit. 'When someone takes us to court over this and wins, then we'll see [about changing the rules],' he is quoted as saying in one newspaper interview (ibid.).

Both the city's senior administrators and executive board members argued, without Mayor Kasl's support, that restrictions on public access to information must be put in place since some contracts with private actors had a confidentiality clause (Bartoníček 1999, 2000). The actual number of such contracts was not revealed, however, nor were simpler rules of access developed for contracts that did not have a confidentiality clause. As a result, speculation once again emerged about the use of public office for private gain in the real estate sphere. Together with Kasl's push to make the voting records of individual executive board members public, the controversy regarding contracts produced serious conflict between most executive board members and the mayor, who began to find himself increasingly politically isolated (Interview 14). In short, while a number of factors had allowed Prague's new mayor to push forward with some success for systematic policies regarding the historic core, political and civil service elites who had been involved in the politics of profit remained resistant to opening up the city's overall development practices to public scrutiny.[18]

Conclusion: Performance Problems and the Prospects for Change

Throughout the 1990s, the politics of preservation and development regarding Prague's historic core was characterized by an ad hoc, closed-door approach to decisionmaking. While the presence of well-developed preservationist institutions and the activity of small but vocal civic groups helped to prevent large-scale redevelopment in the historic core, actual policy consistently diverged from the official goals endorsed by the city council. As a result, while Prague's historic core at the end of the 1990s was indisputably in much better repair than it had been at the beginning of the decade, it had also experienced a highly controversial boom in commercial development and a decline in residential population that attested to the limited ability of politicians to live up to the challenge of systematically managing development pressures.

As in the freeways sphere, the origins of these developments lie in the early post-communist era, when political leaders faced a critical decision point in policy regarding the historic core, a point at which the choices that they made would have major longer-term consequences. While the administrative and public consensus pushed city councillors to pursue the development of a comprehensive strategy for the historic core, high investor interest and underdeveloped regulations separating public from private activity gave them opportunities for private gain. Politicians chose between these options in an unstable and institutionally incoherent context that discouraged them from pursuing longer-range strategies. Ultimately, enough of Prague's political representatives chose opportunities for private gain that the pursuit of systematic and open policymaking with respect to city centre real estate was abandoned.

Once political leaders had turned towards the politics of private gain with respect to Prague's historic core, increasing returns processes began to entrench poor performance for the longer term. The primary increasing returns process at work in this sphere was the development of vested interests in closed, ad hoc decisionmaking. The more that city councillors and bureaucrats chose to pursue private gain, the less attractive any move to open or systematize policy became; the longer that closed, ad hoc policymaking remained the norm, the more politicians and civil servants took advantage of the opportunities that offered. As in the freeways sphere, decisions made early on in the post-communist period had longer-term consequences for the quality of democratic government with respect to preservation and development in Prague's historic core.

The evolution of government performance in these two policy areas, up to the year 2000, was not wholly analogous, however. In the freeways sphere, increasing returns were sufficiently entrenched that the quality of government at the end of the 1990s was little different from what it had been a decade earlier. By contrast, at the end of the 1990s, various factors, both local and national, worked together to create a climate conducive to some change in the politics of real estate development in Prague's historic core. Upon taking office after the November 1998 elections, Mayor Jan Kasl took advantage of these factors to press – with some success – for the adoption of a comprehensive preservation and development policy with respect to the historic core, and also to push – though with less success – for greater transparency in the decisionmaking process.

The beginnings of better government performance with respect to Prague's historic core demonstrate that although performance patterns that emerged early on in the post-communist transformation had staying power, they were not wholly immutable. The contrast between the evolution of politics in the roads and the real estate spheres in the late 1990s does suggest, however, that change in performance patterns is most likely when several factors that promote such change come together. In the freeways sphere, where the challenge to the status quo came primarily from opposition politicians, the patterns of performance developed in the early post-communist period were not broken; at a minimum, such a result would have required a clear electoral victory by the Union for Prague. In the real estate sphere, however, electoral pressure in 1998, national legislative change, a fortuitous confluence of planning processes, and the exhaustion of development possibilities in the historic core together produced an environment in which a new mayor could pursue more systematic and open government with some success, even in the face of considerable opposition from his own colleagues on the city council. Institutional and policy change in the interest of better performance *was* possible in post-communist Prague. Nevertheless, by 2000, it appeared that creating more open, systematic government would likely involve the long-term, piecemeal breaking down of institutionally embedded patterns of performance that emerged early on in the post-communist period. The portrait of post-communist political development revealed in the preceding chapters differs significantly from most accounts of the dynamics of post-communist transformation. The contribution that this study makes to our broader understanding of post-communist transformations is a key theme in the final chapter of this book.

6 Institutional Change and Government Performance: Lessons from Prague

Prague's First Decade of Post-communist Politics: A Balance Sheet

Between 1990 and 2000 the emergence of democracy dramatically changed the politics of urban development in Prague. The basic elements of democratic local government were all firmly established by the end of the decade. Prague had a freely elected municipal government with substantial autonomous powers and resources at its disposal, and it was embedded in a stable democratic national system that ensured legal protection for the activities of a free press and of autonomous societal groups. As happened with many polities in the region, Prague confounded pessimistic early predictions that the broad social and cultural legacies of communism would undermine the transformation to democracy (see, e.g., Jowitt 1992).

Nevertheless, throughout the 1990s Prague's city council continued to have difficulty in governing key aspects of urban development systematically and openly. By the year 2000, there was a widespread sense of malaise and disappointment with the promise of democratic government among the city's politicians and administrators. Comparing local politics in Prague at the beginning of the 1990s and in the year 2000, one city executive board member offered this assessment: 'on the surface, it appears that decisions are made more professionally now, and we have a better sense of where the city should be going. But I'm sorry to say that in my opinion, the proportion of good decisions that are actually carried through has not increased' (Interview 14).

With a few exceptions, most local politicians and bureaucrats interviewed for this project saw difficulties in implementing policy decisions as the main problem with governing Prague. Frustrated with a decade of endemic conflict over urban development issues, many blamed these difficulties on what they saw to be an excessive focus on open policy processes. For example, one member of the executive board noted: 'It turns out that everything is difficult in a democracy. Everyone thinks they have a right to say their piece, even if they know nothing about the issues, so decisions are second-guessed, and it takes forever to get anything done. I guess that's the price you pay for being democratic' (Interview 21).

The analysis presented in this book, however, suggests that the difficulties experienced by Prague's administrative and elected leaders in implementing policy in the late 1990s should not be attributed to excessive democratic openness. On the contrary, in both of the policy spheres examined in this work, the political system in Prague's was marked by the lack of openness to societal interests. Policy was made largely behind doors closed to the public. Electoral processes did not offer voters a choice among clearly differentiated political programs until 1998. Moreover, in one of the policy spheres examined here – preservation and development in Prague's historic core – the city council resisted the formulation of any systematic policy that could guide decisionmaking. The closed and sometimes ad hoc nature of policymaking in Prague made it difficult to develop consensus among state and societal actors about broad policy goals. As a result, conflict was often transferred to the implementation stage. One long-time transport activist captured the frustration and disappointment felt by civic groups after a decade of closed-door policymaking when she said: 'For twelve years we've been trying to get the city government to take quality of life seriously, and sometimes I have this depressing feeling that nothing has changed there, that it's the same closed, ineffective structure it was under communism. The fact that we elect the politicians doesn't seem to make a difference' (Interview 37).

How did these performance difficulties emerge in post-communist Prague? Let us briefly review the argument presented in this book. We have linked Prague's difficulties to the decisionmaking context that the city's new political leaders faced after the local government reforms of 1990. Although these reforms did introduce the foundations for a strong local state, the broader institutional environment was still in flux in the early 1990s. This flux meant that political leaders faced critical decision points, moments at which they had an unprecedented opportunity to shape future outcomes by pursuing strategic reforms. At the same time, the incoherence and fluidity of the institutional context tended to make the pursuit of strategic reforms difficult and unattractive. In the two policy spheres examined in this study, local politicians confronted a disparate mix of institutions that had arisen at different times and that embodied conflicting visions of policy process and substance. They thus lacked an overarching normative consensus that could guide strategic action and faced instead an incoherent cacophony of incompatible demands and conflicting incentives. Moreover, the instability meant that the longer-term outcomes of their decisions were largely unknowable. Together, these factors discouraged Prague's political leaders from pursuing strategic reforms, and encouraged instead the privileging of simple solutions and short-term incentives when making governing decisions. In a polity where many pre-democratic institutions survived, the simple solutions and short-term incentives that presented themselves rarely encouraged the development of a government that performed well.

In both of the policy spheres examined here, decisions made in the early 1990s were subject to increasing returns processes that entrenched their consequences in the institutional landscape of post-communist Prague. In the sphere of freeways development, the first freely elected city council shied away from administrative and policy reform. Instead, it endorsed an only slightly modified version of the city's communist-era plans for its freeways and shut civic groups out of the decisionmaking process. Administrative institutions thus retained their old structure and technocratic orientation, while civic groups remained loosely organized, protest-oriented bodies. A dynamic of mutual delegitimation developed between administrators and politicians, on the one hand, and civic activists, on the other, and each side denied the legitimacy of the other's involvement in freeways policy. This dynamic forestalled any exploration of new policy options by the elites and prevented the meaningful participation of societal actors in planning processes. As the sunk costs of developing the freeways network mounted, moving away from established policy and policymaking patterns became even less attractive. Conflict over the freeways plans was therefore transferred to the implementation stage, and actual construction work on the city's roads network was subject to frequent delays and spiralling costs.

In the case of real estate development in the historic core, the politicians attempted at first to formulate a comprehensive policy that would take into account emerging market realities. Formulating such a policy proved to be a difficult process, however, whereas market pressures for real estate development, in the absence of conflict-of-interest regulations, offered the possibility of immediate material gain. Many city councillors chose the simpler course and began acting as intermediaries on behalf of developers. Doing so gave them a vested interest in maintaining closed, ad hoc decisionmaking procedures. This in turn opened up opportunities for administrative corruption. A gap between policy rhetoric and reality emerged, and individual development projects in the historic core frequently became the subject of conflict between actors who favoured ad hoc, closed-door development and those who pressed for systematic policy guidelines.

If the patterns of politics that emerged in these two policy areas became entrenched, they were by no means destined to remain so indefinitely. The 1998 municipal elections produced the first serious electoral competition among alternative platforms in post-communist Prague, and the Union for Prague (UPP) presented a strong challenge to the hitherto dominant Civic Democratic Party (ODS). Regarding freeways policy, this challenge helped to propel a resurgence of civic protest, which did not, however, result in any significant change in the dynamics of policymaking. Regarding real estate development, however, the UPP's 1998 campaign focus on open government coincided with the exhaustion of development possibilities in the historic core, as well as with the adoption of national access-to-information legislation. Together these factors opened up an opportunity for Prague's new mayor, Jan Kasl, to pursue better performance, even in the face of substantial opposition from many of his fellow ODS politicians. The city's political evolution by the end of the 1990s thus indicated that the patterns of politics that had developed early in the first decade of post-communist transformation were by no means impossible to undo. It did, however, suggest that further evolution towards better democratic performance was likely to be gradual and in face of considerable inertial resistance from within the existing institutional configuration.

The Case of Prague and Post-communist Transformations

The evolution of post-communist political systems in the fifteen years since the collapse of the Soviet bloc is remarkable for its diversity of outcomes. These range from outright authoritarian rule in some of the former Soviet republics to stable democracy across East Central Europe proper. Even within the category of stable democracies, the quality of rule varies widely at both the national and the sub-national levels. Furthermore, the transformation process has rarely been straightforward. Instead of either the rapid consolidation of a new political order or a steady evolution towards it, most post-communist states experienced an initial period of rapid but incomplete reform, followed by periods of retrenchment or even reversal interspersed with further reform. Indeed, even today these processes are by no means complete. In East Central Europe, the recent advent of membership in the European Union has introduced a new set of transformational challenges, while further east, a number of countries that had lapsed into authoritarian or semi-authoritarian rule, such as Georgia, Ukraine, and Kyrgyzstan, have recently experienced a new wave of regime change.

How can social scientists make sense of these diverse and non-linear paths of political transformation in the post-communist world? As noted at the outset of this book, one reaction of researchers has been to withdraw from broader at theorizing about transformation processes to focus instead on understanding the particulars of individual cases or on explaining political outcomes in a single policy sphere. This book, however, has been written with the conviction that there is still much to be gained from searching for broader insights. What such systemic insights can the story of Prague give us?

It might seem at first that there are few broad lessons to be learned from a single case study of a post-communist local government. In the absence of closely comparable studies, we cannot know with confidence the extent to which the dynamics of political transformation observed in Prague have analogues in other post-communist polities. In addition, caution is in order when we attempt to scale up insights from a local government study to the national level. Prague thus cannot serve as the basis for a generalizable model of post-communist political transformations; nevertheless, two features of the present study ensure that it speaks to broader questions.

First, we should recall that Prague is not just any post-communist city. Shortly after the fall of communism it developed some of the strongest and best organized local state structures in the region. As a result, the city's politicians enjoyed greater autonomy from outside influences than did most of their counterparts in the region. This relative autonomy makes it more plausible to compare the case of Prague with national-level cases, while the contrast between a strong local state and rather poor government performance makes Prague a critical case – one that can help us to move beyond state-centred models in thinking about the institutional dynamics of democratic development after communism.

Second, this study has used a rather novel approach in examining the case of Prague. As have a growing number of works on post-communist politics, it has framed the analysis employing assumptions drawn from the historical institutionalist approach to political inquiry, but it differs from most of these works in one important way: Moving beyond a single set of institutions or a single policy sphere, it has examined the transformation process in post-communist Prague in a holistic manner. As a result, it allows us to shed new light on connections between the systemic character of post-communist polities and the behaviour of political leaders.

In the rest of this chapter, I will discuss two ways that this study contributes to our broader understanding of post-communist transformations. First, this case study of Prague helps us to move beyond the somewhat simplistic models of post-communist political development that have dominated academic work until now. Neither the one-shot punctuated equilibrium model, implicit in some of the work on institutional design, nor the evolutionary change model, espoused by some scholars who focus on the legacies of the past, adequately capture the reality of how political systems changed after the fall of communism. This study of Prague suggests the utility of an alternative conceptualization of post-communist transformations that brings together elements of both of these models. This conceptualization sees post-communist transformations as processes marked by an early period of flux that congeals into a new institutional order as the result of a *series* of discrete decisions made by political leaders.

Second, this study gives us some new insight into how and why democratic development might falter in post-communist polities. On the one hand, it highlights the key importance of getting early reforms right, since institutional and policy innovations introduced early on tend to produce increasing returns in the longer run. On the other hand, it also allows us better to understand why the sequencing and substance of early reforms might not be optimal in the first place. It reaffirms the importance of institutional legacies in shaping reform choices, but in addition, it draws our attention to a potential paradox of post-communist transformations: At the very moment that political leaders could have maximum influence over future outcomes, institutional incoherence and instability might discourage them from exercising this influence through strategic action.

Models of Transformation: Towards a New Synthesis

Two approaches to political transformation dominated early research on post-communist politics. The institutional design approach assumed that the adoption of a standard set of correct reforms to basic state structures would lead to a rapid consolidation of democracy. The 'legacies' approach assumed that the negative social and cultural legacies of communism would undermine any efforts at post-communist democracy-building. Both of these approaches, for all their insights, have proved to be of limited value in explaining the diverse transformation trajectories of post-communist states. More recent work has overcome many of the limitations of the earlier research. Central to such recent work is the recognition that transformation processes are shaped by the interplay of institutional design and various legacies of the past. But this new synthesis has not yet led to the emergence of a new conceptualization that takes account of the dynamics of this interplay over time. In its absence, rather simple linear models of political transformation still underpin much of the academic work on post-communist states.

Since the mid-1990s, the leading role of rational choice–inspired research on post-communist institutional design has been displaced by the rise of historically grounded work. This work has successfully addressed at least two of the shortcomings of the early institutional research. First, there has been a fruitful rethinking of the factors that shape initial institutional choices. Many researchers have moved away from the focus on bargaining between establishment and opposition elites and have highlighted instead the role that varied institutional, social, and cultural legacies play in shaping post-communist institutional choices (see, e.g., Bunce 1999; Elster, Offe, and Preuss 1998; Ekiert and Hanson 2003). By acknowledging the differing influence of the past in various post-communist polities, such work has helped our understanding of transformation processes and has identified an important source for the diversity of political outcomes across the region.

Second, recent work on post-communist institutional design has moved away from the initial preoccupation with constitutional issues. Although constitutional design has continued to receive attention (see, e.g., Stanger 2003), most recent research has focused on the design of non-constitutional institutions. Some has examined institutional development in individual arenas of politics, such as the party system (Kitschelt et al. 1999) or administrative structures (Verheijen 1999), while other work has tried to explain patterns of reform in specific policy areas. In the latter category, work on economic reform has been especially voluminous, but many other policy areas have received attention as well. In broadening their empirical focus, scholars of institutional reform in post-communist polities have also implicitly moved beyond the initial preoccupation with the basic stability of democratic rule, and towards the focus of the present volume – the quality of democratic processes and outcomes.

For their part, the scholars who tend to give causal primacy to social and cultural factors have moved beyond the historically grounded pessimism of authors like Ken Jowitt. First, there has been a growing recognition that the legacies of the past are neither uniform across the region nor uniformly negative. Some recent work has argued, for example, that to the extent that communism created well-educated, industrialized, and urbanized societies, it also produced key preconditions for the successful emergence of democracy after communism (Kopstein 2001). Second, under the influence of institutionalist work, some scholars have begun to question the mechanisms through which social and cultural legacies gain causal power in the present. There is increasing recognition in the literature that while social and cultural legacies do have an impact on post-communist political outcomes, their influence tends to be indirect, mediated through the political institutions that constitute the immediate decisionmaking environment of political leaders, and enacted through the governing activity of those leaders (Ekiert and Hanson 2003). As a result, the notion of broad social and cultural legacies as overwhelming and immutable influences on the present has been largely abandoned. In its stead has arisen the notion that social and cultural legacies constitute political resources, frameworks for action, and sources of incentives. These elements influence but do not determine the actions of political leaders, and they are in turn reshaped over time by institutional development processes (Petro 2004).

Recent work on post-communist political transformations has thus increasingly converged around the idea that political outcomes are the product of an interplay between the legacies of the past and post-communist institutional design processes. Yet there has been relatively little work that addresses this interaction over time. Most researchers have focused their attention on accounts of developments in individual policy areas or individual arenas of politics, and as a result, broader questions regarding the dynamics of transformation have taken a back seat. Much work on post-communist politics is therefore still grounded in overly simple underlying models of change.

208   Governing the Post-communist City

Although conceptions of post-communist transformation are more often implicit than explicit in recent work, two models appear to underpin much of it: punctuated equilibrium and evolution. The punctuated equilibrium model suggests that political transformations involve a single 'critical juncture' followed by the consolidation of a new political order. This model was most clearly evident in early work on post-communist institutional design, but it is also implicit in some more-recent institutionalist work. For example, although Elster, Offe, and Preuss reject the notion that institutional design is necessarily followed by the rapid consolidation of a new order, they nonetheless see one moment of institutional design, a singular, quasi-simultaneous turning point, the outcome of which then largely determines subsequent transformation trajectories (1998: 296).

The evolutionary model is most evident in the recent work stemming from the social and cultural legacies tradition. It suggests that post-communist transformations are processes marked by the incremental adaptation of old legacies to new ends. For example, in his study of the Russian region of Novgorod, Petro argues that regional leaders successfully consolidated democracy by 'grafting' new institutional arrangements onto local cultural traditions (2004: 187). There is sometimes a prescriptive element in the work that adopts this model, in that incremental evolution is seen to be the best route towards a successful transformation. For example, Gernot Grabher and David Stark (1998) argue that by reforming post-communist institutions gradually, political leaders can maximize the chances that new institutional arrangements will function well within the context of existing legacies.

In reality, however, most post-communist transformation trajectories do not correspond very neatly to either the punctuated equilibrium or the evolutionary model of change. Most post-communist polities in the former Soviet bloc did indeed experience an initial period of rapid reform, but institutional change was rarely marked by a singular, moment-in-time turning point from which all other developments have flowed in logical consequence. Most of these transformations have involved periods of retrenchment, and in some cases even reversal, in the wake of initial reforms, followed by intermittent periods of further reform. To explain this non-linear character of transformation trajectories better, we need a conceptualization of transformation that takes into account of how institutional choices and the legacies of the past interact over time. The case study of Prague presented here gives us some building blocks for this effort.

This study rests on some assumptions that are worth reviewing briefly here: First, basic state structures do matter for political outcomes, since they largely shape the powers and resources at the disposal of political leaders. Second, a much broader matrix of state and societal institutions also influences the activity of politicians by providing a matrix of incentives that rewards some forms of behaviour over others. Third, these leaders have a bounded, or limited, rationality. Finally, for a number of reasons, the institutional elements of a political system cannot all change at once. Institutional change is asynchronous, and institutional legacies of the past typically remain embedded for some time in a newly emerging political system.

Working with these assumptions, this study of Prague suggests that we might usefully reconceptualize the critical juncture period after the collapse of communism in the Soviet bloc as one in which political leaders encountered multiple critical decision points – that is, multiple opportunities to shape an emerging political system. Over time, as more and more decisions were made, radical reform tended to become more difficult. Early decisions limited the scope of choice for later decisions, and the institutional system became subject to a variety of increasing returns processes that made further reform more difficult and costly. The critical juncture period gave way to an emerging institutional order in which the institutional forms introduced early on in the transformation process tended to persist, regardless of how functional they were from the standpoint of a democracy that could perform well. Further institutional change was by no means impossible at this stage, but barring a major shock that triggered a systemic collapse, such change would tend to be piecemeal, and its proponents would face considerable inertial resistance.

This conceptualization of the dynamics of post-communist transformation is but a sketch based on evidence from a single case study. Nevertheless, it does enable us to synthesize a number of insights that have recently emerged from historical institutionalist work on post-communist political development. When we combine these insights with the evidence from Prague, we can begin to develop a broader understanding of how various factors that shape post-communist political trajectories might fit together. In what follows, we will use the conceptualization outlined above to frame some arguments about why post-communist transformation processes might have suboptimal outcomes. In drawing these arguments together, we can begin to appreciate how the dynamic and evolving interplay of institutions and political actors has contributed to the remarkable diversity of transformation trajectories and outcomes that we have seen since the fall of communism in the Soviet bloc.

Institutions and Agents in Post-communist Transformations: A Dynamic Interplay

We began this book with a puzzle: In the 1990s, Prague's political leaders seemed unable or unwilling to govern systematically and openly, even though they had the powers and resources necessary to do so. Although most post-communist polities have avoided a descent into outright dictatorship, many have faced similar or even greater difficulties than Prague in establishing a well-performing democracy. A growing historical institutionalist literature on post-communist politics identifies ways in which the interaction between institutions and political actors could set a post-communist polity on the road to suboptimal political outcomes. Using the image of transformation dynamics proposed above, and drawing on evidence and insights from the case of Prague, we can begin to see how an evolving institutions–actors interplay can promote or hinder democratic development.

Recent studies of have asked why it is that many post-communist polities experienced partial reform – the introduction of some, but not all of the institutional elements of a well-functioning liberal democracy. As Elster, Offe, and Preuss note, many among the more pessimistic students of post-communist politics initially feared that reform would be derailed by the short-term political costs of a socially painful transformation. In most places, however, this did not happen, because those who suffered most from such reform rarely wielded sufficient political clout to derail it (1998: 272, 306). In a seminal article published in 1998, Joel Hellman argues that these processes were more likely to be stalled by the 'winners' than by the 'losers'. Writing about post-communist economic reform, Hellman observes that initial reforms often delivered concentrated material gains to a small group of actors, such as managers who privatized enterprises into their own hands or business owners who enjoyed monopoly access to certain markets. To the extent that this happened, these early 'winners' subsequently sought to block further reform to preserve a 'partial reform equilibrium' that concentrated gains in their own hands (1998: 204).

This study of Prague has revealed that an analogous mechanism was at work in the city centre real estate sector, where political leaders who chose to take advantage of the non-existence of conflict-of-interest regulations acquired a vested interest in maintaining a partial reform equilibrium that gave them maximum discretion in their decisionmaking. Yet this study also suggests that vested interests are not the only factor that might stall a transformation process. In the sphere of roads policy in Prague, for example a combination of rising sunk costs and the emergence of a dynamic of mutual delegitimation among opposed sets of actors prevented further development of policy processes and substance. In other words, a variety of mechanisms might work to entrench partial reform equilibria for the longer term. Drawing on historical institutionalist language, the conceptualization of post-communist transformations outlined above labels these mechanisms increasing returns processes.

Suboptimal outcomes in post-communist political transformations might be produced by increasing returns processes that lock in the results of early reforms. This observation leads us to look at the nature of early reforms themselves. How could reformers avoid the emergence of negative increasing returns processes that stall the transformation? One possible answer focuses on the speed of reform: Since major reform tends to become more difficult over time, post-communist political leaders should have undertaken all major reforms as quickly as possible, thereby building a new institutional architecture rapidly after the fall of communism. This is the logic that fuelled calls in the early 1990s for 'shock therapy' in the economic sphere – the rapid and wholesale adoption of market institutions (Brada 1993). While this argument has some prima facie attractiveness, the image of transformation introduced above suggests that there are limits to the speed with which reforms can be accomplished. Because the rationality of political leaders is bounded, because they do not have control over all political institutions, and because some reforms depend on the prior outcome of others, post-communist transformations are necessarily multistage processes.

The issue of speed aside, the concrete substance of early reforms, of both the constitutional and the non-constitutional variety, clearly affects the likelihood that negative increasing returns process will set in. Fifteen years of research and empirical evidence show that a strong, well-organized democratic state, in which political leaders have access to adequate material resources and in which the structure of representation does not pit competing governing powers against each other, is a necessary prerequisite for the emergence of a stable democracy that performs well. Our comparative review of post-communist local government in East Central Europe (Chapter 2) underlined the importance of basic state structures. Where local political leaders are hamstrung by inadequate resources and authority, a variety of dependent relationships with higher levels of government or resource-rich local actors tends to become entrenched, hampering the emergence of a well-performing local democracy.

At the same time, this study has highlighted the key role that reforms beyond the basic structure of the state play in shaping the broader matrix of incentives that make systematic, open rule more or less attractive to political leaders. In Chapter 3, we outlined an ideal model of a well-functioning democracy, in which a variety of interdependent institutional arenas produce incentives that encourage high performance. A regulated market economy, an internally consistent and enforceable legal code that protects basic rights and freedoms, a bureaucracy that balances professionalism with openness to societal interests, a programmatic party system, and a vibrant, institutionalized civil society all contribute to the emergence and stabilization of a democracy that performs well. Not all of these arenas are under the direct control of politicians, but our case study of Prague shows that early reforms outside the constitutional sphere can have longer-term impacts that reverbrate through multiple institutional arenas. For example, in our examination of freeways policy we saw that an early decision to exclude civic groups from decisionmaking processes helped to lock in the fragmented, protest-oriented character of those groups in the longer term.

The substance of non-constitutional reforms introduced early on in a post-communist transformation can thus have a major impact on the development of the broad institutional matrix that shapes government performance. However, our conceptualization of transformation allows us to say more than this about the nature of early reforms. Because reform is a multi-stage process, it is not only the substance, but also the *sequence* of reform that matters. This issue has recently begun to receive attention among some scholars. For example, in her important recent work Juliet Johnson (2001, 2003) links the reluctance of Russian banks to focus on stable, long-term investment to the improper order of reform initiatives in the Russian banking sector. By focusing on liberalizing this sector before a legal framework for regulating it had been fully developed, the Russian reforms created a banking system in which short-term investment was more attractive than long-term investment. The banks that evolved within this system in turn developed vested interests that have frustrated efforts at further reform. In the case of Russian banks, then, the emergence of negative increasing returns is directly linked to the order in which various reform initiatives were undertaken.

Evidence from this study of Prague also provides some examples of how the sequence of early reforms matters for longer-term political outcomes. Although we cannot know for certain how different a sequence could have changed the trajectory of Prague, the present analysis suggests some key institutional elements that, if introduced early, might have improved government performance in the longer run. In the sphere of roads policy, a focus on administrative reform in 1991 might have prevented the persistence of closed decisionmaking throughout the rest of the 1990s. The early introduction of conflict-of-interest regulations might have forestalled the emergence of corruption in the real estate sector and might also have contributed to the development of more open government in many other policy areas.

Both the substance and the sequence of early reform efforts influence longer-term transformation trajectories and have an impact on the kinds of increasing returns processes that emerge. That said, we still have only a limited understanding of what exactly constitutes optimal substance and sequence for the development of democracy. Some generalizations from the literature do appear to have strong empirical support: Constitutional arrangements that divide legislative from executive authority tend to produce destabilizing conflict (Linz 1994). Failure to adopt conflict-of-interest regulations early on in a transformation process encourages corruption (Verheijen 1999). Economic liberalization unaccompanied by the development of robust democracy and enforceable commercial regulations produces unstable economies (Hellman 1998). Yet many aspects of the substance and timing of reform escape generalization. As Johnson notes, this may be inevitable. What constitutes an optimal reform program will depend to some degree on the distinct starting point of each post-communist polity, so although we might develop some valid generalizations, no single, comprehensive formula for the substance and sequencing of reform is applicable across the entire post-communist world (Johnson 2003: 312–14).

Keeping this important point in mind, our discussion thus far nonetheless begs another question: What factors make political leaders more or less likely to adopt initial reform strategies that bode well for democratic development in the longer term? This question shifts our focus away from the consequences of post-communist institutional design and towards its causes. The factors that influence initial reform choices have been the subject of extensive study. By drawing attention to asynchronous institutional change and its effects, the case of Prague and the conceptualization of post-communist transformations proposed here allow us to add some new elements to our understanding of post-communist institutional choice.

A significant body of historically grounded comparative work links post-communist institutional choices to the character of institutional, social, and cultural legacies of the communist era. Some strands of this work emphasize the way in which individual institutional legacies shape post-communist reform choices. For example, Valerie Bunce (1999) links the rapid disintegration of several post-communist states in the early 1990s to the inheritance of communist federal institutions that fragmented authority structures, while Tomasz Inglot (2003) argues that communist welfare state institutions produced widespread norms of entitlement that have led to the retention of comprehensive social safety nets in many post-communist states.

Others move beyond the analysis of individual institutions to focus on the way that broad patterns of authority under communism influenced institutional reform processes after the fall of communism. For example, Herbert Kitschelt and his colleagues (1999) link the speed with which programmatic parties emerged after communism to the dominant structure of authority under communism. Still others move beyond institutions altogether. For example, Elster, Offe, and Preuss argue that post-communist institutional choices ultimately depended on the varying degree to which communism in different states produced 'world views, patterns of behavior and basic social and political concepts' that were compatible with the 'functional necessities of a modern, partly industrial, partly already post-industrial society' (1998: 306–7).

The scholarship linking post-communist reform patterns with legacies of the past thus identifies a number of kinds of legacies, ranging from the institutional inheritance to broad social and cultural inheritances. As Ekiert and Hanson (2003) suggest, the various kinds of legacies are not mutually exclusive causal influences. Rather, we can think of social and cultural legacies as macro-level factors that shape the range of reform possibilities in the early post-communist period by providing a broad landscape of social cleavages and dominant norms of political behaviour. These cleavages and norms are in turn reflected and embedded in the various state and societal institutions that structure the immediate decisionmaking environment in which post-communist political leaders can embark on a reform process. Whether we focus primarily on the influence of institutional legacies or on the influence of broad social and cultural legacies ultimately depends on the extent to which we are interested in highlighting proximate or 'deeper' causation in post-communist transformations (Kitschelt 2003).

The large and diverse scholarship on legacies and institutional choices permits few generalizations; it does, however, provide additional support for two broad observations mentioned earlier. First, some – but by no means all – of the legacies of the past can in fact support the construction of a new democratic political order. Second, the extent to which these legacies are usable in the development of democratic institutions, and do not instead constitute burdens to be overcome, depends at least in part on the extent to which a polity has a history of liberalizing reform prior to the fall of communism (Ekiert 2003). In this manner, the likelihood that early post-communist reforms will set a polity on the road to well-performing democracy is influenced by developments that occurred well before the fall of the old communist regime.

As a single case study that focuses on institutional rather than on social or cultural legacies, this study of Prague cannot speak to all elements addressed in the literature on legacies and institutional design. However, in highlighting the asynchronous nature of post-communist institutional change, it gives us some new insight into how institutional legacies in particular can shape the resolution of critical junctures in the early post-communist period. First, it demonstrates that even within the context of a single case, the effects of institutional legacies can vary across different policy areas and over time. Second, it draws attention to the independent effects that the existence of an unstable mix of old and new political institutions might have on the decisionmaking behavior of political leaders in the early post-communist period.

As we saw in Chapter 2, institutional legacies were key to the outcomes of the 1990 local government reforms in Prague. The inheritance of a well-developed communist-era metropolitan administration provided a base of organizational resources on which a new model of a unified city could be built. Furthermore, the historical example of a unified Prague before communism made a strong metropolitan model more attractive, as it provided a precedent and a template for reform. As a result, the stalemate between those who called for a unified city and those who demanded radical decentralization was resolved in favour of the former, and Prague emerged from the 1990 reforms with one of the strongest local state structures in the region.

Beyond the realm of constitutional design, however, the impact of institutional legacies on the reform process in Prague was quite different. We should recall that the historical institutionalist framework posits two distinct ways in which institutions influence political outcomes: They distribute powers and resources that influence the feasibility of various courses of action, and they embed norms of political behaviour, producing a matrix of incentives that makes various courses of action more or less attractive to political leaders. In the wake of the 1990 local government reforms, Prague's new political leaders had the powers and the resources they needed to pursue institutional and policy reform in the interest of systematic and open government. However, the broader institutional context in which they operated provided them with a decidedly mixed set of incentives.

The decisionmaking environment for Prague's first elected post-communist leaders included state and societal institutions that had arisen at various times in the city's past and embodied a variety of disparate norms of political behaviour. Administrative institutions and legal frameworks remained little changed since the communist era, and the embedded norms of bureaucratic-administrative rationality associated with the previous state-dominated political system still prevailed. They privileged the development and implementation of systematic long-range policies, but were not adapted to function in the emerging democratic and market environment. Civic groups and the city's dominant political movement had arisen during the protest wave that toppled communism. As a result, they embraced the ideal of open government but had little capacity for systematic policy development.

Although the particular mix of institutional incentives present in early post-communist Prague was probably unique to that city, the conceptualization of transformation as a process marked by asynchronous institutional change suggests that politicians across much of the post-communist world probably did face similarly conflicting incentives early on. What factors influenced how political leaders responded to such conflicting incentives? One response to this question would be to focus, as some of the writers discussed above have done, on the relative balance of democracy-supporting versus democracy-impeding norms in the institutional environment. Clearly, this is a key factor. If, for example, Prague's administrative institutions had experienced sustained interaction with civic groups prior to the fall of communism, the development of open government in the roads sector might have been less difficult, and the outcomes of early decisions in this sphere might have been quite different. However, this study has highlighted the potential significance of another set of factors: the systemic characteristics of the decisionmaking environment.

A number of writers have drawn attention to the fluid and unstable nature of the early post-communist political environment. Usually, this instability is noted as a source of unexpected outcomes, which indeed it may be. For example, Kitschelt suggests that the volatile environment characteristic of the early transition period means that unpredictable factors – such as the appearance of the right leader at the right time – might have major consequences for future outcomes, and that therefore there might be an element of 'quasi-randomness' to post-communist political development for which no systematic theory can account (2003: 75, 78; see also Johnson 2001: 262).

The present study, however, highlights the potential impact of systemic instability on the way in which political leaders make early critical decisions in the first place. First, the unpredictability of outcomes may shorten the time horizons of decisionmakers early in the transformation, since politicians will be less inclined to invest effort in systematic reform strategies whose success they are highly unsure of. Second, as Kitschelt notes, 'in times of regime crisis, political actors often may not have the time and the access to gather the information that would allow them to choose their best course of action' (2003: 52). In other words, the need to deal simultaneously with multiple critical decisions may strain the information-processing capabilities of boundedly rational actors, encouraging them to seek simple, immediately rewarding solutions to complex problems. As Paul Pierson observes, 'even if some of the mechanisms discussed by rational choice theorists are operative in everyday politics, they will often be especially fragile or altogether absent precisely at moments of institutional formation' (2000b: 482).

This study has identified another feature of the early post-communist institutional environment that might also limit the inclination of actors to engage in strategic reforms. As boundedly rational actors, political leaders seek overarching normative frameworks that can guide and give purpose to their actions. But early on in a transformation process, asynchronous institutional change tends to produce a decisionmaking environment that embeds a variety of mutually incompatible norms of political behaviour – what I have called an institutionally incoherent environment. Such an environment does not provide political leaders with a readily identifiable normative framework that they can use to guide strategic action. Instead, it presents them with a bewildering cacophony of competing norms out of which a clear direction for strategic action becomes difficult to identify, further reinforcing the tendency towards governing behaviour that privileges immediate, short-term solutions and gains.

Systemic instability and institutional incoherence can have independent impacts on the way that political leaders choose from among institutional incentives early on in a post-communist transformation. In both of the policy areas examined in this study of Prague, systemic instability and institutional incoherence encouraged the city's new political leaders to seek simple, short-term solutions to the multiple governing challenges that they faced in the early days. In an environment where many political institutions continued to embed pre-democratic norms, this focus on the short term produced decisions that in turn entrenched government performance problems in the city for the longer term.

In sum, this study of Prague highlights a previously neglected set of factors that may help to explain the emergence of partial reform equilibria. Early on in a transformation, when political leaders face a multiplicity of critical junctures, the systemic characteristics of the decisionmaking environment may discourage them from pursuing the strategic reforms necessary to complete the institutional architecture of a well-functioning democracy. The very lack of established order that gives political leaders such extraordinary influence over future outcomes in the initial stages of the transformation process may at the same time also limit their ability and inclination to engage in strategic reform. Insofar as this is the case, the longer-term outcomes of a transformation process have much to do with the structure of short-term incentives that politicians encounter in dealing with the multiple critical decision points of the early post-communist period. In re-evaluating the divergent transformation trajectories of post-communist states, scholars would do well to pay close attention to the systemic character of the institutional environment in which early reform decisions were made.

That said, we know that many early post-communist governments *did* engage in long-range strategic reform. What factors enabled these leaders to overcome the lure of short-term incentives? Our case study cannot provide definite answers to this question, but does suggest some possibilities. First, the experience of Prague suggests that the partisan organizational resources available to politicians may be an important factor. In Prague, the dominant post-communist political party, the Civic Forum / ODS, was initially structured in a highly decentralized way, making the development of a partisan governing platform very difficult. As a result, political leaders lacked an autonomous organization that could serve as a focal point for the emergence of a strategic governing agenda.

Adequate partisan organization may make it possible to develop a strategic reform agenda, but it by no means ensures that such an agenda will emerge, nor does it ensure that any such agenda will be focused on building the institutional architecture of a democracy that performs well. For this, political leaders require in the first instance a normative and practical framework for reform that is compatible with democratic development. Insofar as politicians cannot identify such a framework in their immediate institutional environment, their ability to draw on normative and practical frameworks derived from other settings may become key to facilitating strategic action.

One possible source of such frameworks is the inheritance from the past. In his study of Novgorod, Russia, Nicolai Petro (2004) argues that the cultural myth of Novgorod as a bastion of democracy in medieval times was successfully used by the region's post-communist leaders to frame a publicly acceptable reform strategy. This study of Prague provides another example of the use of such an inherited framework: The existence of a democratic metropolitan authority in Prague before 1938 was successfully used to help construct a new post-communist state structure. In some cases, however, the past may not offer frameworks for action that are easily compatible with democratic development. Then, the extent to which political leaders can engage in strategic action that promotes democratic development may depend on their ability and willingness to adapt frameworks transferred from other places.

Across the post-communist world, many political leaders have done precisely this: they have used frameworks derived from other settings to structure their efforts at strategic reform. Early on in the transition, this phenomenon was especially common in the economic sphere, where the wholesale rejection of central planning and the promise of foreign assistance led to the widespread adoption of market reform frameworks imported from abroad. But the use of imported frameworks was common in other areas of reform as well, especially among national governments in the East Central European countries that have now gained admission to the European Union. Such adaptation is not without its risks. As the contrasting fate of economic 'shock therapy' in Poland and Russia indicates, whether an imported reform agenda will have the intended effects depends on the political environment into which it is inserted. Much depends on how political leaders adapt frameworks derived from other settings to local conditions. Nevertheless, this study suggests that in the early post-communist period, the local political environment sometimes provided no coherent cues for political action, and in these cases, political leaders needed to draw on normative or practical frameworks derived from other settings to provide a foundation for strategic reform.

Fifteen years after the fall of communism in the former Soviet bloc, the transformation of post-communist polities continues. Decisions made in the early post-communist period have not entirely determined longer term development trajectories. Yet barring a wholesale loss of system legitimacy, such as that experienced recently in Georgia and Ukraine, major reform has tended to become more difficult with time, as the institutional architecture of the political system has congealed into a durable form. In many post-communist polities, including Prague, significant reforms in more recent years have come only when a favourable confluence of factors has opened up a window of opportunity that new political leaders can use to dislodge institutionally entrenched patterns of political interaction. The success of post-communist transformations is strongly shaped by decisions made early on in the transformation process. Whether those critical early decisions set a polity on the road to well-performing democracy may in turn depend on whether political leaders can transcend the lure of short-term gains and draw inspiration from other places and times to govern for the future in the midst of a complex and confusing transformation.

Appendix: Data on Interviews

Interviews with key actors in Prague politics in the 1990s were an important source of information for this book. A total of forty-three confidential interviews with forty-two individuals were conducted between June and November 2000. Three interviews included two respondents at once, while two respondents were interviewed twice, and one three times. Respondents included ten current or former local politicians (three city councillors and seven executive board members, including two former mayors); eleven members of interest groups and/or community groups (seven community activists, two developers, and two individuals who work in a support function for community activists); and twenty-one current or former employees in local government bodies (including both managerial staff and professional staff, such as urban planners). Interviews were open-ended, framed by a set of broad guiding questions. They lasted anywhere from thirty minutes to four hours, with an average interview lasting about an hour and a quarter. With eight exceptions, where interviewees asked that I take written notes, interviews were tape-recorded. In the list below, interview subjects are listed by the identifying number used in the text; their role in municipal politics is described in general terms in order to preserve confidentiality.

Interview List

ID#	General description of interview subject	Interview date
1	Transport planner, Transport Engineering Institute (UDI)	8 June

2	Manager, civil society support NGO	20 Oct.
3	Two land use planners, City Development Authority (URM), Prague Monument Preserve Studio	24 Oct.
4	City councillor, Union for Prague (UPP)	14 Sept.
5	City councillor, Civic Democratic Party (ODS)	12 Sept.
6	Activist working in freeways sector	6 June
7	Administrator, Borough of Prague 1 Municipal Property Office	13 July
8	Land use planner, URM	5 Sept.
9	Former executive board member, ODS	2 Nov.
10	Second interview with subject of Interview 9	3 Nov.
11	Third interview with subject of Interview 9	7 Nov.
12	Administrator, Prague Department of Transport	10 July
13	Administrator, Prague Department of Public Relations (OSV)	2 Nov.
14	Executive board member, ODS	6 Nov.
15	Administrator, Department of Land Use Decisions (OUR)	7 July
16	Retired transport planner, URM	24 Aug.
17	Land use planner, URM, Prague Monument Preserve Studio	30 Oct.
18	Two transport planners, URM	1 Sept.
19	Activist and former historic preservation administrator	20 Sept.
20	Former executive board member, ODS	12 Oct.
21	Executive board member, ODS	29 June
22	Lawyer representing civic groups	14 Oct.
23	Property developer specializing in work for foreign investors	27 June
24	Administrator, Department of Historic Preservation (OPP)	5 Oct.
25	Activist, environmental education association	12 Oct.
26	Former executive board member, ODS	30 Aug.
27	Transport planner, URM	26 June
28	Former executive board member, ODS	13 Nov.
29	Transport planner, URM	8 June
30	Manager, Chamber of Commerce	22 Aug.
31	Administrator, Department of Transport	12 July
32	Preservation professional, OPP	11 Oct.
33	Activist working in freeways sector	26 Oct.

34	Second interview with subject of Interview 33	9 Nov.
35	Activist in local tenants' association	5 July
36	Land use planner, URM	9 Aug.
37	Activist working in freeways sector	3 Oct.
38	Two administrators, Borough of Prague 1 Land Use Development Department	7 Sept.
39	City councillor, Freedom Union (US)	27 Oct.
40	Executive board member, ODS	12 June
41	Second interview with subject of Interview 40	30 Oct.
42	Preservation professional, Prague Institute for Monument Preservation (PUPP)	13 Sept.
43	Property developer	2 Nov.

Notes

All translations from Czech-language sources quoted in the text are by the author.

1 Introduction

1 I use the term 'East Central Europe' narrowly to denote Poland, Hungary, and the Czech and Slovak republics. When speaking more broadly of former Soviet bloc states I use the term 'post-communist' countries.

2 Major studies of government performance in Western democracies include Putnam (1993), Levy, Mettsner, and Wildavsky (1974), Fried and Rabinowitz (1980), and Weaver and Rockman (1993).

3 For further discussion of these concepts, see Linz and Stepan (1996: Chapter 1) and Petro (2004: Chapter 1).

4 The two exceptions that I am aware of are both studies of sub-national government in former communist states: Stoner-Weiss (1998) and Soos, Toka, and Wright (2002).

5 Compare, e.g., the standards used in Putnam (1993) with those developed in Weaver and Rockman (1993).

6 Throughout the book, I will use the terms 'political leaders' and 'elected officials' interchangeably. I treat political elites who do not hold elected office as a separate category of actors, since they do not have the same access to the formal levers of decisionmaking as elected officials do.

7 Some writers on government performance do use this standard. It is perhaps most strongly represented in the work of Weaver and Rockman, who among their ten key tasks for 'governmental effectiveness' include the abilities to set and maintain priorities, to coordinate conflicting objectives, to ensure implementation, and to ensure policy stability (1993: Chapter 1).

8 The Rose-Ackerman (2005) volume mentioned earlier is an important exception to this generalization in the post-communist field; indeed, her analysis of the quality of post-communist democracies focuses largely on the character of policy processes.

9 In addition to the state-centred writing, there is an extensive body of economics writing on post-communist market reform and the design of economic institutions (see, e.g., Aslund 1994; Brada 1993). While this literature produced some important hypotheses about the links between economic and political reform, I do not engage with it here, as it is not central to my argument.

10 Peter Hall defines institutions as 'rules, compliance procedures, and standard operating practices that structure the relationship between individuals in various units of the polity and economy' (1986: 19). Orren and Skowronek observe that to separate political institutions from other broad social and economic structures, we need to define them as structures explicitly designed for political purposes (1994: 326).

11 Legal statutes are the one set of political institutions discussed in this book that do *not* constitute organizations with members.

12 For a recent, and extensive, exposition of the argument that institutions contribute to the structuring of preferences, see North (2005: esp. Chapter 3).

13 I would like to thank one anonymous manuscript reviewer for clarifying my thinking on this issue.

14 Blair Ruble's study (1993) of Yaroslavl, Russia, provides one local-level cautionary tale about the dangers of engaging in extensive legislative and administrative reform before constitutional structures are stabilized. Local institutional reform at the beginning of the 1990s was significantly undermined by subsequent federal-level changes in the powers and organization of Russian municipalities.

15 Examples of the former focus include Coulson (1995), Zsamboki and Bell (1997), Regulska (1997), and Kirchner (1999). Policy research is dominated by an extensive literature on national and local reforms in housing policy. See, e.g., Bodnar (1996), Eskinasi (1995), Hegedus and Tosics (1998), and Struyk (1996).

16 Such literature is somewhat better established in the study of post–Soviet Russia. See, e.g., Ruble (1993), Bater et al. (1998), Stoner-Weiss (1998), and Petro 2004.

17 This is reflected in differential budget figures. For example, Czech municipalities only have a few selected responsibilities in health care delivery, and in 1997 they spent only 3.6% of their budgets on health care. Hungarian

local governments, with broad health care responsibilities, spent 18.2% of their budgets on health care in the same year (International Monetary Fund (IMF) 2000).

18 The increased political significance of local government in recent years is not limited to East Central Europe. Around the world, national fiscal strain and the desire to encourage local solutions to local problems are combining to produce a decentralization of political responsibilities and political conflict to local government (Teune 1995; Borja and Castells 1997).

19 Figures are calculated from IMF (2000). The East Central European average covers Poland, Hungary, and the Czech and Slovak republics; the Western average covers Germany, France, the United Kingdom, and the United States. The strongest outliers within each country group, respectively, are the centralized Slovak Republic, at 7.8%, and the decentralized United States, at 43.1% (this figure includes state governments in the U.S. federal system).

20 See, e.g., Fried and Rabinowitz (1980), Putnam (1993), and Stoner-Weiss (1998); for a significant exception that studies performance at the national level, see Weaver and Rockman (1993).

21 See Maier, Hexner, and Kibic (1998: Chapter 3), for extensive treatment of the built form of Prague's communist-era housing estates and the problems arising from it.

22 At this time, the Czech Republic was still one of two units in a federal Czechoslovakia, the other being the Slovak Republic. As the federal capital, Prague was thus also a government hub for the Slovak lands. It lost this status with the split up of the Czechoslovak Federation in 1993, but a continued Czech–Slovak customs union helped to ensure that the economic impact of the split on Prague was not significant.

23 Nonetheless, there is variation in the degree of dominance of East Central European capitals in their respective national urban systems. In 1991, Budapest contained 19.5% of Hungary's population; 11.8% of the Czech Republic's population lived in Prague; 8.4% of Slovakia's lived in Bratislava; and only 4.3% of Poland's lived in Warsaw (however, the latter figure is distorted since Warsaw, unlike the other cities, has populous suburbs outside the city limits; Surazska 1996: 368). With the exception of Slovakia, whose capital has grown considerably, national and capital city populations have both been more or less stable since the fall of communism, so these figures remain accurate.

24 In Prague, e.g., unemployment in 1998 stood at 0.3%, compared with a national average of 5% (Maier et al. 1998: 91).

25 In the housing sector liberalization was slower, as post-communist national

governments tended to see rental housing as a social 'shock absorber,' and rent controls thus remained extensive across the region for much of the 1990s (Hegedus and Tosics 1998: 163).

26 A common exception to this trend was relatively high investment in mass transit.

2 The Structure of Government in Prague: Building a Strong Local State

1 Unfortunately, I could not find reliable time-series data on the Slovak Republic for either this Table or 2.2, so the comparison is restricted to three states.

2 Given Warsaw's fragmented, multi-tiered local government system (see below in text) comprehensive fiscal data on this city are, unfortunately, hard to come by.

3 It should be noted that while the three countries have been broadly similar in wealth throughout the 1990s, Poland's GDP per capita has been some-what lower than that of the Czech Republic or Hungary. The figures should be interpreted with this point in mind.

4 Average is for France, Germany, the United Kingdom, and the United States for 1997–98. Calculated from International Monetary Fund (IMF 2000) and OECD on-line database.

5 According to the Czechoslovak Federal Constitution of 1969, which was retained until the partition of the country in 1993, municipal government laws were the prerogative of the national councils of the two constituent republics, Czech and Slovak. Local government in the Czech and Slovak republics thus began to develop independently from the beginning of the post-communist era, rather than after the division of the country three years later. The term 'national government' as it is used in this text refers to the Czech national government, not the Czechoslovak federal government. As of 1992, the average Czech municipality had only 1,800 inhabitants, compared with 3,300 in the case of Hungary and 15,000 in Poland (Balder-sheim et al. 1996).

6 The names of these bodies changed repeatedly over time. To simplify mat-ters, I always refer to the directly elected body as the city council and to the indirectly elected body as the executive board, since the functions of these bodies remained similar over time, despite the name changes.

7 By this time, few Jews lived in the old ghetto. Most of Prague's large Jewish population had moved to other parts of the city after residency laws confin-ing them to the ghetto were repealed in the 1820s. Subsequently, over the

course of the nineteenth century, the area had become run down and was populated by the city's marginal poor. The controversy surrounding the ghetto's razing had to do with concerns that the city was destroying its medieval architectural heritage, concerns that are discussed further in Chapter 3.

8 This portrait of local administrative institutions as substantially autonomous from communist Party organs stands in contrast to the common vision among analysts of communist-era civil servants in East Central Europe as 'party servants, serving neither the state nor the public, but implementing Communist Party decisions' (Berčík and Němec 1999: 186). Whether Prague's or the Czech Republic's civil service was something of an exception to this rule, or whether the common vision is based on received wisdom rather than thorough research, remains an open question beyond the scope of this project.

9 All references in the following discussion are to paragraphs in the Czech National Council Law on Municipalities, no. 367/1990.

10 Technically, land use planning was also at first a transferred power of state administration. Unlike other transferred powers, however, land use plans were subject to the approval of municipal councils. Their transferred status was because many small municipalities did not have the staff to prepare land use plans on their own and thus had to rely on the national administration to do so. In Prague, where the Chief Architect's Office (UHA) existed for this purpose as a municipal organization, planning was from the outset for all intents and purposes an 'own power' of the municipality. All municipalities received own power over land use planning as of July 1998 (Tůnka and Sklenář 1999: 9).

11 All references in the following discussion are to paragraphs in the Czech National Council Law on the Capital City of Prague, no. 418/1990.

12 The term 'development program' is roughly synonymous with what would in English be called a 'strategic plan,' which lays out longer-term policy goals for urban development. The term was deliberately left vague to allow for the later introduction of national legislation giving formal recognition to municipal strategic plans. However, such legislation was never introduced, so development programs / strategic plans remained discretionary policy documents without any legal standing (Interview 36; see also Chapter 3).

13 In addition, the city regained ownership of a wide range of other service enterprises. In 2000 the *Directory of Municipal Organizations* (which only noted enterprises directly controlled by the city, rather than by the boroughs) listed 13 theatres and 9 other cultural organizations, 11 health and safety–related organizations, 36 social service organizations such as shel-

ters and old age homes, 7 colleges, and 12 other organizations (Information Centre of the Department of External Affairs 2000).

14 Title to some of this property, particularly vacant land with development potential, remained in dispute even after it had been formally given to the city. For example, some of the land that the city got from communist-era housing construction firms was subject to restitution claims into the latter part of the 1990s (Kvačková 1996a). However, overall the evidence that I have found suggests that such problems, while real, were not widespread for long, and that by the mid-1990s the city had a strong base of secure and usable property.

3 Institutions and Political Actors in Early Post-communist Prague

1 For an outstanding and exhaustive analysis of these phenomena in post-communist Russia, see Reddaway and Glinski (2001).
2 In Slovakia protest was led by a parallel but autonomous movement, Public Against Violence.
3 Prague was not an exception in this regard. Baldersheim et al. observe that across much of East Central Europe new local elites initially had little in common except for opposition to communist rule and a lack of prior political experience (1996: Chapter 4).
4 District Forums often produced quite detailed borough-level electoral programs, although a lack of clear borough powers and the inexperience of new politicians often resulted in policy 'wish lists' that later turned out to be beyond the power of boroughs to pursue.
5 Some of these institutions, especially the UDI, did retain other roles, such as the design of regulatory arrangements like traffic lights and parking (see Dratva 1996; Nerad 1996).
6 Reference is to paragraphs in the Czechoslovak Federal Assembly Law on Land Use Planning and Building Code, no. 50/1976.
7 I use the term 'civic groups' to denote local citizens' groups or community organizations in Prague. This terminology corresponds to the term used in Czech for these groups, občanské sdružení.
8 The majority of Prague's historic core falls within the jurisdiction of the Borough of Prague 1.

4 Planning and Developing the Main Road Network

1 For example, one of the reports noted that in contrast to Prague, developing an inner-city freeways system in a German city 'would be very difficult due to citizen protest' (Leutzbach 1990: 5).

2 Kořán remained in office until he was recalled by city council and replaced by Milan Kondr in September 1991.

3 Polák was deputy mayor for transport until he was replaced by Pavel Holba in April 1993, in one of the many executive board reshuffles that marked the 1990–94 period.

4 In the ZKS plans the inner ring road was merged with the middle ring in the west and the north, while in the east it was to be routed along the already-existing North-South Artery.

5 According to one interviewee, the fact that council had split early in 1991 into a large number of small parties or factions contributed to this result, since its fragmentation made the articulation of an alternative position all the more difficult (Interview 33).

6 Although civic activists assumed that bribery and/or lobbying by construction firms played a role in the decision to pursue the HUS freeways plan, there is little evidence that this was the case (these issues are discussed at greater length below).

7 Short-term parking allows for more traffic throughput than does long-term parking, since more vehicles can pass through any given spot in one day.

8 Although this repair campaign offered an ideal opportunity to monitor the impact of road narrowing and closures on traffic in the city centre, the city's transport bodies did not take advantage of this opportunity (Interview 8).

9 The figures used here are calculated on the basis of maps produced by the city's Transport Engineering Institute (UDI). Figures represent the sum of daily traffic volumes on the five busiest north-south roads in the city centre: Vaničkova, Karmelitská, Smetanovo nábřeží, Opletalova, and the North-South Artery.

10 The protest movement had focused in particular on the segment of the western city ring road that was to run under Stromovka Park, while in the 1990s construction proceeded on the segments immediately to the south; however, the completion of the western city ring road entailed the eventual construction of the Stromovka segment as well.

11 The remaining transport investment funding was allocated as follows: 12.5% went to the construction and repair of smaller roads, 42.8% went to subway construction, and 5% went to the construction of tram lines (calculated from City of Prague Department of Finance 2001).

12 As of 1997 the overall cost of completing the city's proposed freeways network was estimated at Kc60–65 billion (about U.S. $2.5 billion; Hrbek 1997).

13 For example, František Polák, deputy mayor in charge of transport issues in the early 1990s, became press spokesman for Metrostav in the second half of the decade.

14 The absence of evidence regarding the informal lobbying activity of design

and construction companies does not mean, of course, that such lobbying played no role. All we can say is that it appears to have played a smaller role than many opponents of freeways development in Prague assumed.

15 That the draft offered three possible routings of the city's outer ring road in the southeast was the result of a number of factors. In 1994 the national government took over responsibility for financing and building the outer ring road; but its planning remained within the competence of the city. The original plans for the freeways, which routed the outer ring road next to a large housing estate on the southeast periphery of Prague, led in the early 1990s to the emergence of the protest group Optim-Eko, which had strong support among local residents (see, e.g., Brabec 1993). Given the financial involvement of the national government in the outer ring road, the controversy went to a national-level assessment committee, which recommended an alternative routing farther away from residential areas (Murphy 1997). Both routings, along with a third one, were then presented in the conceptual draft of the city's land use plan, and the city council ultimately adopted the option endorsed by the national assessment committee. Several factors contributed to this outcome, which stands in contrast to the city ring road cases discussed later on in this chapter. The involvement of national actors was clearly a major factor; additional factors include the ambitions of the then-mayor of Prague, Jan Koukal, to win a seat on the national Senate in the district that included the proposed freeway (see Roztočil 1996) and the fact that the road was not slated for construction until fifteen to twenty years later, which gave supporters of the original routing the hope of reversing the decision in the future (Interview 29).

16 This party had been formed in December 1997 as a splinter faction of the ODS both nationally and locally.

17 Formerly the governing coalition allies of the ODS, the ODA moved to the opposition at the end of 1997.

18 In the Czech Republic politicians can 'cumulate' posts, so that Bursík could simultaneously be both a Prague city councillor and the national environment minister.

19 For planning permits, this was the Ministry for Local Development; for construction permits, this was the Ministry of Transport (Interview 15).

20 The committee did, at first, also consider a 'zero variant.' This option, however, did not take into account the possibility of building the city's ring road system without the western city ring, but rather considered the implications of building no freeways at all in the whole city. In any event, the option was withdrawn from consideration before the committee had completed its work (Brno Technical University 1994: 6, 48).

21 The southern extension was eventually completed in the summer of 2004.
22 The request for an Environmental Impact Assessment (EIA) was successful.
    The EIA was completed by the Ministry of the Environment in 2002, and
    recommended against construction of this segment of the ring road.
    Buoyed by this decision, SOS Praha continued to campaign against the con-
    struction of the northern extension, and it was joined in this campaign by
    political representatives of some of the boroughs. However, the EIA recom-
    mendation was not binding, and the city maintained its commitment to
    building the northern extension and issued planning permits for all parts of
    the extension in 2003. Despite continued campaigning and appeals by
    opponents, by 2006 the northern extension had proceeded to the construc-
    tion permits stage. Barring an unprecendented appeals victory by oppo-
    nents at this stage, construction of the extension seemed likely to begin in
    2007 (Municipal Districts of Prague Suchdol, Dolní Chabry, and Lysolaje
    2006; České Dálnice 2006).

5 Preservation and Development in Prague's Historic Cove

1 One institution, the Prague division of the State Institute for the Reconstruction of Historic Cities and Monuments (SURPMO), was transferred to
   national-level control (Interview 32).
2 Furthermore, boroughs could develop even more detailed 'regulation
   plans' for areas in their jurisdiction, specifying development parameters
   down to the level of individual buildings (Tůnka and Sklenář 1999: 15).
3 Along with rent controls, tenants retained strong protection against evic-
   tion in the post-communist Czech Republic, since landlords had to offer
   them replacement flats if they did evict them. Although this fact acted as
   something of a brake on the conversion of residential space to commercial
   space, it also led in some cases to landlords going to extremes such as cutting off heat and water in winter to remove sitting tenants with regulated
   rents. Luděk Sýkora (1993) has analysed the consequences of the dual regu-
   lated/deregulated rent sector in Prague and the resulting 'rent gap' in a
   series of outstanding articles. See Sýkora 1993, 1995, 1999.
4 As might be expected, informants interviewed for this project noted that
   the pursuit of private gain affected the work of political leaders in areas
   well beyond the sphere of real estate development in the historic core, since
   a preoccupation with informal development deals drew the overall attention of city councillors and executive board members away from the pressing issues that the city faced (Interview 10; Interview 20).
5 The 1985 guidelines remained on the books until 1997, when they were for-

mally cancelled, but after the adoption of the Plan of Stabilized Zones in 1994 they were no longer legally valid (Interview 24).

6 As was the case in the historic core, this designation was not followed by the adoption of any guidelines regarding what the objective of the 'historic' designation was, so the only effect of the designation was to involve the PUPP and the OPP in a broader range of development decisions (Interview 10).

7 Although this research identified a number of individuals who were seen by many interview subjects as being corrupt, the names of these individuals have been omitted in the text.

8 We should recall here that the executive board had 15 members between 1990 and 1994, and 12 members thereafter.

9 These numbers were compiled by the Prague civic group Zelený Kruh (Green Circle) in 1999 on the basis of data from the *National Business Registry*, and thus do not include any informal activity.

10 Working out a detailed plan for the historic core became more difficult in 1998, since an amendment to the national Law on Land Use Planning and the Building Code prohibited the development of addenda to existing plans. The city would thus have to develop a detailed plan for the historic core as a fully fledged land use plan 'nested' within the broader city land use plan (Prague Executive Board 1999). Although this complicated the process of developing such a detailed plan for the historic core at the end of the 1990s, it by no means explained the inaction of city council between 1993 and 1998.

11 In theory, boroughs could develop highly detailed 'regulation plans' for small areas that would stipulate building guidelines and the residential/ non-residential function of each piece of property. During the 1990s, the Borough of Prague 1 developed such regulation plans for three small areas within the Prague Monument Preserve. However, in the absence of a broader plan for the whole area approved by city-wide institutions, Prague 1 could not enforce these documents (Interview 38).

12 The Borough of Prague 1 is entirely within the Prague Monument Preserve; about one-quarter of the Borough of Prague 2 is also within the preserve.

13 In a few cases where the city did make substantial money, the figures were released, e.g., in March 1994 city council approved the sale of a prime vacant property in the historic core to a foreign bank for Kc212 million (U.S. $5.9 million; Lidové Noviny 1994).

14 The bulk of the 7.4% in 1993 came from the privatization of several large municipal companies that year, rather than from real estate deals (see Schreib 1993c).

15 Since the city council had not explicitly commissioned a land use plan for the historic core, the plan still carried the title 'Updated Urban Study of the Prague Monument Preserve,' even though it in fact had all of the elements of a detailed land use plan and was intended to function as such if approved by council.

16 The historic core had a total of 3,670 buildings.

17 Although conditions seemed promising in 2000–2001 for the adoption of a detailed land use plan for the historic core, the draft document never made it to the council, and it was not adopted as policy. Detailed analysis of why this occurred is beyond the scope of this study, which ends in 2000. The failure to adopt a land use plan for the historic core almost certainly had much to do with the resignation from office of its main political champion, Jan Kasl, in May 2002.

18 Kasl's unsuccessful campaign to make the decisionmaking process more transparent appears to have contributed to his decision to resign as mayor in May 2002. In November 2000 Kasl's fellow ODS councillors publicly threatened to have him recalled for his 'uncommunicative' governing style (Lidové Noviny 2000b). The threat was not acted on, but relations between Kasl and his ODS colleagues continued to deteriorate. In March 2002 Kasl spoke openly to the media about his desire to root out corruption among his colleagues; two months later, he resigned as mayor and left the ODS. In explaining his resignation, he said that 'I no longer want to be part of something that I cannot influence. I think it has become clear that it is impossible to run the city with people from the Prague ODS ... [I have] definitively lost hope that the party will, in the end, embark on a process of internal transformation' (Kolář 2002). Shortly thereafter Kasl founded a new political party, the European Democrats, which came second in the November 2002 municipal elections. Even though his push for transparency appears to have contributed to Kasl's downfall as mayor, many of his policy innovations – such as detailed preservation guidelines for the OPP and the establishment of a public relations department (OSV) – survived his move to the political opposition.

References

Achremenko, Michal. 1997. Pražané mají své akcie i na radnici (Praguers also have shares at city hall). *Lidové Noviny*, 21 March, 15.

Adamková, Alena. 1992. Socialní smír zaplatí cestující (Commuters to pay for social contract). *Ekonom* 41: 42–3.

Aslund, Anders. 1994. Lessons in the first four years of systemic change in Eastern Europe. *Journal of Comparative Economics* 19: 22–38.

Balcar, Zdeněk. 1996. Vývoj názorů na řešení komunikační sítě hl. m. Prahy (The evolution of opinions on the development of Prague's transport network). *Silniční Obzor* 57(3): 83–5.

Baldersheim, Harald, Michal Illner, Aurun Offerdal, Lawrence Rose, and Pawel Swianiewicz. 1996. New institutions of local government: a comparison. In *Local democracy and the processes of transformation in East-Central Europe*, ed. Harald Baldersheim et al., 23–41. Boulder: Westview.

Baldersheim, Harald, and Michal Illner. 1996. Local democracy: The challenges of institution-building. In *Local democracy and the processes of transformation in East-Central Europe*, ed. Harald Baldersheim et al., 1–22. Boulder: Westview.

Bárta, Gyorgyi. 1998. Industrial restructuring or deindustrialisation? In *Social change and urban restructuring in Central Europe*, ed. by Gyorgy Enyedi, 189–208. Budapest: Akademiai Kiado.

Bartoníček, Radek. 1999. Do smluv města mohou nahlédnout jen poslanci (City contracts can only be seen by councillors). *Mladá Fronta Dnes*, 2 Oct., 2.

– 2000. Poslanci napadli uzavřenost radnice (Councillors attack the closed nature of city hall). *Mladá Fronta Dnes*, 28 Jan., 2.

Bater, James, Vladimir Amelin, and Andrey Degtyarev. 1998. Market reform and the central city: Moscow revisited. *Post-Soviet Geography and Economics* 39(1): 1–18.

Bečková, Kateřina. 1993. Před popravou domu v Klimenstké (Awaiting the

execution of the building on Klimentská Street). *Lidové Noviny,* 20 Feb., 10.
– 2000. Sto let Klubu za Starou Prahu v sedmi kapitolách (A hundred years of
the Club for Old Prague in seven chapters). In *Sto let Klubu za Starou Prahu*
(A hundred years of the Club for Old Prague), ed. Katerina Bečková, 27–87.
Prague: Schola Ludus – Pragensia.

Berčík, Peter, and Juraj Němec. 1999. The civil service system of the Slovak
Republic. In *Civil service systems in Central and Eastern Europe,* ed. Tony
Verheijen, 183–201. Cheltenham: Edward Elgar.

Biegel, Richard. 1999. Bestie nad Prahou (A beast over Prague). *Respekt* 4: 9,
11.

Blažek, Bohuslav. 1994. Praha 2010: Od problémů ke strategickému plánu
(Prague 2010: From problems to a strategic plan). *Technický Magazín* 11.

Blažek, Bohuslav, Jan Kasl, and Milan Turba. 1994. Praha 2010: Město na
křizovatce (Prague 2010: City at the crossroads). *Technický Magazín* 21.

Blažek, Jiří. 1996. Financovaní místních rozpočtů v České Republice od roku
1996 (Local government finance in the Czech Republic since 1996). In
Geografická organizace Společnosti a transformační procesy v České Republice (The
geographical organization of society and transformation processes in the
Czech Republic), ed. Martin Hampl et al., 333–42. Prague: Přírodovědecká
Fakulta Univerzity Karlovy.

Blažek, Jiří, Martin Hampl, and Luděk Sýkora. 1994. Administrative system
and development of Prague. In *Development and administration of Prague,* ed.
Max Barlow, Petr Dostál, and Martin Hampl, 73–87. Amsterdam: Institut
voor Sociale Geografie.

Bodnar, Judit. 1996. 'He that hath to him shall be given': Housing privatization
in Budapest after state socialism. *International Journal of Urban and Regional
Research* 20(4): 616–36.

Borja, Jordi, and Manuel Castells. 1997. *Local and global: Management of cities in
the information age.* London: Earthscan.

Bosáková, Renata. 1999. Financování hlavního města Prahy a jeho městských
částí (Financing the capital city of Prague and its boroughs). Master's thesis,
Department of Geography, Charles University, Prague.

Brabec, Jan. 1993. Máme tady všechno, i bazén s diskotekou (We have all we
need here, even a pool with a disco). *Respekt* 47: 7, 9.

Brada, Josef C. 1993. The transformation from communism to capitalism: How
far? How fast? *Post-Soviet Affairs* 2(9): 87–110.

Brdečková, Tereza. 1995. Praha proti pražanům (Prague against praguers). *Respekt* 14: 9–11.

Brno Technical University. 1994. *Posouzení variant dopravního řešení v severozá-
padní části města Prahy* (Evaluation of options for transport infrastructure

development in the northwest sector of the city of Prague). Brno: Vysoké učení technické v Brně, Fakulta stavební.

Brunnell, Laura. 2000. Partners in performance: State–society relations in post-communist Poland. Doctoral dissertation, University of Colorado, Boulder.

Bunce, Valerie. 1999. *Subversive institutions: The design and destruction of socialism and the state*. Cambridge: Cambridge University Press.

– 2003. Rethinking recent democratization: Lessons from the postcommunist experience. *World Politics* 55 (Jan.): 167–92.

Čápová, Hana. 1994. Magistrát a dolarové dluhopisy (The Magistrát's hard currency bonds). *Respekt* 42: 4.

Čenovská, Libuše. 1989. Jednání pokračují (Negotiations continue). *Tribuna* 39: 7.

Červenka, Jan. 1995. Je to kolaps (It's gridlock). *Dobrý Večer*, 1 June, 1.

České Dálnice. 2006. *Rychlostní silnice MO*. Internet document accessed on 5 Dec. 2006 at: http://www.ceskedalnice.cz/rmo.htm

City Development Authority of the Capital City of Prague (URM). 1994. *Varianty městského okruhu v úseku Malovanka – Pelc Tyrolka: Studie* (Routings of the city ring road in the Malovanka – Pelc Tyrolka segment: Study). Prague: Útvar Rozvoje Města, June.

– 1996a. Strategický plán hl.m. Prahy: Workshop 2 – doprava. Výsledky a závěry workshopu (Strategic plan of the capital city of Prague: Workshop 2 – transport. Workshop outcomes and conclusions). Unpublished document.

– 1996b. Strategický plán hl.m. Prahy: Workshop 4 – ochrana a rozvoj. Výsledky a závěry workshopu (Strategic plan of the capital city of Prague: Workshop 4 – preservation and development. Workshop outcomes and conclusions). Unpublished document.

– 1998a. *Územní plán hl.m.Prahy – návrh: městské části* (Capital city of Prague land use plan – draft: Boroughs). Prague: Útvar Rozvoje Města.

– 1998b. *Územní plán hl.m.Prahy – návrh: průvodní zpráva* (Capital city of Prague land use plan – draft: Summary report). Prague: Útvar Rozvoje Města.

– 1999a. Zadání aktualizace urbanistické studie Pražské památkové rezervace (Assignment for the updated urban study of the Prague Monument Preserve). Appendix 2 to Prague Executive Board document 3835.

– 1999b. *UPn PPR – informační materiál pro workshop – koncepce dopravní obsluhy* (Land use plan for the Prague Monument Preserve – background information for workshop – traffic servicing conception). Prague: Útvar Rozvoje Města.

– 1999c. Strategický plán hl.m. Prahy: Návrh strategických priorit a programů pro první etapu realizace (Strategic plan of the capital city of Prague: Draft strategic priorities and programs for the first phase of implementation). Duplicated document.

– 1999d. *Regionalní operační program regionu NUTS 2 hl.m. Praha* (Regional operating program for the NUTS 2 region of the capital city of Prague). Prague: Útvar Rozvoje Města.

– 1999e. *UPn PPR – závěry workshopu 15. – 16. 4. 1999 – koncepce památkové ochrany* (Land use plan for the Prague Monument Preserve – conclusions of workshop held 15–16 April 1999 – historical preservation conception). Prague: Útvar Rozvoje Města.

– 2000. *Pražská Památková rezervace - aktualizace urbanistické studie: průvodní zpráva* (The Prague Monument Preserve - updated urban study: Summary report). Prague: Útvar Rozvoje Města.

City of Prague. 1997a. S automobily se žije těžko, bez nich také (It's hard to live with cars, but also without them). Public information bulletin, *Večerní Praha*, 24 Nov., 8.

– 1997b. Půjčka znamená šanci přežít (A loan is a chance for survival). Public information bulletin, *Mladá Fronta Dnes*, 28 July, 5.

– 1998. Praha disponuje řadou cenných lokalit, jejichž rozvoj může pomoci přetíženému centru (Prague has at its disposal several valuable areas whose development can help the overburdened core). Public information bulletin, *Večerní Praha*, 24 July, 6.

– 2000a. *Strategic plan for Prague*. Prague: Útvar Rozvoje Města.

– 2000b. Pod Letnou povede další tunel (Another tunnel to lead under Letná). Public information bulletin, *Mladá Fronta Dnes*, 20 July, 18.

City of Prague, Department of Finance. 1995. Unaudited consolidated revenue and expenditure statements – City of Prague and Boroughs. Duplicated document.

– 1998. Rozpočet 1997 (Budget 1997). Duplicated document.

– 2001. Vývoj dopravních investic hl.m. Prahy v letech 1991–2000 (Development of the capital city of Prague's transport investments in the years 1991–2000). Prepared for M. Horak in Feb. 2001.

City of Prague, Department of Historic Preservation (OPP). 2000. Zadání pro zpracování koncepce účinnější péče o památkový fond v hl.m. Praze (Assignment for the development of a strategy for the better care of monuments in the capital city of Prague). Duplicated document.

Civic Democratic Party (ODS). 1991. *Stanovy* (Statutes). Cheb: Typos.

– 1994a. *Komunální volební program ODS v Praze* (Municipal electoral program of the ODS in Prague). Cheb: Typos.

– 1994b. *Prahu do pravých rukou: Pražský volební magazín ODS* (Prague into the right hands: The ODS Prague electoral magazine). Prague: Adverta.

– 1997. Jednací řád regionálního sdružení ODS hl.m. Prahy (Rules of procedure of the regional ODS association for the capital city of Prague). Duplicated document.

– 1998. *S námi proti hazardu do Pražského zastupitelstva: komunální volební program* (With us without risk into Prague city council: Municipal electoral program). Prague: Občanská Demokratická Strana, Oct.

Civic Forum. 1990. Cíle Pražského OF (Goals of the Prague Civic Forum). Duplicated document.

Coufalová, Martina. 1998. Mám jednu ruku dlouhou (I have a long hand). *Reflex* 28: 28–33.

Coulson, Andrew. 1995. From democratic centralism to local democracy. In *Local government in Eastern Europe*, ed. Andrew Coulson, 1–19. Aldershot: Edward Elgar.

Crawford, Beverley, and Arend Lijphart. 1997. Old legacies, new institutions: Explaining political and economic trajectories in post-communist regimes. In *Liberalization and Leninist legacies*, ed. Beverley Crawford and Arend Lijphart, 1–39. Berkeley: University of California Press.

Czech Association of Construction Engineers. 1990. Základní Komunikační Systém v Praze: posouzení (Prague's Basic Communications System [ZKS]: evaluation). Duplicated document.

Czech National Council. 1987. Zákon České Národní Rady o státní památkové péči c.20/1987 (Czech National Council Law on State Historic Preservation, no. 20/1987). In *Sbírka Zákonů 1987* (Collected Laws 1987). Prague: Federální Statistický Úřad.

– 1990. Vládní návrh: Zákon České Národní Rady o hlavním městě Praze (Government draft: Czech National Council Law on the Capital City of Prague). In *Praha: jaká byla, je, bude* (Prague: what it was, is, will be), 18–28. Prague: Pražská rada občanského fóra.

– 1992. Zákon České Národní Rady o obcích, c.367/1990 (Czech National Council Law on Municipalities, no. 367/1990). In *Sbírka Zákonů 1992* (Collected Laws 1992). Prague: Ministry of the Interior.

– 1993. Zákon České Národní Rady o hlavním městě Praze, c.418/1990. (Czech National Council Law on the Capital City of Prague, no. 418/1990.) In *Sbírka Zákonů 1993* (Collected Laws 1993). Prague: Ministry of the Interior.

– 1998. Zákon o Územním Plánování a Stavebním Řádu, c.50/1976 (Law on Land Use Planning and the Building Code, no. 50/1976) [amended version, no. 197/1998]. In *Sbírka Zákonů 1998* (Collected Laws 1998). Prague: Ministry of the Interior.

Czech Statistical Office. 1993. *Statistical yearbook of the Czech Republic*. Prague: Czech Statistical Office.

– 1996. *Population trends in the capitals of East-Central Europe*. Prague: Czech Statistical Office.

– 1997. *Numeri Pragenses 1997*. Prague: Czech Statistical Office.

– 1999. *Numeri Pragenses 1999*. Prague: Czech Statistical Office.

Dahl, Robert A. 1961. *Who governs?* New Haven: Yale University Press.

– 1989. *Democracy and its critics*. New Haven: Yale University Press.

Demszky, Gabor. 1998. Perspectives on Budapest. In *The transfer of power: Decentralization in Central and Eastern Europe*, ed. Jonathan Kimball, 59–78. Budapest: Local Government and Public Service Reform Initiative.

Denemark, Martin. 1994. ODA chce Primátora (ODA wants the mayor's chair). *Dobrý Večer*, 1 June, 2.

Devas, Nick. 1995. Local government finance in Hungary: Issues and dilemmas. In *Local government in Eastern Europe*, ed. Andrew Coulson, 214–37. Aldershot: Edward Elgar.

Di Palma, Giuseppe. 1990. *To craft democracies: An essay on democratic transition*. Berkeley: University of California Press.

Dobrý Večer. 1994. Předběžné výsledky komunálních voleb 1994 v Praze (Preliminary results of 1994 municipal elections in Prague). *Dobrý Večer*, 22 Nov., 5.

Doláková, Natálie, and Michaela Šárová. 1994. Patnáctka pod stromeček (Fifteen for Christmas). *Večerní Praha*, 17 Dec., 8.

Dostál, Petr, and Martin Hampl. 1994. Changing economic base of Prague. In *Development and administration of Prague*, ed. Max Barlow, Petr Dostál, and Martin Hampl, 29–46. Amsterdam: Institut voor Sociale Geografie.

Drasnářová, Klára. 1992. Bude městem pro lidi? (Will it be a city for people?). *Lidové Noviny*, 3 June, 2.

Dratva, Tomislav. 1996. Řízení a regulace městského silničního provozu v Praze (The management and regulation of urban road transport in Prague). *Silniční Obzor* 57(3): 81–2.

Dryzek, John, and Stephen Holmes. 2002. *Post-communist democratization: Discourses across thirteen countries*. New York: Cambridge University Press.

Dušková, Zuzana, ed. 1997. *Hlavní město Praha v prvních letech obnovené samosprávy* (The capital city of Prague in the first years of renewed self-government). Prague: Institut městské informatiky hl.m.Prahy.

Dvořák, Václav. 1994. Nepoušťejte auta zpátky na severojižní magistrálu (Do not let cars back on the North-South Artery). *Respekt* 31: 4.

Ebel, Robert, and Peter Simon. 1995. Financing a large municipality: Budapest. In *Decentralization of the socialist state*, ed. Richard Bird, Robert D. Ebel, and Christine Wallich, 119–52. Washington: International Bank for Reconstruction and Development.

Eckstein, Harry. 1998. Congruence theory explained. In *Can democracy take root in post-Soviet Russia? Explorations in state–society relations*, ed. Harry Eckstein, Frederic J. Fleron Jr, Erik P. Hoffmann, and William M. Reisinger, 3–33. Lanham, MD: Rowman and Littlefield.

Ekiert, Grzegorz. 2003. Patterns of postcommunist transformation in Central and Eastern Europe. In *Capitalism and democracy in Central and Eastern Europe: assessing the legacy of communist Rule*, ed. Grzegorz Ekiert and Stephen Hanson, 89–119. Cambridge: Cambridge University Press.

Ekiert, Grzegorz, and Stephen Hanson. 2003. Time, space and institutional change in Central and Eastern Europe. In *Capitalism and democracy in Central and Eastern Europe: Assessing the legacy of communist rule*, ed. Grzegorz Ekiert and Stephen Hanson, 15–48. Cambridge: Cambridge University Press.

Elster, Jon, Claus Offe, and Ulrich K. Preuss. 1998. *Institutional design in postcommunist societies: Rebuilding the ship at sea*. Cambridge: Cambridge University Press.

Enyedi, Gyorgy. 1996. Urbanization under socialism. In *Cities after socialism*, ed. Gregory Andrusz, Michael Harloe, and Ivan Szelenyi, 100–18. Oxford: Blackwell.

– 1999. Governing metropolitan Budapest. Draft paper, Central European University. Duplicated document.

Eskinasi, Martijn. 1995. Changing housing policy and its consequences: The Prague case. *Housing Studies* 10(4): 533–48.

Eurostat. 2001. *Regional statistics database.* Statistics on per capita GDP of selected East Central European cities. Prepared for M. Horak in Feb. 2001.

Exner, Jiří. 1992. What is Prague? Draft ideological concept of socio-economic development of Prague, the capital city. Duplicated document.

Fišer, Petr. 1995a. Jakou bychom si přáli budoucnost pro Prahu? (What kind of future do we imagine for Prague?). *Český Týdeník*, 27 June, 8.

– 1995b. Jakým městem se chce Praha stát? (What kind of city does Prague want to become?). *Český Týdeník*, 4 July, 15.

Fisher, Duncan. 1993. The emergence of the environmental movement in Eastern Europe and its role in the revolutions of 1989. In *Environmental action in Eastern Europe*, ed. Barbara Jancar-Webster, 89–113. Armonk: M.E. Sharpe.

Fried, Robert C., and Francine F. Rabinowitz. 1980. *Comparative urban politics: A performance approach*. Englewood Cliffs: Prentice-Hall.

Frýšarová, Renata. 1995. Strahovský automobilový tunel nesmí ohrozit zdraví Pražanů (The Strahov automobile tunnel must not threaten the health of Praguers). *Právo*, 20 Sept., 1.

Geddes, Barbara. 1997. A comparative perspective on the Leninist legacy in

Eastern Europe. In *Liberalization and Leninist legacies,* ed. Beverley Crawford and Arend Lijphart, 142–83. Berkeley: University of California Press.

Geussová, Milena. 1990. Jak se ruší KNV (The abolition of the regional national committees). *Lidové Noviny,* 14 Nov., 10.

Ghanbari-Parsa, Alan R., and Ravi Moatazed-Keivani. 1999. Development of real estate markets in Central Europe: the case of Prague, Warsaw and Budapest. *Environment and Planning A* 31: 1383–99.

Grabher, Gernot, and David Stark. 1998. Organizing diversity: Evolutionary theory, network analysis and post-socialism. In *Theorising transition,* ed. John Pickles and Adrian Smith, 54–75. London and New York: Routledge.

Grospič, Jiří. 1983. *Politické a státní zřízení ČSSR* (The political and state system of the Czechoslovak Socialist Republic). Prague: Svoboda.

Hall, Peter. 1986. *Governing the economy.* New York: Oxford University Press.

Hamburg-Consult. 1990. Stanovisko k budoucímu vývoji dopravy v hlavním městě Praze, se zvláštním zřetelem k výstavbe základního komunikačního systému (Assessment of future development of transport in the capital city of Prague, with particular reference to the construction of the Basic Communications System). Duplicated document.

Handl, Erich. 1992. Krize pod Strahovem (Crisis under Strahov). *Mladá Fronta Dnes,* 12 Feb., 5.

Hay, Colin, and Daniel Wincott. 1998. Structure, agency and historical institutionalism. *Political Studies* 46: 951–7.

Hegedus, Joszef. 1999. Hungarian local government. In *Decentralization and transition in the Visegrad: Poland, Hungary, the Czech Republic and Slovakia,* ed. Emil Kirchner, 132–58. New York: St Martin's Press.

Hegedus, Joszef, and Ivan Tosics. 1998. Towards new models of the housing system. In *Social change and urban restructuring in Central Europe,* ed. Gyorgy Enyedi, 137–67. Budapest: Akademiai Kiado.

Hellman, Joel. 1998. Winners take all: The politics of partial reform in postcommunist transitions. *World Politics* 50(2): 203–34.

Holmes, Stephen. 1996. Cultural legacies or state collapse? Probing the postcommunist dilemma. In *Post-communism: Four perspectives,* ed. Michael Mandelbaum, 22–76. New York: Council on Foreign Relations.

Holub, Petr. 1994. Do poslední cihly (Down to the last brick). *Respekt* 4: 7 and 9.

Honajzer, Jiří. 1996. *Občanské Fórum: vznik, vývoj, a rozpad* (Civic Forum: Emergence, development and disintegration). Prague: Orbis.

Horáček, Ladislav, ed. 1998. *Dějiny Prahy II: Od sloučení Pražských měst v roce 1784 do současnosti.* (History of Prague II: From the unification of Prague's towns in 1784 to the present). Prague: Paseka.

Horak, Martin. 1998. Transformation of Czech housing policy and its consequences: Evidence from Prague's rental sector. Unpublished paper, University of Toronto.

– 2000. Media review: Purpose, scope, structure and analysis. Project conducted as part of research for doctoral dissertation, June 2000.

Horský, Jiří, and Jiří Schmidt. 1991. Pravidla hry (Rules of the game). *Respekt* 12: 15.

Horyna, Mojmír. 1990. Malá Strana 1989 (Lesser Quarter 1989). *Lidové Noviny,* 9 Jan., 12.

Hospodářské Noviny. 1993. Podniky dluží Pražské radnici miliony za pronájem obecního majetku (Enterprises owe Prague city hall millions in rent for municipal property). *Hospodářské Noviny,* 9 Sept., 1.

– 1999. Neexistující územní plán je hrozbou (The lack of a land use plan is a threat). *Hospodářské Noviny,* 18 Jan., 4.

Hrbek, Michal. 1997. První etapa expresního okruhu by měla být hotova v roce 2001 (The first phase of the outer ring road should be complete in 2001). *Právo,* 1 Feb., 7.

Hrdlička, František, and Olga Táborská. 1994. Kdybych byl Primátorem (If I were mayor). *Dobrý Večer,* 4 Oct., 13.

Hrubý, Dan, and Petr Studnička. 1993. Až budou dva tisíce botiček (Until we have two thousand wheel locks). *Reflex,* 12 May, 36–8.

Hrůza, Jiří. 1992. Urban concept of Prague. *Sborník České Geografické Společnosti* 97(2): 75–87.

Hušek, Matěj. 1999. Stavba hotelu Four Seasons údajně zničí cennou architekturu (Four Seasons hotel building will allegedly destroy valuable architecture). *Zemské Noviny,* 22 March, 3.

Imrych, Robert. 1994. Hotel Four Seasons – věc veřejná (Four Seasons hotel – a public affair). *Lidové Noviny,* 25 Nov., 4.

Independent Committee for the Evaluation of ZKS (IEC). 1990. *Posouzení Základního Komunikačního Systému hl.m. Prahy: Společné Stanovisko* (Evaluation of the Basic Communications System [ZKS] of the capital city of Prague: Final report). Duplicated document.

Information Centre of the Department of External Affairs of the Capital City of Prague. 2000. *Informační bulletin magistrátu hl.m. Prahy* (Information bulletin of the magistrate of the capital city of Prague). Prague: Informační středisko odboru vnějších vztahů.

Inglot, Tomasz. 2003. Historical legacies, institutions, and the politics of social policy in Hungary and Poland, 1989–1999. In *Capitalism and democracy in Central and Eastern Europe: Assessing the legacy of communist rule,* ed. Grzegorz Ekiert and Stephen Hanson, 210–47. Cambridge: Cambridge University Press.

International Monetary Fund (IMF). 1999. *International financial statistics yearbook 1999*. Washington, DC: author.

– 2000. *Government finance statistics yearbook 2000*. Washington, DC: author.

Janderová, Kristina, and Tomáš Brych. 1999. Radní si často přivydělavají tisíce korun (Executive board members often earn thousands of crowns extra). *Blesk*, 4 March, 3.

Janík, Miloslav. 1998a. Pražskému grémiu se nelíbí tunel blízko centra města (Prague Panel disagrees with tunnel close to city centre). *Mladá Fronta Dnes*, 11 July, 2.

– 1998b. Stavba tunelu Mrázovka nabrala zpoždění (The construction of the Mrázovka Tunnel has been delayed). *Mladá Fronta Dnes*, 21 July, 2.

– 1999. Výstavba tunelu Mrázovka vadí občanským sdružením (Civic groups bothered by construction of the Mrázovka Tunnel). *Mladá Fronta Dnes*, 15 Nov., 1.

Janík, Miloslav, and David Konečný. 1998. Unii pro Prahu povede proti Koukalovi Bursík (Bursík will lead the Union for Prague [UPP] against Koukal). *Mladá Fronta Dnes*, 30 Sept., 1–2.

Janouškovec, Jiří. 1984. Protože proto (Just because). *Tribuna* 18: 16.

Johnson, Juliet. 2001. Path contingency in postcommunist transformations. *Comparative Politics* 33(3): 253–74.

– 2003. 'Past' dependence or path contingency? Institutional design in postcommunist financial systems. In *Capitalism and democracy in Central and Eastern Europe: Assessing the legacy of communist rule*, ed. Grzegorz Ekiert and Stephen Hanson, 289–318. Cambridge: Cambridge University Press.

Jowitt, Kenneth. 1992. *New world disorder: The Leninist extinction*. Berkeley: University of California Press.

Judge, Eamonn. 2000. The development of sustainable transport policies in Warsaw: 1990–2000. Paper presented at the Planning Research Conference, 27–9 March, London School of Economics.

Kádner, Tomáš, and Tomáš Kašpar. 1991. Organizační řád ODS Města Prahy (Organizational structure of the Prague city ODS). Duplicated document.

Keating, Michael. 1991. *Comparative urban politics*. Aldershot: Edward Elgar.

King, Charles. 2000. Post-postcommunism: Transition, comparison, and the end of Eastern Europe. *World Politics* 53 (Oct.): 143–72.

Kirchner, Emil, ed. 1999. *Decentralization and transition in the Visegrad: Poland, Hungary, the Czech Republic and Slovakia*. New York: St Martin's Press.

Kirchner, Emil, and Thomas Christiansen. 1999. The importance of local and regional reform. In *Decentralization and transition in the Visegrad: Poland, Hungary, the Czech Republic and Slovakia*, ed. Emil Kirchner, 1–18. New York: St Martin's Press.

Kitschelt, Herbert., 2003. Accounting for postcommunist regime diversity: What counts as a good cause? In *Capitalism and democracy in Central and Eastern Europe: Assessing the legacy of communist rule*, ed. Grzegorz Ekiert and Stephen Hanson, 49–86. Cambridge: Cambridge University Press.

Kitschelt, Herbert, Zdenka Mansfeldová, Radoslaw Markowski, and Gabor Toka. 1999. *Post-communist party systems: Competition, representation, and interparty cooperation.* Cambridge: Cambridge University Press.

Klapalová, Martina. 1998a. Ministerstvo brání osm propouštěných památkářů (Ministry defends eight fired preservationists). *Mladá Fronta Dnes,* 26 May, 1–2.

– 1998b. Magické a tajemné Kafkově Praze hrozí přeměna v tuctové velkoměsto (Kafka's magical and mysterious Prague threatened by transformation into standard metropolis). *Mladá Fronta Dnes,* 4 March, 20.

– 1998c. Památková rada Primátora měla první zasedání (Mayor's monuments council had its first meeting). *Mladá Fronta Dnes,* 24 July, 2.

– 2001. Hotel Four Seasons otevřen, nábřezí poškozeno (Four Seasons hotel opens, embankment damaged). *Mladá Fronta Dnes,* 9 Feb., 1.

Koelble, Thomas. 1995. The new institutionalism in political science and sociology. *Comparative Politics* 27: 231–43.

Kolář, Petr. 2002. Pražský primátor Kasl rezignuje a opustí ODS (Prague Mayor Kasl resigns and will leave ODS). *Lidové Noviny,* 29 May, 1.

Kolářová, Hana. 1989. Stromovka je symbol (Stromovka is a symbol). *VTM* 19: 16–21.

Kolomazníková, Jarmila, and Miloslav Janík, 1997. Význam stavby se projeví teprve za několik let (The utility of the project will not be apparent for several years). *Mladá Fronta Dnes,* 20 Oct., 3.

Konečný, David. 1998. Rozděleni volebních obvodů narazilo na tvrdou kritiku (Division of electoral districts strongly criticized). *Mladá Fronta Dnes,* 23 July, 1–2.

Konečný, David, and Jana Šprunkova. 1997. Hotel Four Seasons nebude platit pět let ani korunu (Four Seasons hotel will not pay a dime for five years). *Mladá Fronta Dnes,* 30 July, 1–2.

Kopstein, Jeffrey. 2001. Where is Europe? Democratic consolidation and EU enlargement: A review essay. Unpublished manuscript.

Kordovský, Petr. 1990. A co čeští architekti, pane Primátore? (And what about Czech architects, Mr. Mayor?). *Literární Noviny,* 25 June, 6.

Kornai, Janos. 1980. *The economics of shortage.* Amsterdam: North-Holland.

Kostlan, František. 1993. Hotel na Alšove nábřeží a záhadné synergie (The hotel on Alsovo embankment and mysterious synergies). *Telegraf,* 5 March, 4.

Kosutová, Táňa. 1997. Praha na přelomu tisíciletí (Prague at the turn of the millennium). *Ekonom* 23: 72.

Kotchegura, Alexander. 1999. A decade of transition over: What is on the administrative reform agenda? In *Civil service systems in Central and Eastern Europe*, ed. Tony Verheijen, 9–14. Cheltenham: Edward Elgar.

Kovářová, Karolina, and Kristína Janderová. 1998. Památkáři prohlašuji, ze jejích ústav památky neochranuje (Preservationists declare that their institute does not protect historic buildings). *Mladá Fronta Dnes*, 12 March, 1.

Krasner, Stephen. 1984. Approaches to the state: alternative conceptions and historical dynamics. *Comparative Politics* 16(2): 223–46.

Krásný, Pavel. 1996. Prahou obchází strašidlo automobilismu (Prague visited by the ghost of automobilism). *Fórum Architektury a Stavitelství* 2 (March): 9–11.

Krejčí, Petr. 1994. Předcasná hysterie kolem hotelu (Premature hysteria about hotel). *Lidové Noviny*, 16 Dec., 7.

Krygier, Martin. 1997. Virtuous circles: Antipodean reflections on power, institutions, and civil society. *East European Politics and Societies* 11(1): 36–88.

Kubieláš, Pavel. 1992. Strahovský tunel v dohlednu (Strahov Tunnel completion on the horizon). *Český Deník*, 17 Nov., 3.

Kubik, Jan. 2003. Cultural legacies of state socialism: History making and cultural-political entrepreneurship in postcommunist Poland and Russia. In *Capitalism and democracy in Central and Eastern Europe: Assessing the legacy of communist rule*, ed. Grzegorz Ekiert and Stephen Hanson, 317–51. Cambridge: Cambridge University Press.

Kuncová, Monika. 1993a. Zanesení Prahy na seznam UNESCO princ Charles neovlivnil (Prince Charles had no influence on Prague's admission to UNESCO list). *Právo*, 28 Jan., 2.

– 1993b. Reorganizace na Pražské radnici (Reorganization at Prague city hall). *Právo*, 10 Feb., 6.

– 1994. Za posledních pět let měla Praha údajne přijít o desítky miliard korun (Prague has allegedly let tens of billions of crowns slip away over the past five years). *Právo*, 29 Sept., 6.

– 1997. Za hrozbou škrtnutí Prahy ze seznamu UNESCO stojí patrně turistická lobby (Tourism lobby apparently behind the threat to remove Prague from UNESCO list). *Právo*, 10 Sept., 4.

Kvačková, Radka. 1991a. Chybí pět miliard (Five billion crowns short). *Lidové Noviny*, 20 Dec., 1.

– 1991b. Jištěná regulérnost (Due process assured). *Lidové Noviny*, 14 Oct., 3.

– 1992. Bitva o majetek (Battle over property). *Lidové Noviny*, 3 April, 2.

– 1993. Spor o dům z přelomu století (Controversy around turn-of-the-century building). *Lidové Noviny,* 17 Feb., 3.

– 1994. Návrhy na hotel u Karlova mostu budou moci posoudit i občané (Citizens will also get a chance to see proposals for the hotel by Charles Bridge). *Lidové Noviny,* 6 Dec., 11.

– 1996a. Jisté je to, co nakoupil Primátor Baxa (What Mayor Baxa bought is secure). *Lidové Noviny,* 8 Oct., 4.

– 1996b. Praha ma z akcií dvacet milionů (Prague makes twenty million on its shares). *Lidové Noviny,* 14 Oct., 4.

– 1997. O Špalíček neni rvačka (No rush for Spalíček building). *Lidové Noviny,* 16 Jan., 3.

Kylařová, Jitka. 1999. *Předpisy o výstavbe na území hl.m. Prahy, Díl I* (Regulations regarding construction on the territory of the capital city of Prague, Part I). Prague: Ministerstvo pro Místní Rozvoj.

Ledvinka, Václav, ed. 2000. *Osm století Pražské samosprávy* (Eight centuries of Prague self-government). Prague: Scriptorium.

Ledvinka, Václav, and Jiří Pešek. 1990. Praha – tradice a budoucnost správy města (Prague – tradition and future of the city's administration). In *Praha: jaka byla, je, bude* (Prague: What is was, is, will be), 4–11. Prague: Pražská rada občanského fóra.

Leo, Christopher. 1996. City politics in an era of globalization. In *Reconstructing urban regime theory: urban politics in a global economy,* ed. Mickey Lauria, 77–98. Thousand Oaks, CA: Sage.

Leutzbach, Wilhelm. 1990. Připomínky k dalšímu vývoji dopravy v hlavním městě Praze, se zvláštním zřetelem k výstavbě komunikační sítě (Notes on future development of transport in the capital city of Prague, with particular reference to the construction of the freeways network). Duplicated document.

Levitas, Tony. 1999. The political economy of fiscal decentralization and local government finance reform in Poland 1989–99. Draft USAID Project Report 180–0034. Duplicated document.

Levy, F.S., Arnold J. Mettsner, and Aaron Wildavsky. 1974. *Urban outcomes: Schools, streets and libraries.* Berkeley: University of California Press.

Lidové Noviny. 1988. Chudinka Staroměstska radnice (Poor Old Town Hall). *Lidové Noviny,* April, 16.

– 1989. Technokracie v praxi (Technocracy in practice). *Lidové Noviny,* June, 2.

– 1990a. Obce a magistráty (Municipalities and Magistráts). *Lidové Noviny,* 14 July, 1–2.

– 1990b. Protest (Protest). *Lidové Noviny,* 20 July, 8.

– 1990c. Předvolební řeč čísel (Pre-election numbers). *Lidové Noviny,* 13 Nov., 3.

- 1990d. OF nejvíce hlasů a mandátů (Civic Forum gets most votes and seats). *Lidové Noviny,* 28 Nov., 1.
- 1990e. J. Kořán Primátorem (J. Kořán elected mayor). *Lidové Noviny,* 13 Dec., 2.
- 1991a. Děleni mezi radnicemi (Division among the boroughs). *Lidové Noviny,* 19 June, 2.
- 1991b. Jde hlavně o pozemky (The main issue is land). *Lidové Noviny,* 28 June, 12.
- 1991c. Metro az později (Metro will be delayed). *Lidové Noviny,* 5 Aug., 2.
- 1991d. Město pro lidi (A city for people). *Lidové Noviny,* 24 Sept., 2.
- 1994. Velké stavební akce v centru Prahy (Large construction projects in the centre of Prague). *Lidové Noviny,* 30 June, 1.
- 1995. Four Seasons: méně pokojů, menší nájemné (Four Seasons: Fewer rooms, lower rent). *Lidové Noviny,* 11 Feb., 3.
- 2000a. Pražský magistrát hodlá své smlouvy dále tajit (Prague Magistrate intends to keep its contracts secret). *Lidové Noviny,* 6 Jan., 13.
- 2000b. Boj o křeslo pražského primátora se přiostřil, opozice se ODS směje (Battle over the Prague mayor's chair intensifies; opposition laughs at ODS). *Lidové Noviny,* 24 Nov., 1.

Linková, Jana. 1994. Na obranu svých občanů (In defence of its citizens). *Zemské Noviny,* 31 March, 12.

Linz, Juan. 1994. Democracy, presidential or parliamentary: Does it make a difference? In *The failure of presidential democracy: The case of Latin America,* ed. Juan Linz and Arturo Valenzuela, 3–87. Baltimore: Johns Hopkins University Press.

Linz, Juan, and Alfred Stepan. 1996. *Problems of democratic transition and consolidation.* Baltimore: Johns Hopkins University Press.

Lochmanová, Zdenka, and Martin Sysel. 1998. Strahovský tunel opět s odkladem (Strahov Tunnel faces more delays). *Právo,* 9 April, 4.

Lukeš, Zdenek. 1990. Ještě jednou causa Stromovka (The Stromovka controversy revisited). *Tvorba* 4: 7.

- 1993. Jak usmrtit dům (How to kill a building). *Lidové Noviny,* 13 Feb., 11.

Maier, Karel, Milan Hexner, and Karel Kibic. 1998. *Urban development of Prague: history and present issues.* Prague: České vysoké učení technické v Praze.

Málek, Daniel. 1997. Smíchov očekává dopravní zácpy (Smíchov anticipates traffic jams). *Mladá Fronta Dnes,* 24 Nov., 3.

Marcuse, Peter. 1996. Privatization and its discontents: Property rights in land and housing in the transition in Eastern Europe. In *Cities after socialism,* ed.

Gregory Andrusz, Michael Harloe, and Ivan Szelenyi, 119–91. Oxford: Blackwell.

Marvan, Lukáš. 1993. Zůstane Praha Prahou? (Will Prague remain Prague?). *Lidová Demokracie*, 9 April, 7.

Mejstřík, Martin. 1995. Mezi památkári a pražským magistrátem propukl boj (War breaks out between historical preservationists and the Prague Magistrát). *Český Týdeník*, 26 Sept., 8–9.

– 1996. Four Seasons napodruhé (Four Seasons, take two). *Český Týdeník*, 14 March, 9.

Mladá Fronta Dnes. 1991. Pražský Primátor odvolán (Prague mayor recalled). *Mladá Fronta Dnes*, 13 Sept., 1–2.

– 1994. Koukal se obává, ze známí lide obecní politice nerozuměji (Koukal fears that celebrities don't understand municipal politics). *Mladá Fronta Dnes*, 29 Nov., 3.

– 1996a. Nový systém pražské integrované dopravy (Prague's new integrated transit system). *Mladá Fronta Dnes*, 25 April, 3–6.

– 1996b. Porota vybrala vítězný návrh na stavbu hotelu Four Seasons (Jury selects winning proposal for Four Seasons hotel building). *Mladá Fronta Dnes*, 5 Nov., 4.

– 1999a. Sdružení chteji, aby policie stíhala ty, co navrhli silnici (Civic groups want police to prosecute those who planned freeway). *Mladá Fronta Dnes*, 28 Aug., 13.

– 1999b. Hotel Four Seasons bude vybudován do dvou let (Four Seasons hotel to be complete within two years). *Mladá Fronta Dnes*, 26 Aug., 5.

– 2000. Tunely na okruhu mohou být pozdeji (Tunnels on the ring road may be built later). *Mladá Fronta Dnes*, 22 July, 2.

Mott MacDonald Europe. 1991. Prague transportation system: Preliminary overview. Duplicated document.

Municipal Districts of Prague Suchdol, Dolní Chabry, and Lysolaje. 2006. *North-Western Segment of Prague Ring Road, Czech Republic*. Memorandum to European Commission, accessed on 8 Oct. at http://www.volny.cz/szokruh/mem_eu_0602.htm

Murphy, David. 1997. David and Goliath face off in Prague 4. *Prague Post*, 9 July, 6.

Musil, Jiří. 1987. Housing policy and sociospatial structure of cities in a socialist country: The example of Prague. *International Journal of Urban and Regional Research* 11: 27–36.

– 1993. Changing urban systems in post-communist societies in Central Europe: Analysis and prediction. *Urban Studies* 30: 899–905.

Nachtigall, František. 1998a. Smíchov jako nova dominanta (Smichov as a new focus). *Blesk*, 15 Jan., 3.

– 1998b. Duel: Koukal zápolí s Bursíkem (Duel: Koukal fights Bursík). *Blesk*, 22 Oct., 4.

Nerad, Jaroslav. 1996. Parkování v Praze z retrospektivy práce UDI Praha (Parking in Prague from the historical perspective of UDI Prague). *Silniční Obzor* 57(3): 88–90.

North, Douglass. 2005. *Understanding the process of economic change*. Princeton: Princeton University Press.

Novotný, Ivan. 1997. Praha, nemocné srdce Evropy (Prague, the ailing heart of Europe). *Týden*, 19 April, 4–5.

Orren, Karen, and Stephen Skowronek. 1994. Beyond the iconography of order: Notes for a 'new institutionalism.' In *The dynamics of American politics*, ed. Lawrence Dodd and Calvin Jillson, 311–30. Boulder: Westview.

Ostrom, Vincent, Robert L. Bish, and Elinor Ostrom. 1988. *Local government in the United States*. San Francisco: Institute for Contemporary Studies.

Painter, Joe. 1995. Regulation theory, post-Fordism and urban politics. In *Theories of urban politics*, ed. David Judge, Gerry Stoker, and Harold Wolman, 276–95. London: Sage.

Paroubek, Jiří. 1999. Praha hledá cestu jak financovat své projekty (Prague is looking for a way to finance its projects). *Metro*, 22 Sept. 15.

Parsons, Wayne. 1995. *Public policy*. Aldershot: Edward Elgar.

Pečínka, Bohumil. 1998. Když vítěz není vítěz (When the winner is not the winner). *Respekt* 32:3.

Perknerová, Kateřina. 1993. Primátor Jan Koukal (ODS) je spokojen s postavením na úrovni ministra (Mayor Jan Koukal (ODS) is satisfied with his standing in the national cabinet). *Právo*, 5 Nov., 1 and 25.

Pešek, Jiří, Draha Pithartová, and Věra Pospíšilová. 1990. Velké téma: Praha (Feature: Prague). *Lidové Noviny*, 24 Aug., 4.

Peterka, Martin. 1990. Praha v obležení (Prague under siege). *Respekt* 17: 9.

Petro, Nicolai. 2004. *Crafting democracy: How Novgorod has coped with rapid social change*. Ithaca: Cornell University Press.

Pickel, Andreas. 2002. Transformation theory: Scientific or political? *Communist and Post-communist Studies* 35(1): 105–14.

Pickvance, Chris. 1996. Environmental and housing movements in cities after socialism: The cases of Budapest and Moscow. In *Cities after socialism*, ed. Gregory Andrusz, Michael Harloe, and Ivan Szelenyi, 232–67. Oxford: Blackwell.

Pierson, Paul. 2000a. Increasing returns, path dependence, and the study of politics. *American Political Science Review* 94(2): 251–67.

– 2000b. The limits of design: Explaining institutional origins and change. *Governance* 13(4): 475–99.

Plechát, Jiří. 1990. Potřebujeme Národní Výbory (We need the national committees). *Respekt* 16: 9.

Plicka, Ivan. 1990. Nezávislá komise o ZAKOSu (The independent committee on ZKS). *Respekt* 27: 14.

– 1991. ZAKOS (ZKS). *Respekt* 22: 15.

Pokorný, Dušan. 1990. Bude stát národní muzeum na Václavskem náměstí? (Will the national museum stand on Wenceslas square?) *Praha 90*, April, 8–11.

Polák, František. 1991. Letter to City Councilor Zdeněk Meisner regarding the latter's concern over revisions to the ZKS freeways system. Duplicated document.

Pomahač, Richard. 1993. Administrative modernization in Czechoslovakia between constitutional and economic reform. *Public Administration* 71(Spring/Summer): 55–63.

Pospíšilová, Věra. 1990. Čí bude Praha? (To whom will Prague belong?). *Lidové Noviny*, 4 Aug., 1.

Prague City Committee of the Czech Union for Nature Protection. 1989. Souhrn argumentů proti vedení SDO ZKS v úseku Argentinská – Špejchar uzemím Stromovky (Summary of arguments against building the ZKS middle ring road between Argentinská Street and Špejchar through the territory of Stromovka Park). Duplicated draft text.

Prague City Council. 1991. Členové zastupitelstva hl.m. Prahy – rozdělení v klubech (Members of the Prague city council – division into caucuses). Duplicated document.

– 1993. Uzemní a Hospodářské zásady k novému uzemnímu planu hlavního města Prahy (Land use and economic principles for the new land use plan of the capital city of Prague). Duplicated document.

– 1994. Seznam členů zastupitelstva hlavního města Prahy. (Directory of city councillors of the capital city of Prague). Duplicated information brochure.

– 1996. *Zásady dopravní politiky hlavniho města Prahy* (Principles of transport policy of the capital city of Prague). Prague: Sofiprin.

– 1999. K návrhu územního plánu sídelního útvaru hl.m. Prahy (Regarding the land use plan of the settlement area of the capital city of Prague). Prague City Council information package no. Z-893.

Prague City Information Institute. 1999. *Praha: životní prostředí 1999* (Prague: Environment 1999). Prague: IMIP.

Prague Executive Board. 1991a. Zpráva o rozvoji dopravní infrastruktury v Praze: pracovní verze (Report on the development of transport infrastructure in Prague: Working draft). Duplicated document.

- 1991b. Zpráva o výstavbě dopravního systému v Praze (Report on the construction of Prague's transport system). Duplicated document.
- 1999. K návrhu zadání aktualizace urbanistické studie Pražské památkové rezervace (Regarding the assignment for an updated urban study of the Prague Monument Preserve). Prague Executive Board document 3835.

Prague National Committee. 1989. Poslanci národního výboru hlavního města Prahy (Deputies of the national committee of the capital city of Prague). Duplicated information brochure.
- 1990a. Poslanci národního výboru hlavního města Prahy (Deputies of the national committee of the capital city of Prague). Duplicated information brochure.
- 1990b. Usnesení číslo 21/17/P k informativní zprávě o posouzení základního komunikačního systému v Praze (Resolution no. 21/17/P re: report on the evaluation of Prague's Basic Communications System). Duplicated document.

Prague Transit Company. 1996. *Vyroční zpráva 1995* (Annual report 1995). Prague: author.
- 1998a. *Vyroční zpráva 1997* (Annual report 1997). Prague: author.

Právo. 1998. Koukal stáhl kandidaturu (Koukal withdraws his candidacy). *Právo*, 26 Nov., 1–2.
- 1998b. Jak se bude vyvíjet hlavní město do roku 2010 (How the capital city will develop until 2010). *Právo* series of articles on the land use plan, June–Oct.

Przeworski, Adam. 1991. *Democracy and the market: Political and economic reforms in Eastern Europe and Latin America.* Cambridge: Cambridge University Press.

Pucher, John, and Christian Lefevre. 1998. *The urban transport crisis in Europe and North America.* London: Macmillan.

Putnam, Robert. 1993. *Making democracy work.* Princeton: Princeton University Press.

Reddaway, Peter, and Dmitri Glinski. 2001. *The tragedy of Russia's reforms: Market bolshevism against democracy.* Washington, DC: United States Institute of Peace Press.

Regulska, Jana. 1997. Decentralization or (re)centralization: Struggle for political power in Poland. *Environment and Planning C: Government and Policy* 15: 187–207.

Rose-Ackerman, Susan. 2005. *From elections to democracy: Building accountable government in Hungary and Poland.* Cambridge: Cambridge University Press.

Rothschild, Joseph. 1989. *Return to diversity: A political history of East Central Europe since World War II.* Oxford: Oxford University Press.

Roztočil, Martin. 1996. Pražský Primátor by měl být zemským hejtmanem (Prague's mayor should be a regional prefect). *Denní Telegraf*, 9 Nov., 3.

Ruble, Blair. 1993. *Money sings: The changing politics of urban space in post-Soviet Yaroslavl*. Washington, DC: Woodrow Wilson Center Press.

Růžička, Michal. 1991. Praha: gordický dopravní uzel (Prague: The Gordian knot of transport). *Lidové Noviny*, 31 Aug., 5.

Sadílek, Josef. 1998. Řešení sítě hlavních komunikací v uzemních plánech hl.m. Prahy (The development of the Main Road Network in Prague's land use plans). *Silniční Obzor* 59: 37–43.

Šálek, Marek. 1999. Stop (Stop). *Týden* 21: 39–44.

Santoška Citizens' Initiative. 1991. Kronika občanské iniciativy Santoška (Chronicle of the Santoška Citizens' Initiative). Duplicated document.

Šárova, Michaela. 2000. Dostavba tunelu Mrázovka má roční zpozdeni (Construction of the Mrázovka Tunnel is a year behind schedule). *Zemské Noviny*, 25 July, 9.

Schmidt, Jiří. 1993. Čtvrtý týden ve funcki (The fourth week in office). *Český Deník*, 11 June, 3.

Schreib, Luděk. 1991. Kolik máme? (How much do we have?). *Večerní Praha*, 25 Oct., 2.

– 1992. Volby nám nepomohou (Elections won't help us). *Večerní Praha*, 29 Sept., 3.

– 1993a. Velký třesk na radnici (Blow-up at city hall). *Večerní Praha*, 30 April, 1.

– 1993b. Nové památkové zóny (New historic zones). *Večerní Praha*, 14 Oct., 4.

– 1993c. S náměstkem primátora T. Kaiserem o hospodaření s městským majetkem (Deputy Mayor T. Kaiser on the subject of managing municipal property). *Večerní Praha*, 20 July, 5.

– 1998a. Vyřeší budoucí Primátor dopravní kolaps v našem hlavním městě? (Will the future Mayor resolve the transport crisis in our capital city?). *Večerní Praha*, 30 Oct., 20–1.

– 1998b. Jednání o Primátorovi a vedení radnice začíná (Negotiations over the mayor and the leadership of city hall begin). *Večerní Praha*, 16 Nov., 3.

– 1999. Kasl: územní plán schválíme (Kasl: We will approve the land use plan). *Večerní Praha*, 20 July, 6.

– 2000. Nový poradní sbor primátora (The mayor's new advisory council). *Večerní Praha*, 8 Feb., 7.

Shapiro, Ian. 1996. *Democracy's place*. Ithaca: Cornell University Press.

Shugart, Matthew. 1997. Politicians, parties and presidents: An exploration of post-authoritarian instiutional design. In *Liberalization and Leninist legacies*, ed. Beverley Crawford and Arend Lijphart, 40–90. Berkeley: University of California Press.

Simon, Herbert. 1985. Human nature and politics: The dialogue of psychology with political science. *American Political Science Review* 79: 293–304.

Šindelářová, Milena. 1990. Bitva (nejen) o Vinohrady (A battle for (not only) Vinohrady). *Respekt* 35: 8–9.

Škrdlant, Tomáš. 1990. Anatomic ZÁKOSu (Anatomy of the ZKS). *Lidové Noviny*, 21 Sept., 11.

Slonek, Petr. 1999a. Vystavbě tunelu Mrázovka v současnosti nic nebrání (Nothing stands in the way of Mrázovka tunnel construction anymore). *Večerní Praha*, 12 April, 3.

– 1999b. Ekologove protestovali proti dálnici (Environmentalists protest against freeway). *Blesk*, 26 May, 1.

Smith, David M. 1996. The socialist city. In *Cities after socialism*, ed. by Gregory Andrusz, Michael Harloe, and Ivan Szelenyi, 70–99. Oxford: Blackwell.

Šnajdr, Pavel. 1999. Územní plán hlavního města byl schválen (The capital city's land use plan has been approved). *Hospodářské Noviny*, 10 Sept., 7.

Solař, Miloš. 1999. Chybějící koncepce památkové ochrany je dlouholetou pražskou bolestí (The lack of a preservation policy is a long-standing headache for Prague). *Mladá Fronta Dnes*, 16 Nov., 14.

Soos, Gabor, Gabor Toka, and Glen Wright, eds. 2002. *The state of local democracy in central Europe.* Budapest: Local Government and Public Service Reform Initiative.

SOS Praha. 1999. Kontakty na angažované združení koalice SOS Praha (Contacts for groups involved in SOS Prague). Duplicated document.

– 2000. Podnět ve věci stanovení posuzování vlivů na životní prostředí dle zákona 244/92 Sb. Stavby: 'Městský okruh – Myslbekova – Prašný most – Špejchar – Pelc Tyrolka' na území Praha 1, Praha 6, Praha 7, Praha 8, Praha–Troja (Petition in the matter of conducting an environmental impact assessment according to law 244/1992, regarding the 'City ring road – Myslbekova – Prašný most – Špejchar – Pelc Tyrolka' project on the territory of Prague 1, Prague 6, Prague 7, Prague 8, and Prague–Troja). Duplicated document.

Šprunková, Jana, and Karolína Kovářová. 1998. Obecní volby (Municipal elections). *Mladá Fronta Dnes*, 18 Nov., 7–10.

Stanger, Allison. 2003. Leninist legacies and legacies of state socialism in postcommunist Central Europe's constitutional development. In *Capitalism and democracy in Central and Eastern Europe: Assessing the legacy of communist rule*, ed. Grzegorz Ekiert and Stephen Hanson, 182–209. Cambridge: Cambridge University Press.

Štětka, Jan. 1992. Tanec kolem památek (The historical preservation dance). *Český Deník*, 22 Dec., 5.

Stone, Clarence. 1989. *Regime politics: Governing Atlanta 1946–1988*. Lawrence: University of Kansas Press.

Stoner-Weiss, Kathryn. 1998. *Local heroes: The political economy of Russian regional governance*. Princeton: Princeton University Press.

Štursa, Jan, et al. 1988. Pražská Stromovka ohrožena (Prague's Stromovka in danger). *Tvorba* 13: 5.

Šubrt, Pavel. 1997. Nutný a nechtěný (Necessary and unwanted). *Týden*, 13 Dec., 4–5.

Surazska, Wisla. 1996. Transition to democracy and the fragmentation of a city: Four cases of Central European capitals. *Political Geography* 15(5): 365–81.

Svobodné Slovo. 1995. Bitva o hotel Four Seasons pokračuje (The battle over the Four Seasons hotel continues). *Svobodné Slovo*, 11 Jan., 1 and 4.

Swianiewicz, Pawel, Gejza Blaas, Michal Illner, and Gyorgy Peteri. 1996. Policies: Privatizing, defending the local welfare state, or wishful thinking? In *Local democracy and the processes of transformation in East-Central Europe*, ed. Harald Baldersheim, 161–96. Boulder: Westview.

Sýkora, Luděk. 1993. City in transition: The role of rent gaps in Prague's revitalization. *Tijschrift voor Economische en Sociale Geografie* 84(4): 281–93.

– 1994. Local urban restructuring as a mirror of globalization processes: Prague in the 1990s. *Urban Studies* 31(7): 1149–66.

– 1995. Prague in the 1990s: changing planning strategies in the context of transition to market economy. In *European cities, planning systems and property markets*, ed. J. Berry and S. McGreal, 321–44. London: E. and F.N. Spon.

– 1998. Commercial property development in Budapest, Prague and Warsaw. In *Social change and urban restructuring in Central Europe*, ed. Gyorgy Enyedi, 109–36. Budapest: Akademiai Kiado.

– 1999. Changes in the internal spatial structure of post-communist Prague. *GeoJournal* 49(1): 79–89.

Sýkora, Luděk, and Iva Šimoničková. 1994. From totalitarian urban managerialism to liberalized urban property market: Prague in the early 1990s. In *Development and administration of Prague*, ed. Max Barlow, Petr Dostál, and Martin Hampl, 47–72. Amsterdam: Institut voor Sociale Geografie.

Sýkora, Luděk, Jiří Kamenický, and Petr Hauptmann. 2000. Changes in the spatial structure of Prague and Brno in the 1990s. *Acta Universitatis Carolinae Geographica* 1: 61–77.

Táborská, Olina, and František Hrdlička. 1995. Kauza od Vltavy (A Vltava affair). *Dobrý Večer*, 23 Feb., 6.

Teune, Henry. 1995. Local government and democratic political development. *Annals of the American Academy of Political and Social Sciences* 540: 11–23.

Thelen, Kathleen, and Sven Steinmo. 1992. Historical institutionalism in comparative politics. In *Structuring politics: Historical institutionalism in com-*

parative analysis, ed. Sven Steinmo, Kathleen Thelen, and Frank Longstreth, 1–32. Cambridge: Cambridge University Press.

Tichý, Zdeněk. 1991. Pomáhat, nebo obchodovat? (To help, or to do business?). *Lidové Noviny*, 15 May, 11.

Transport Engineering Institute of the Capital City of Prague (UDI). 1991. *Dopravně inženýrské posouzení výhledové koncepce Hlavní Uliční Síťe v Praze* (Transport engineering evaluation of the Main Road Network [HUS] proposal for Prague). Prague: UDI Praha.

– 1998. *Ročenka dopravy Praha 1997* (Transport yearbook: Prague 1997). Prague: UDI Praha.

– 2000. *Ročenka dopravy Praha 1999* (Transport yearbook: Prague 1999). Prague: UDI Praha.

Tůnka, Martin, and Tomáš Sklenář. 1999. *Pořizování územně plánovací dokumentace v souvislosti s novelou stavebního zakona* (Preparing land use planning documentation in the context of the amended building law). Prague: ARCH.

Turková, Monika. 1994. Do dvou let se na Alšově nábřeží objeví hotel Four Seasons (Four Seasons hotel to appear on Alšovo Embankment within two years). *Český Deník*, 5 Feb., 3.

Union for Prague (UPP). 1998. *Program rozvoje Prahy 1998–2002* (Program for the development of Prague 1998–2002). Prague: Unie pro Prahu, Oct.

Váchová, Lucie. 1990. Demolice podle plánu (Demolition by design). *Respekt* 20: 14.

Vašků, Václav. 1990. Open letter from 10 civic groups to the Prague executive board regarding implementation of the independent committee's proposals on ZKS. Duplicated document.

Vavírková, Miroslava. 1989. Jak budeme chodit a jezdit Prahou? (How will we walk and drive in Prague?). *Práce*, 27 Sept., 1.

Večerní Praha. 1990a. Komise k tunelu (The committee on the tunnel). *Večerní Praha*, 12 Feb., 1.

– 1990b. Tramvají pod kopec (By tram under the hill). *Večerní Praha*, 17 Dec., 3.

– 1991a. Otazníky (nejen) nad Bořislavkou (Questions (not only) about Bořislavka). *Večerní Praha*, 24 Sept., 7.

– 1991b. 'Velká' a město (Large [privatization] and the city). *Večerní Praha*, 3 Oct., 3.

– 1991c. Majetek spíše ano (Tentative yes to property). *Večerní Praha*, 29 Nov., 1.

– 1992. Budeme jezdit hůře? (Will we ride worse?). *Večerní Praha*, 30 Oct., 4.

– 1994a. Zástupci Pražanů zasednou (Prague's representatives take their seats). *Večerní Praha*, 1 Dec., 2.

– 1994b. Radní se představují (Executive board members introduce themselves). *Večerní Praha*, 21 Dec., 4.

Verheijen, Tony, ed. 1999. *Civil service systems in Central and Eastern Europe.* Cheltenham: Edward Elgar.

Vlček, Tomáš. 1990. Praha s prsty památkářů (Prague with the preservationist touch). *Lidové Noviny,* 26 May, 8.

Volejník, Ondřej. 1995. Metrostav nesouhlasí se stanoviskem městského hygienika ke zprovoznění Strahovského tunelu (Metrostav opposes the city hygienist's position regarding the opening of the Strahov Tunnel). *Telegraf,* 16 May, 3.

Votoček, Jan. 1994. Dvě protichůdné koncepce rozdělování majetku v Praze (Two opposed visions of dividing property in Prague). *Český Deník,* 14 Feb., 10.

Walsh, Annemarie Hauck. 1969. *The urban challenge to government.* New York: Praeger.

Weaver, R. Kent, and Bert Rockman. 1993. *Do institutions matter? Government capabilities in the United States and abroad.* Washington DC: Brookings Institution.

Weiss, Martin. 1991. Fatální zpoždění: zákon o majetku obcí (Fatal delay: The law on municipal property). *Respekt* 11: 4.

Wollner, Marek. 1993. Zákon o střetu zájmů trpí socialistickým dedictvím (Law on conflict of interest suffers from the socialist legacy). *Lidové Noviny,* 8 April.

Yin, Robert K. 1994. *Case study research.* Thousand Oaks, CA: Sage.

Žaloudek, Ivo. 1994. Je nutné vyjasnit statut hlavního města (It is necessary to clarify the statute of the capital city). *Denní Telegraf,* 10 Oct.

Zavoral, Petr. 1996. Pražané by měli šetřit na nová auta (Praguers will have to save up for new cars). *Český Týdenik,* 5 March.

Zelený Kruh. 1999. No title (List of formally declared business activities of Prague councillors compiled on basis of national business registry). Duplicated document.

Zemanová-Kopecká, Radka, and Eva Kubátová. 1999. Radnici zaznělo výhrůžně: Příště sem přijdem zas! (City hall hears threat: We will return here!). *Večerník Praha,* 25 June, 3.

Zemské Noviny. 1994. Každá z pražských etap měla svého Primátora (Each of Prague's stages of development has had its mayor). *Zemské Noviny,* 26 Oct., 7.

Zsamboki, K., and M. Bell. 1997. Local self-government in Central and Eastern Europe: Decentralization or deconcentration? *Environment and Planning C: Government and Policy* 15: 177–86.

Index

policy, 10–11
policy-making accountability, 8
political institutions: defined, 18–19, 226n10; and government performance, 17, 26–8, 75–82, 210–20; as influences on political behaviour, 19–20
political leaders: defined, 225n6; and government performance, 10–12. *See also* city council; executive board
political parties: as components of political society, 76–7; in early post-communist Prague, 81–6; government performance and, 76–7, 219. *See also individual parties*
political society. *See* political parties
Pomahač, Richard, 90
post-communist politics: analytical approaches to, 2–4; early scholarly work on, 13–18, national vs local studies of, 28–2. *See also* transformations, post-communist
powiat, 48
Prague: communist-era development of, 34–5; elections in (*see* elections); growth of city boundaries, 57–8; finances, 44–6, 67–70; historical development of, 32–7; local government history to 1939, 49–53; local government history 1939–89, 53–8; local government structure after 1990, 62–74; metropolitan government in, 48–9, 51–2, 62–7; municipal property in, 65–6, 70–3, 160, 183–90; political parties in early post-communist, 81–6; post-communist growth of, 37–9; rationale for studying, 28–2, 204–5; territorial organization of, 64–7;

theories of post-communist transformation and, 203–5, 209–20; urban zones of, 35–6. *See also* administration (Prague); boroughs; city council; executive board; government performance in Prague; historic core; land use planning (Prague); transport infrastructure
Prague 1, Borough of, 159–60, 179, 181, 183, 234nn11–12
Prague 2, Borough of, 132, 159–60, 181, 183, 234n12
Prague 5, Borough of, 152, 155, 180
Prague 6, Borough of, 153
Prague 7, Borough of, 153, 156
Prague 8, Borough of, 154
'Prague 2010,' 146–8
Prague Castle, 103
Prague Centre of State Monument Preservation and Nature Protection (PSSPPOP), 56, 101–2, 161
Prague Council of Cities and Towns (PROM), 62–3
Prague Institute for Monument Preservation (PUPP), 161–2, 166–7, 169–72, 182, 195
Prague Monument Preserve (PPR), 102–3, 159–61, 166, 170–1, 173, 177–9, 181, 193–4
Prague Monument Preserve Studio, 167
Prague Monuments Council, 101, 161, 170, 195
Prague Mothers, 97, 123
Prague Panel, 187, 189–90
Přemyslid dynasty, 32
Preuss, Ulrich, 15, 208, 210, 214
Principles of Transport Policy for the Capital City of Prague, 130–3

private gain, pursuit of. *See* corruption

privatization, real estate, 71–2, 105–6, 160, 164–5

property, municipal. *See* Prague property restitution, 70–1

public transit, 113, 130–1

punctuated equilibrium, 21–5, 205

PUPP. *See* Prague Institute for Monument Preservation

Putnam, Robert, 7, 10–11, 31

real estate development: in early post-communist Prague, 99, 105–6, 167–9; local government control over, 160–2; in historic core (*see* historic core)

Report on the Development of Transport Infrastructure in Prague, 119

Ritz-Carlton, 188–9

roads. *See* Basic Communications System; Main Road Network; Stromovka freeway; western city ring road

Rockman, Bert, 225n7

Rose-Ackerman, Susan, 8–9, 12, 226n8

Royal Way, 103

Ruble, Blair, 226n14

Rudolf II, 33

rule of law, 76–7

Russia, 15, 20, 212–13, 220, 226n14

Santoška Citizens' Initiative, 97

Second World War, 34, 99

seniority system in administration, 88–9

sequencing of reform, 212–13

shock therapy, 211, 200

Skowronek, Stephen, 18, 24, 27

Slovakia, 29–30, 35

Smíchov, 152–3, 163, 180

Soos, Gabor, 28

SOS Praha, 144–5, 156, 233n22

Soviet bloc, 2, 8, 15, 203, 210, 220

Společnost Praha, 163, 167, 170, 176

Stark, David, 23, 208

state, the: and political institutions, 18–19; strength of, 15, 20, 211–12

state, the local: strength of, 32, 42–3, 49, 73–5, 204

State Institute for the Reconstruction of Historic Sites and Buildings (SURPMO), 101–2

Stepan, Alfred, 20, 76–8

Stoner-Weiss, Kathryn, 11

Strahov Tunnel, 94, 120, 133, 152, 164–5

strategic planning: in Czech Republic, 229n12; and freeways development, 147–9; and historic core, 180–1, 191–2; in 1990s Prague, 145–9, 180–1, 191–2

Strategic Planning Section (USK), 147, 180

Stromovka freeway, 94–9, 112–13, 115, 119–20, 133, 152–4, 231n10

SubTerra, 134

sunk costs, 128, 157, 202

Supreme Court, 156

Sýkora, Luděk, 71, 179, 233n3

subway, 34, 87, 89, 91, 130–1, 133, 231n11

successor elite, 15

systematic government: definition of, 11–13; in Prague (summary), 200–3; institutions and, 76–82; local state structure and, 43, 46–7. *See also* government performance;